Paris and the
Ile de France

Further titles available
in the
Phaidon Cultural Guides
series:

Athens and Attica
Austria
Florence and Tuscany
France
Germany
Great Britain and Ireland
Greece
Holland
Italy
Jerusalem and the Holy Land
The Loire Valley
Provence and the Côte d'Azur
Rome and Latium
Spain
Switzerland

Paris and the Ile de France

A Phaidon Cultural Guide

with over 275 colour illustrations
and 6 pages of maps

Phaidon

Contributors: Franz N. Mehling, Maria Paukert M.A., Bernhard Pollmann

Photographs: Marion Müllmayer

Maps: Herbert Winkler, Munich

Ground-plans: Karl Schneider, Solms

Phaidon Press Limited, Littlegate House, St Ebbe's Street, Oxford OX1 1SQ

First published in English 1987
Originally published as *Knaurs Kulturführer in Farbe: Paris und Ile de France*
© Droemersche Verlagsanstalt Th. Knaur Nachf. Munich 1986
Translation © Phaidon Press Limited 1987

British Library Cataloguing in Publication Data

Paris and the Ile de France.—(A Phaidon
    cultural guide)
    1. Paris (France)—Description—Guide-
    books
    I. Knaurs Kultürführer in Farbe, Paris und
    Ile de France. *English*
    914.4'3604838   DC708

    ISBN 0-7148-2446-1

Translated and edited by Babel Translations, London
Typeset by Hourds Typographica, Stafford
Printed in West Germany by Druckerei Appl, Wemding

Cover illustration: Paris, Notre-Dame (photo: © Tony Stone Associates Ltd.)

Preface

The Ile de France is the historic core of the French Republic. Set in the Paris Basin, it is traversed by the rivers Seine, Marne and Oise. Its hub is Paris, the capital of France and the economic and cultural centre of the country. The city is the seat of the supreme political and ecclesiastical authorities, and of the principal educational institutions and economic organizations of the nation as well as of important international bodies.

Paris has long been admired as one of the most beautiful and most interesting European capitals; it is also the undisputed home of refined taste and *savoir vivre*. It was and still is a magnet for writers, artists, Bohemians, idealists, dreamers, refugees and victims of persecution, and also for the droves of tourists who flock to the city from all quarters of the globe. They come to be inspired, to be captivated by the unique magic of this metropolis, which has been the setting for countless novels, stories, and tales. They long to be caught up in the everyday life of the city, and to succumb to the enchantment of the famous sights, some of them, such as Notre-Dame and the Musée du Louvre, housing priceless treasures from a glorious past, others, such as the Eiffel Tower, the Centre Beaubourg and the new Forum des Halles, breathing the spirit of modernity and still providing subjects for painters of genius and amateur daubers alike, for draughtsmen, and for eager photographers.

The Ile de France contains also Versailles, the dream palace of the Sun King, which became, with its splendour and magnificence, the model for many a palace in other countries. The hunting-lodge of Fontainebleau built in the sixteenth century owed its earliest fame to the Italian painters working here, who are known as the first School of Fontainebleau. It was here that Napoleon I renounced his imperial power and took leave of his beloved soldiers. The little château of Malmaison was for many years the residence of his first wife, the lively and pleasure-loving Empress Josephine, whom he divorced because she had borne him no child. The abbey church of Saint-Denis houses the royal tomb monuments of eleven centuries.

The Ile de France has also a great number of other fine churches, sumptuous palaces and residences, museums and monuments. Many of these may be unfamiliar, but all are well worth a visit. The present guide will introduce the sightseer both to the well-known and to the little-known gems of art and architecture which the capital of France and its surroundings have to offer.

The Ile de France section starts on page 138. As with other guides in the series, the text in this section is arranged in alphabetical order of place name for easy reference. The link between places which are geographically close but separated in the text because of the alphabetical arrangement is provided by the maps on pages 256–9. They show all the principal towns described in the text and also, in the same colour, those subsidiary places mentioned in the environs section at the end of each entry.

The heading to each entry gives the name of the town and, below, its geographical region (department) and a reference to the map section, giving page number and grid reference. Within each entry the sights are printed in bold type: less significant objects of interest appear under the heading **Also worth seeing** and places in the vicinity under **Environs.** At the end of the book is an index of places mentioned in the text and a glossary of technical terms.

Paris

Organization of the Paris article:

Paris

p.256–259

' . . . Paris is a feast for life,' declared Ernest Hemingway (1899–1961). And the composer Frédéric Chopin (1810–49) said 'Paris is where you find the greatest luxury, the greatest misery, the greatest virtue, the greatest vice . . . Paris is everything you want it to be. You can enjoy yourself, be bored, laugh, weep, simply do as you please. . . ' We have to agree with them, and with all the others who have celebrated the French capital in words or music, or who set outstanding novels, stories and films there.

There was a time when French, 'the language of the birds', was the official court language of all the large and small principalities and kingdoms of Europe; it is said that Frederick the Great of Prussia (1712–86) spoke it better than German. Similarly the French court was the model for every-

Arc de Triomphe de l'Etoile at night

thing concerning style and art, and, first in Paris and then in Versailles, was seen as the fountainhead of fashion, refinement and gallantry, in short, of 'savoir vivre'.

Paris is still a city of fashion: it produced the two-pieces which have outlasted every trend and the famous perfumes of Mme Chanel (1883–1971), now sold world-wide. This will be confirmed by anyone who has glanced into the windows of the great French couturiers like Dior, or the foreign houses for whom Paris is still an absolute must, and also by lovers of the tantalizing perfumes which are almost all created here. Paris is a city of the arts, and the cradle of many styles, particularly in Modern Art, Impressionism, Symbolism, Cubism and Surrealism, and evidence of this is afforded by the numerous large and small galleries and museums. Paris is a city of literature and the theatre, as is shown by names such as Molière, (1622–73), Racine (1639–99), Anouilh (b.1910), Ionesco (b.1912), Balzac (1799–1850), Dumas père (1824–95) and Dumas fils (1824–95), Zola (1840–1902) and many others.

But Paris is also a city of frivolity and the demi-monde: history books tell of the liberality of the court of the 'Roi Soleil', and writers like Balzac and Dumas fils portray most vividly the glitter and misery of the famous courtesans of the city. The famous and notorious can-can, also a product of Paris, created a scandal of gigantic proportions, and the dance can still be seen in the city today. But even people who are interested in none of these things can hardly resist the charm of Paris. They will love the great boulevards and the little streets lined with old houses, cafés large and small, cheap and expensive restaurants, and will be captivated by the quays and bridges of the Seine, the incomparable blue of the Parisian sky, the bustle, and the quiet, found here after dark. They will be enchanted by the metropolitan charm and intimate flair of this city, two characteristics which are present side by side. They will be impressed by monuments ancient and modern, combining to form a harmonious overall picture.

History and Cultural History

The pre- and early history of Paris is shrouded in mystery. In the 3C BC pre-Celtic tribes settled in the area of the present city.

350 BC: The Celtic tribe of the Anavisi (later: Parisians) conquered the area; their settlement, later to become Paris, adopted the name *Lutuhezi* = Celtic 'water-dwelling'.

250 BC: The Parisians established their major settlement on the island in the river Sequana (Seine), the modern Ile de la Cité. At the end of the 2C and beginning of the 1C BC the Parisians joined the neighbouring Celtic tribe of the Senoni, but then became dependent upon them; however they had the right to mint their own coins and struck some in gold. (The Romans later adopted *Lutetia*, the Celtic form of the name Lutuhezi, and *Parisia* is not in evidence as the name of the town until the 4C AD).

53 BC: Paris is mentioned for the first time in writing in Caesar's 'Gallic Wars'. While Gaul was under Roman rule, Caesar summoned a Gallic 'assembly to Lutetia in the region of the Parisians; these were the tribe neighbouring the Senoni, and had earlier been members of the same state, but now did not seem to be involved in their plans for revolt (against the Romans)' (6.3.4–5).

52 BC: The Parisians were involved with the general Gallic rebellion against Rome under the leadership of the Arvernian king Vercingetorix. Caesar, in chapters 57–58 of the 'Gallic Wars', describes the defence of the city under the Aulercan Camulogenus, 'who despite his great age was called to this office because of his outstanding knowledge of military

Eiffel Tower and Paris at night ▷

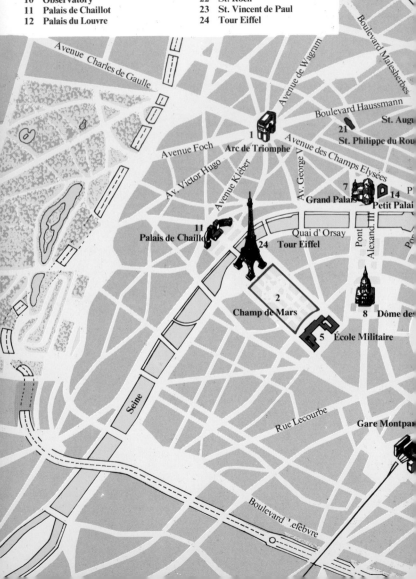

Map of Paris

Avenue Charles de Gaulle

Avenue de Wagram

Boulevard Berthier

Boulevard Malesherbes

Boulevard Haussmann

St. Augu

21

St. Philippe du Rou

1

Arc de Triomphe

Avenue Foch

Avenue des Champs Elysées

Av. Victor Hugo

Avenue Kléber

Av. George V

7

Grand Palais

14 P

Petit Palai

11

Palais de Chaillot

Quai d'Orsay

Pont Alexandre III

Po

24 Tour Eiffel

2

Champ de Mars

8 Dôme des

5 École Militaire

Seine

Rue Lecourbe

Gare Montpar

Boulevard Lefèbvre

Cimetière de Montmartre

3

16 Sacré-Cœur

Boulevard Ncy

Boulevard de Clichy

Boulevard de

Rue La Fayette

23 **St. Vincent de Paul**

20 **St. Laurent**

Magenta

Rue Réaumur

Sébastopol

ncorde **22** **St. Roch**

19 **St. Eustache**

Boulevard de

12 **Palais du Louvre**

Quai des Tuileries

Pont Royal

Pont Neuf

Boulevard du Palais

Boulevard St. Germain

9 **Notre-Dame**

Pont de Sully

Rue de Lyon

Palais du Luxembourg

13

Boulevard Saint Michel

Raspail

18 **St. Étienne-du-Mont**

15 **Panthéon**

Pont d'Austerlitz

Boulevard de l'Hôpital

Seine

Cimetière Montparnasse

Boulevard de Port Royal

10 **Observatory**

Av. de Chois

Pont Nationa

affairs,' and the conquest by the Romans under the legate Titus Labienus, after the Parisians had themselves set fire to the city.

51 BC: Caesar ordered the rebuilding and fortification of Lutetia on the island in the Seine and on the W. bank of the river and stationed a river flotilla here (hence the ship in the Parisian coat of arms). Buildings in the new Roman city included a forum (now the Rue Soufflot), three thermae (baths; Cluny, Collège de France and Rue Gay-Lussac), a theatre (between the Boulevard Saint-Michel and the Rue Racine), an amphitheatre (Rue Monge) and a temple (to the Roman god Mercury, now Montmartre). It began to play a major role as a trading town and river port; the 'nautae Parisiaci', Parisian sailors, were famous, although Paris was never as important as Lyon or Reims in Roman times.

AD 250: According to the historian Gregory of Tours, Pope Fabian sent the priest Dionysius (Denis) to Gaul as a missionary bishop, with seven companions. Denis, whose cathedral probably stood on the Ile de la Cité, was martyred *c.* 280 at the foot of Montmartre. Later to become the French national saint, he was buried in a chapel in Catuliacum (modern Saint-Denis).

360: Lutetia became a focal point in history for the first time: Julian the Apostate, who had been appointed Caesar (co-regent to the Emperor) in Gaul, was proclaimed Emperor by his soldiers in Lutetia. It was around this time that the city was given the name of the tribe: a council report dating from AD 360 contains the phrase 'apud Parisiam civitatem'.

451: Tradition has it that this was the year in which Paris was spared from attack by the Huns under Attila as the result of a plea by St.Genoveva (Geneviève). In the same year Roman, Burgundian, Visigothic and Frankish troops under the leadership of the Roman imperial general Aetius defeated the Huns under Attila in the battle of the Catalaunian Plains.

Geneviève's reputation for holiness increased further when she travelled the Seine from town to town during a famine, and came back with twelve ships full of grain. In 460 she built a church over the tomb of Denis and his companions, and King Dagobert I later founded the abbey of Saint-Denis on the same spot. Geneviève died on 3 January 512 and is honoured as the patroness of Paris. Her church was profaned when it became the Panthéon during the revolution in 1791, and in 1793 her bones were burned in public.

486: The Merovingian King Clovis I defeated Syagrius, the Roman ruler of the area, around Soissons (near Reims, also including the region around Paris) and the remaining Roman rulers of Northern Gaul. The victory over Syagrius opened up the Somme and Seine areas, the later kingdom of Neustria, to Clovis I, and brought him the Roman 'fiscus', the state domain: roughly 20 per cent of the total area conquered.

498: Clovis I had himself and 3,000 of his warriors baptized (it is not certain in which town; probably Reims). This was the decisive step to union of the Franks and the Gallo-Romans.

508: Clovis I made Paris his residence. The Franks' takeover of land in Gaul led to a clash of two entirely different cultures. The linguistic barriers were quickly overcome: the Frankish rulers adopted Latin, but gave the new empire a 'Frankish' name: Francia. The two cultures influenced each other mutually: the Franks were romanized, and the acceptance of Christianity was an essential part of this. Generally speaking, states founded at the time of the migration of the peoples were based on territory seized from landowners originally resident there, but Clovis simply took over the Roman 'fiscus'; the possessions of the Gallo-Roman provincial aristocracy remained un-

Rodin, Thinker, Musée Rodin ▷

touched, and the established nobility and clergy were given new civil and ecclesiastical functions. Former Roman towns became bishoprics and centres of spiritual and cultural life, alongside the monasteries and imperial residences: they incude Paris, Trier, Metz, Verdun, Soissons, Orléans, Autun. A firm alliance grew up between the old-established Gallo-Roman clergy and the Merovingians; the Gallo-Romans were experienced writers and administrators, and soon became indispensable to the new empire.

Merovingian art: The art of the Merovingian period has no particular stylistic unity. Its basis was in the Germano-Frankish tradition, elements from the period of the migration of the peoples, and elements of provincial Roman and early Christian style. The church above all was the driving force in this art, that is to say the urban and aristocratic seats of bishops and the monasteries, and finally the residences of the kings. Church architecture was dominated by the basilica, with dome towers between nave and apse. Churches were generally sited by a manor house or a graveyard ('ad sanctos'). As they were largely built in wood, they were rebuilt in the Carolingian and Romanesque periods, and thus few of them have survived. Stone building dates from the 6&7C.

Merovingian literature: Hagiography, the description of the lives of saints, became the commonest literary form. The most striking example of Merovingian piety, with its strong inclination to belief in miracles and distinctive cult of saints, are the 'Miracle Books' of Bishop Gregory of Tours. The 'Vita of St.Columba', written in the first quarter of the 7C, has a special place among the books of saints. Common to this and other works is not only the religious background, but an interest in reflecting contemporary history. For this reason they are outstanding sources for details of everyday life in the Merov-

ingian period. The second great literary genre was history. The key work here is the 'History of the Franks' by Bishop Gregory of Tours, who has already been mentioned. The second important work of history of the period was completed *c.* 660; it is the 'Four Books of Chronicles' of the historian known as Fredegar.

511: After the death of Clovis in this year, the empire was divided among his four sons: Childebert established his residence in Paris, Theoderich I in Reims, Chlodomer in Orléans and Chlothar I in Soissons. Childebert commissioned a massive cathedral dedicated to St.Stephen on the site of the later church of Notre-Dame. Other churches and monasteries were also founded. The division of the kingdom of the Franks was consistent with old Germanic law: the 'health' of the royal line should remain fruitful without limitation. Despite the division, the ideal of empire was not called into question; the four kings retained an essentially identical foreign policy. In 531 Theoderich and Chlothar defeated Thuringia, and the conquest of the empire of Burgundy was complete by 534. From 536 a large part of S. Germany between the Neckar and the Danube came under Frankish rule. Bavaria remained relatively independent, and N. Germany also avoided domination by the Franks. In 537 the Ostrogoth king Witigis handed over Provence to the Franks in exchange for assistance in the struggle against Byzantium, thus giving the Franks access to the Mediterranean. In 539 Theoderich attacked Italy, defeated the Ostrogoths and the Byzantines, and for a time conquered Venetia and parts of Liguria. An attempt on the empire of the Visigoths (Saragossa was besieged in 542) failed, however. In 561, on the death of Chlothar I, who had managed to unite the empire under a single ruler once more, the Franks

The Panthéon ▷

were the only great power in Western Europe to be taken seriously.

561: This year saw the beginning of a confused period. After the death of Chlothar I the empire was divided among his four sons, and when one of them died in 567 it was once more divided among the remaining three. The subdivisions of Neustria (capital Paris), Austrasia (Reims/Metz) and Burgundy (Orléans) came into being. Politics were dominated for almost half a century (until 613) by quarrels over the original fourth part of the empire. The principal protagonists in this period were not the kings and child kings, but the inimical queens Fredegunde of Neustria and Brunhilde of Austrasia/Burgundy. The history of the times, written by Bishop Gregory of Tours, is a horrific story of assassination, intrigue, quarrels between relations, fornication, excess and treachery. Inner conflict led to endangered frontiers: the Bretons invaded increasingly frequently in the West, the Lombards raided the S., Frankish counter-attacks were unsuccesful; the E. front was threatened by the Avars.

613&14: The mayors of the palace established themselves as the real holders of power. In 613 Chlothar II came to power as the result of a revolt among the nobility and had Queen Brunhilde tortured to death. The period of confusion seemed to be over, but as little as a year later the Frankish nobility forced Chlothar to issue the 'Edictum Chlotharii' in exchange for their help when he took over power; power in the state was transferred largely to the land-owning nobility, and the palace mayors, administrators of the royal household and leaders of the king's mounted retinue, secured wide-ranging powers for themselves. Territorial struggles broke out again in 639, this time not between the kings, but between the palace mayors.

Social structure: In the Merovingian empire the king ruled over a kind of military aristocracy recruited from the Frankish retinue, and the nobility whose titles depended on his service, active largely as adminstrators, and mainly Gallo-Roman. Both groups owned land presented by the king for services rendered. As a result of the division of empire and quarrels between individual kings, the military aristocracy and the adminstrative nobility became more and more important; power passed increasingly from the crown to the nobility.

The ecclesiastical aristocracy also had rich possessions. From the 7C they were frequently exempted from taxation and received royal privileges. In the 7C the practice was established that bishops were nominated by kings, often regardless of their ecclesiastical capabilities. This led to the increasingly national nature of the Merovingian church, and the clergy were less and less under papal control.

687: This year saw the beginning of the rise of the Carolingians. The power struggle between Austrasia and Neustria was resolved by the victory at Tertry of the Austrasian mayor of the palace Pépin of Héristal. He united Austrasia and Neustria under his rule and took over real power in the Frankish kingdom, leaving the Merovingian kings as mere puppets: 'rotten kings' was the judgement of a contemporary biographer. The mythic 'king's health' of the Merovingians remained uncontested, however.

Pépin of Héristal's victory at Tertry transferred the Frankish power base from Neustria (Paris) to Austrasia, from the West to the East. The rise of the Carolingians, whose ancestor was Pépin of Héristal, began in Metz and Trier, between Rhine, Moselle and Maas. Pépin's great-grandson was Charlemagne, who gave his name to the Carolingian dynasty. Despite the transfer of power the economic rise of Paris continued.

714: After the death of Pépin of Héristal his illegitimate son Charles Mar-

Notre-Dame, St-Etienne portal ▷

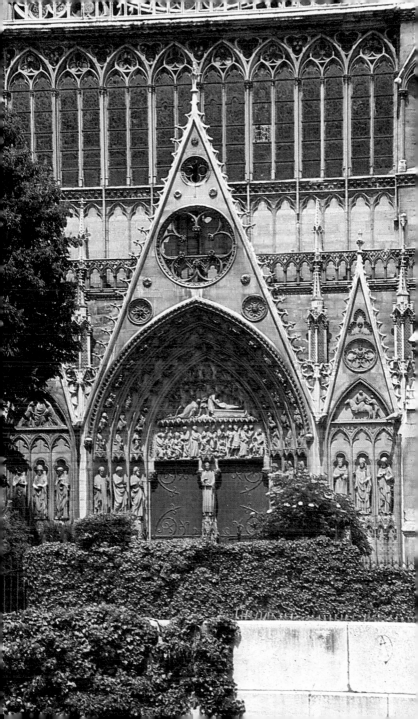

tel, the 'Hammer', established himself as mayor of the palace of the entire Frankish empire and further extended the power of the Carolingians. He strengthened Frankish domination in Bavaria, Alemania and North Friesland, stopped the western march of the Muslims in Tours and Poitiers in 732, and was known from then onwards as the 'saviour of the West'. He ruled from 737 without a Merovingian shadow king. In 739 Pope Gregory III sought his protection against the Lombards, and thus recognized the mayor of the palace as the real ruler of the Frankish empire. The system of fiefs was also developed under Charles Martel: his retinue were given the fief of land in return for military services rendered.

751: An 'instruction' from Pope Zacharias led to the last Merovingian shadow king's being shorn of his hair and sent into a monastery: the Merovingian 'king's health', of which the external sign was splendid hair, was extinguished. Mayor of the place Pépin the Short had himself anointed king in the Old Testament manner by Boniface, the 'Apostle of the Germans'. Thus the Carolingians, originally mayors of the palace, became kings. The anointing was repeated in 754 in Rome, by Pope Stephen II.

768: Pépin the Short, the first Frankish king of the Carolingian dynasty, died in Saint-Denis, near Paris. His successors were his sons Charlemagne and Karlmann. Charlemagne became sole ruler after the death of Karlmann in 771. His residence was not Paris, but Aix-la-Chapelle; Paris became the residence of a count.

845: The Normans conquered and plundered Paris for the first time. Further raids followed in 856 and 861. In the same year the Irish philosopher Johannes Scotus Eriugena was called to the court school in Paris by the West-Frankish king and Holy Roman Emperor Charles the Bald. Scotus wrote his magnum opus, the five books of 'De divisione naturae' in which he described the world as a manifestation of the person of God.

866: Robert the Strong, the first Duke of Francia to be named as such,

Saint-Germain-en-Laye, Château Museum, Brassempouy Venus (l), Espelugues horse (r)

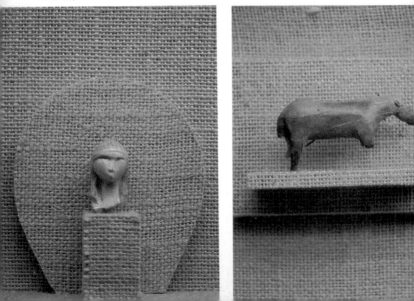

defeated the Normans at the Loire. The Duchy of Francia was one of France's greatest medieval crown fiefs; at the height of its power it included the counties of Paris, Orléans, Melun and Estampes, and fiefdom over the counties of Anjou, Touraine, Blois, Chartres, Gatinais, Maine and Senlis. Robert the Strong was at the same time the first named Capetian, later the royal house. The first three generations of Capetians are also called Robertines after him.

885&886: Count Odo (Eudes) of Paris, the son of Robert the Strong, defended the fortified city successfully against the Normans for the first time (the siege lasted thirteen months).

888: After the deposition of Charles the Fat the Western Frankish leaders chose Count Odo of Paris as the first non-Carolingian to be king of the Western Frankish empire. Odo was faced with violent resistance from the great vassals and the Normans, until in 893 Archbishop Fulko of Reims crowned Charles II, known as the Simple, as king. In 897 Odo handed over to him by treaty all the land between the Seine and the Maas.

911: The West Frankish king Charles the Simple recognized by treaty the Danish Normans' acquisition of land in the Seine estuary. Rollo, the leader of the Normans, was granted the land in fief and committed himself to the defence of the realm. This was the origin of Normandy, and marked the end of Norman raids on Paris.

921: King Charles the Simple, as 'rex Francorum occidentalium' ('King of the Western Franks') and King Henry I, as 'rex Francorum orientalium' ('King of the Eastern Franks') recognized the independence of the Western and Eastern Frankish empires in the Treaty of Bonn. From this point it is possible to speak of the kingdom of 'France'.

922: The French nobles proclaimed Robert I, Odo's younger brother, king of France in Reims. At first Robert had declared himself subject to the Carolingian Charles III, but rose against him in 920. This second attempt by the Capetians to seize the crown of France ended a year later: on

Jouarre, St-Paul chapel, crypt, St-Ozanne

16 June 923 Robert fell in the Battle of Soissons against Charles.

946: Hugo the Great, Duke of Francia and Count of Paris, the son of Robert I, drove out the Carolingian King Louis IV; the German King Otto I, related by marriage to Hugo and Louis, undertook a French campaign and restored Louis to his former rights.

987: After the death of King Louis V, to whom he had been guardian, Hugo Capet, successor since 956 of Hugo the Great as Count of Paris and Duke of Francia, was chosen King of France by the electoral assembly of the great crown vassals in Senlis, and crowned in Reims. He founded the Royal dynasty of Capetians. The name is derived from 'cappa', the ecclesiastical garment which Hugo had worn as lay abbot of the monastery of Saint-Martin in Tours. His predecessors were known as 'Robertines'.

Although Hugh Capet and his successors reigned mainly from Orléans, Hugo pronounced Paris capital of France, extended the city and granted it new privileges. A royal Prévôt (pro-

Saint-Denis, Charlemagne's crown

vost) took over the administration of civil and criminal justice, the right to exploit taxes and leadership of the police; a merchant Prévôt was responsible for the administration of the city.

1070: Under Philip I the kings of France visited the capital, Paris, more frequently, but the actual residence remained in Orléans.

1108: Louis VI, the Fat (le Gros) succeeded his father as king. In numerous struggles he defeated his unruly vassals in his possessions of Ile de France and Orléanais, and created the basis of a strong kingdom. The reign of Louis VI was the start of the confirmation of Capetian power.

1113: Louis VI founded the abbey of Saint-Victor. The philosophical and theological school of Saint-Victor, named after this Augustinian abbey, strove to unite the academic disciplines of scholasticism and theological mysticism. The most important protagonists were Guillaume de Champeaux (d.1154), Hugues de Saint-Victor (1096–1141) and Richard de Saint-Victor (d. Paris 1173).

1137: Louis VII, the Young, succeeded his father on the throne. He married Duchess Eleanor of Acquitaine, whose court in Poitiers became a centre of courtly culture (troubadour poetry). His adviser, Abbott Suger of Saint-Denis, exercised a decisive influence on French politics. Building of the monastery of Saint-Denis also began in his reign; the monastery was to be a major influence on the development of Gothic architecture. In 1152 Louis VII and Eleanor were separated; she then married Henry Plantagenet, Count of Anjou (King Henry II of England from 1154). This marriage increased English influence on the continent, but also led to numerous wars between France and England. Henry II swore an oath of fealty to his French possessions in 1154, but war soon broke out, resulting in the loss of western and south-western France to England.

1141: Louis the Young granted the citizens of Paris a concession to build a harbour by the Place de Grève.

1142: Death of the theologian and philosopher Peter Abelard, the principal exponent of early scholasticism; a year before his teachings had been pronounced heretical at the Council of Sens. Abelard, who taught dialectics and theology in Paris and other places, had collected numerous pupils around himself in the French capital, including the later Pope Celestine II, Peter Lombard and Berengar of Tours, the scholasticists, and Arnold of Brescia, the preacher of reform. Abelard is famous for his love of the seventeen-year-old Héloïse; her uncle, Canon Fulbert, had Abelard castrated to make him canonically incapable of achieving ecclesiastical honours.

1160: Death in Paris of the Italian scholasticist and Bishop of Paris Peter Lombard. His theological work 'The Four Books of Sentences' laid the basis of dogma for subsequent centuries.

1163: Laying of the foundation stone of the Gothic cathedral of Notre-Dame (completed in the 13C). The school of Notre-Dame was named after it; this was a group of composers (chorales) which existed from c. 1160 to 1250; outstanding figures were Leoninus and Perotinus Magnus.

1170: Confirmation of the merchants' freedom privileges; they gradually established communal autonomy. Paris was not formally granted a charter.

1180: Accession of Philip II (Philip-Augustus). He is considered the architect of French unity. By 1206 he had driven the English from their French possessions. French dominance in Europe began after Philip's victory over King John Lackland at Bouvines in 1216.

1200: Philip-Augustus had the streets of Paris paved, built the old Louvre ('Louverie' = hunters' meeting-place) as his castle and built a wall around the N. part of the town (1190–1210), which had c. 100,000 inhabitants.

The monastic and episcopal schools in the city, which were already famous for teachers like Peter Lombard and Peter Abelard, were united c. 1200 as a 'studium generale' (university); it soon had 20,000 students and achieved an outstanding reputation, particularly in the field of theology.

1217: The Mendicant Order of Dominicans (Jacobins) opened its first school in Paris, followed by the Franciscans (Cordeliers).

1223: Louis VIII, the Lion, succeeded his father Philip-Augustus as king of France without election, thus establishing hereditary monarchy in France.

1229: The Albigensian Wars, which had broken out in 1209, were ended by the Treaty of Paris between the French crown and Count Raymond VIII of Toulouse. Victories over the Albigensians were the basis of the power of the French crown in S. France; this victory was also the victory of the 'langue d'oïl' (French as it was spoken N. of the Loire, centred in

Musée de Cluny, originals from the Gallery of Kings

Musée Rodin, the Burghers of Calais, Rodin

Paris, over the 'langue d'oc' (the language of the S.).

1230: Arrival of the German Dominican Albertus Magnus in Paris; he held the chair of theology at the university from 1244–8.

1236: The English scholastic philosopher and theologian Alexander of Hales, the founder of the older Franciscan School, joined the Franciscan Order in Paris. He spent almost all his life in Paris, where he studied and taught (d.1245 in Paris).

1240: Saint Louis introduced an appeal court in Paris, swore in notaries, gave artists and craftsmen a constitution with rules and organized a police force. He also commissioned the Gothic Sainte-Chapelle.

1250: The city finally settled into the tripartite structure by which it is still to a large extent dominated: the Cité with royal and episcopal residences, the 'Ville', the merchant and bourgeois area on the right bank of the river, and the 'Université' on the left bank (the modern Quartier Latin).

1252: Thomas Aquinas, Dominican, scholasticist philosopher and theologian, who had studied under Albertus Magnus in Paris, started teaching in Paris (1252–6 and 1269–72).

1257: Robert le Sorbon, Saint Louis' court chaplain, established an institute for poor students of theology (Pope Clement IV's confirmatory Bull dates from 1268). As the Sorbonne this college became one of the most famous schools of theology, and later universities, in the world. In the same year the Italian theologian, philosopher and mystic John of Fidanza (St.Bonaventure) became the seventh general of the Franciscan Order, which he directed principally from Paris.

1296: Upkeep of roads, the town wall, quays, harbours, fountains and the

Joan of Arc

Temple de l'Oratoire, Colligny monument

sewerage system became the responsibility of a council of twenty-four. Paris had *c.* 130,000 inhabitants, which made it one of the most populous cities in Europe.

1302: Philip IV, the Fair, finally moved Parliament, the supreme court, to Paris.

1307: Philip the Fair, in a single day's raid, had all the Knights Templar arrested and their assets confiscated. The reason for this move was rumours about heresy, immorality and unnatural ritual in the Order.

1328: With the death of Charles IV, the last of the Capetian kings, the House of Valois came to power, in the person of Philip VI, nephew of his predecessor Philip the Fair. The House of Valois ruled until 1589.

1337: Beginning of the Hundred Years War between England and France; it continued until 1453, and Paris suffered a great deal in the course of it. The war was caused by the English King Edward III's claim to the throne of France.

1348: The Black Death claimed a third of the inhabitants of Paris.

1349: King Philip VI acquired the Dauphiné from the Count of Vienne and conferred it upon the heir to the throne as an apanage to secure succession according to rank. From then onwards the heir to the French throne was known as the Dauphin.

1356: The French were heavily defeated at the Battle of Maupertuis by the English under Edward, the Black Prince. King John the Good was taken prisoner by the English, and his son Charles the Wise took over the business of government.

As a result of this defeat Paris became the centre of the first great rising of the Third Estate against the crown:

Etienne Marcel, Prévôt of the merchants of Paris, at an assembly of the Estates of the Empire in Paris, demanded an end to the malpractices of feudal kingship, dismissal of numerous royal officials and the establishment of a board to supervise finance, made up from the Estates; Marcel received firm support from the Bishop of Laon. Charles the Wise conceded at first, but then resisted Marcel's attempts to subjugate the king's power to the Estates of the Empire. Marcel then took over the city, with the help of Charles the Bad of Navarre, supported by a band of armed craftsmen and workers, and murdered Marshalls Clermont and Conflans before the eyes of the Dauphin on 22 February 1358. Five months later Marcel was killed by Jean Maillart, the leader of the moderate party, with a battleaxe, and Paris surrendered to the Dauphin.

1357: Etienne Marcel bought the house 'aux Piliers' on the Place de la Grève, to serve as the seat of the city representatives. The Hôtel de Ville was later built on this site.

1358: The Jacquerie peasants' revolt (Jacques Bonhomme is a name associated with simpletons) seized Paris, the Ile de France and other areas of Northern France. The peasants, exploited by the nobility, brought to their knees by the ravages of war with the English and terrorized by robber bands, rose in May 1358 against the nobility, who had not even been able to defend them against the English. The Jacquerie began in the Ile de France, but soon spread to Picardy, Champagne and the Orléanais. Palaces were stormed, and the nobility fell. Many cities sympathized with the peasants, but Etienne Marcel, leader of the Estates' revolt in Paris (see 1536), made the mistake of declaring solidarity with them without offering sufficient support. The nobility, on the other hand, united against the common danger

◁ *Carnavalet, Louis XIV*

and the ill-fed and imperfectly armed peasants were mercilessly mown down. Result: great tracts of land were depopulated, the peasants became even more serf-like and the nobility increased in confidence.

1367: Charles V had the N. ring wall of the city, which now had 140,000 inhabitants, extended (1367–82), and commissioned a deep outer moat.

1370: Laying of the foundation stone of the Bastille, a fortress which was to become a symbol of Royal despotism. New city gates were also built from 1370 onwards: Porte Sainte-Antoine by the Bastille, Porte du Temple near the old Templar building, Porte Saint-Martin, and the Portes Saint-Denis, Montmartre and Saint-Honoré.

1382: Maillotin uprising in protest against new tax demands. (The leaders were called Maillotins after the lead hammers which they used as weapons.) The revolt was bloodily crushed, the city constitution was suspended and Prévôts and magistrates were not appointed again until 1411.

After this the king abandoned his residence in the Palais in the Cité and moved to the Louvre, which new building had almost turned into a fortress, and to the Hôtel Saint-Pol near the Bastille. For emergencies he had caused Vincennes to be extended as fortress on the scale of a small town (completed 1373; at the time the most modern fortress in Europe).

1411: Start of the civil war between the Armagnacs (supporters of the Duke of Orléans) and the Burgundians (the Duke of Burgundy's party); Paris took the side of Burgundy. This bloody civil war was sparked off by the enmity between the duchies of Burgundy and Orléans, which had led to the murder of the Duke of Orléans in 1407. Duke John the Fearless of Burgundy admitted having commissioned the deed, which he defended as tyrannicide in a speech in Paris. King Charles the Mad did not declare him-

Blaise Pascal monument ▷

self unequivocally for either party during the conflict.

1413: The people stormed the Bastille, under the leadership of the butcher and skinner Simon Caboche, in order to compel Charles the Mad to reform taxation in favour of the lower classes and small businesses. The revolutionaries, known as Cabochiens after their leader, conducted a reign of terror in Paris and had the Armagnacs (followers of the Duke of Orléans) slaughtered en masse, including the Regent, Count Bernard of Armagnac; the Dauphin was driven out of Paris.

1419: Duke John the Fearless of Burgundy was murdered in the course of peace negotiations with the Dauphin Charles (VII). The Burgundians, who had occupied Paris, concluded an alliance with the English.

1420: The Burgundians handed Paris over to the English. The city remained an English possession until 1436.

1429: Joan of Arc successfully stormed Paris. She was wounded at the Porte Saint-Honoré.

1436: The Count of Dunois regained Paris from the English; Charles VII did not move his court back to Paris, but continued to reside in Troyes. There was no court life in Paris for more then a hundred years (until 1528).

1453: End of the Hundred Years War between France and England, with no formal peace treaty. The English had lost all their territories in France with the exception of Calais.

1463: The poet François Villon, the first French lyricist of modern times, (d. *c.* 1493 in Paris) was exiled from Paris for ten years for killing a priest. Nothing was heard of him after this date. His main work was the ballad

Jacques Louis David 'Coronation of Napoleon' (r), above (r:) 'General Bonaparte' (l:) 'Empress Josephine' by Pierre-Paul Prud'hon (all in the Louvre) ▷

Bibliothèque Nationale, Voltaire (l), Versailles, Louis XVI in the Salon d'Apollon (r)

collection known as the 'Grand Testament'.

1464: Introduction of letter post.

1470: First printing press installed in the Sorbonne, about twenty-five years after the invention of printing by Johannes Gutenberg.

1528: Francis I made Paris the capital of France again. Numerous Renaissance palaces sprang up in and around Paris. The king lived in the Hôtel de Tournelles and the Louvre.

1534: Ignatius Loyola, the priest and mystic who had already been summoned before the Inquisition on numerous occasions, founded the Society of Jesus (Jesuits), together with six companions; the Society was soon to dominate the Counter-Reformation in Europe.

1540: Death in Paris of the Italian painter Rosso Fiorentino, the founder of the Fontainebleau School.

1546: Start of the rebuilding of the Louvre as a modern palace.

1547: Death of Francis I, in whose reign absolutist tendencies had been strengthened. He was succeeded by his son Henry II, who was married to Catharine de'Medici. He was strongly influenced by his mistress, Diane de Poitiers.

1549: The poet Joachim du Bellay, with Pierre Ronsard the most important of the 'Pléiade' poets, published his pamphlet 'Deffence et Illustration de la langue françoise', in which he suggested that French, hitherto despised as barbaric, was a suitable vehicle for artistic expression. Du Bellay's manifesto for a French national language was the herald of French classicism.

1553: Death of the poet François Rabelais, author of 'Gargantua et Pantagruel'.

Versailles, Marie Antoinette and Children

1559: King Henry II sustained a fatal wound in a tournament in Paris, which led to the imposition of a ban on jousting. He was succeeded by his son Francis II, who was married to Mary Queen of Scots, under the guardianship of Catharine de'Medici. After Francis' death in 1560 the minor Charles IX became king.

1561: Death of the typographer Claude Garamond in Paris (Garamond, Antiqua, Cursive, Grecs du Roi and other typefaces).

1563: Queen Catharine de'Medici had the Tuileries built as a dower house about 1,500 yards W. of the Louvre. The building of this little palace ouside the city walls stimulated the

Carnavalet, portrait of Mme Récamier (1777–1849), an adversary of Napoleon I ▷

rise of the Faubourg Saint-Honoré (Saint-Roch chapel built in 1578).

1572: Murder in Paris at the so-called Parisian Blood Wedding (St.Batholomew's Eve) of about 3,000 Huguenots, including their leader Gaspard de Coligny. Queen Catharine de'Medici was responsible for the massacre.

1578: King Henry II commissioned the Pont Neuf (1578–1607), the longest bridge in Paris. It connects the two banks of the Seine via the tip of the Ile de la Cité.

1585: After the death of the last Valois heir to the throne the so-called War of the Three Henries broke out: the Huguenot leader King Henry of Navarre, a Bourbon, had the strongest claim to the throne, but was not a Catholic. In order to gain the crown the Catholic Duc de Guise, Henry I of Lorraine, concluded an alliance with Catholic Spain and brought about the deposition of the reigning King, Henry III.

1588: King Henry III was driven from Paris in the so-called Revolt on the Barricades. He fell into the hands of his opponent Henri de Guise, but was able to murder him.

1589: King Henry III, the last ruler of the House of Valois, and in league with the Huguenots, was murdered at the siege of Paris, then dominated by the Catholics under the fanatical Jacques Clément. King Henry of Navarre was not able to enter the city until 1594.

1590: Death in Paris of the sculptor Germain Pilon, supreme master of French sculpture between Mannerism and baroque. His principal work is the marble tomb of King Henry II and Catharine de'Medici in Saint-Denis. In the same year the distinguished surgeon Ambroise Paré died in Paris: he had improved the treatment of gunshot wounds (treatment with ointment instead of hot oil), and invented artificial limbs and other orthopaedic apparatus.

1594: Henry of Navarre embraced Catholicism with the words 'Paris vaut bien une messe', whereupon Catholic-dominated Paris opened its gates to him. The former Huguenot leader was crowned as Henry IV. He was the founder of the Bourbon dynasty, which reigned until the Revolution in 1789, and then from 1814–48.

1598: King Henry IV guaranteed equal rights and freedom of belief to the Huguenots by passing the Edict of Nantes. The Edict marked the end of the Huguenot wars.

1599: The office of 'Grand Voyeur de France' was created, alongside the Prévôts; his duties included supervision of public streets and squares. Replanning of the city started under King Henry IV.

1605: Construction of the first covered sewer in Paris (égout de Ponceau). The Place Royale (now Place des Vosges) was the first square in Paris to be regular in design. The Hôtels of the nobility grew up around it, forming the Marais district.

1610: King Henry IV murdered in Paris by the Catholic fanatic François Ravaillac. Louis XIII, a minor, was under the guardianship of his mother, Maria de'Medici, and did not actually accede to the throne until 1617.

1615: Queen Maria de'Medici built the Palais du Luxembourg as a dower house.

1622: Paris became an archbishopric. Until this date it had been dependent on Sens.

1624: Cardinal Richelieu took over the business of government as First Minister of King Louis XIII. His goal was the achievement of French hegemony in Europe. Within France he strengthened the centralized power of the king and established a structure of absolute rule (centralization, restriction of the privileges of the nobility, military and political elimination of Protestantism). Cardinal Richelieu was the first of a line of great leading French statesmen.

1626: Angélique Arnaud, who had become abbess of the convent of Port-Royal at the age of ten, became abbess of the Parisian daughter convent of

Port-Royal, which she made into a centre of Jansenism.

1630: Richelieu had the castles of the nobility razed to the ground and forbade duelling. The nobility was stripped of power.

1635: Richelieu founded the 'Académie Française' for the cultivation of the French language in Paris by expanding a private association; it became the supreme authority on French language and literature.

After litigation between the cathedral chapter and the royal bridgebuilders, the nobility began to settle on the Ile Saint-Louis, S. of the noble Marais quarter.

1639: The Italian philosopher and Utopian Tommaso Campanella died in a dungeon in Paris; he had written his major work 'Civitas Solis' while behind bars. Many important French works were published abroad during the period of absolutism, for example the philosophical treatise 'Discours de la Méthode' by René Descartes, containing the key sentence 'Cogito ergo sum' ('I think therefore I am'; published anonymously in Leyden in 1637).

1642: After the death of Cardinal Richelieu, Cardinal Jules Mazarin took over the business of government, ruling from 1643 on behalf of Louis XIV, a minor. In the same year Jean-Jaqcues Olier became the incumbent of Saint-Sulpice. He founded the Society of the Priests of Saint-Sulpice (Sulpicians), the members of which undertook world-wide missionary work. At this time Paris was the centre of a spiritual rebirth of French Catholic theology, known as the Ecole Française. The Eudists and the Oratory, two communities of priests, also disseminated the thinking of the Ecole Française.

1648: Revolt of the masses ('Day of the Barricades') against the rule of the Queen Mother Anne of Austria and the chief minister Cardinal Mazarin. The Parisian parliament (court), the population of Paris and the French aristocracy combined as the Fronde in revolt against absolute monarchy. The Fronde rebellion, which lasted until 1653, was the last revolt of the Estates against absolute monarchy.

In the same year the painter-brothers Antoine and Louis le Nain, famous

Carnavalet, model of the Bastille destroyed in 1789

for their pictures of peasants, religious pictures and portraits, fell victim to the plague in Paris.

1649: The royal family fled to Saint-Germain in the face of fighting on the French barricades (now Saint-Germain-en-Laye).

1651: Louis XIV was declared of age and took over the business of government. After the collapse of the Fronde rebellion, the court moved back to Paris from Saint-Germain. In 1653 Cardinal Jules Mazarin, who had fled after the Fronde rebellion of January 1649, returned from exile in Cologne. Absolute monarchy emerged from the rebellion even stronger.

1661: On the death of Cardinal Mazarin, Louis XIV took up the reigns of power. In the same year work started on the palace of Versailles, the high baroque and neoclassical style of which set the pattern for baroque palaces throughout Europe.
In the same year Louis ordered the arrest of finance minister Nicolas Fouquet, accused of embezzling enormous sums.

1666: Minister Colbert founded the 'Académie Royale des Sciences'. Six

Ecole des Beaux Arts

years earlier he had founded the 'Académie de France' in Rome. The 'Académie d'Architecture' was founded in 1671, under the direction of François Blondel.

1673: Molière, comic dramatist and actor, the founder of classical French comedy and one of the greatest modern European comic writers, died on stage in Paris.

1680: Louis XIV moved the seat of government to Versailles. With the exception of the Régence period (1715–23) the kings of France lived in Versailles until the time of the Revolution. Although the Roi Soleil did not live in Paris his building activities left their mark on the city: he had the city wall pulled down and built promenades (boulevards) in its place, the Tuileries gardens and the great Avenue des Champs-Élysées were laid out, the first street lighting was installed in Paris, and almost 150 new streets and fountains were built, the Saint-Denis, Saint-Antoine, Saint-Martin and Saint-Bernard gates were beautified by the addition of triumphal arches, sick soldiers were accommodated in the Hôtel des Invalides, vagabonds and beggars found refuge in the Hôpital Général, fallen women were placed in the Hôpital de la Salpêtrière.

1685: Louis XIV revoked the Edict of Nantes, which caused a mass exodus of Huguenots from France to Germany and Holland.

1687: Death in Paris of the composer Jean-Baptiste Lully, founder of French opera and a national style in French music. His orchestral style retained a firm hold well into the 18C.

1715: Louis XIV died in Versailles after reigning for fifty years; he left the state finances in complete disarray. He was succeeded by his great-grandson Louis XV, at first under the regency of Duke Philip II of Orléans (until 1723, the so-called Régence). The Regent made Paris his seat, and so the nobility settled in the exclusive Faubourg Saint-Germain.

1720: Financial measures taken by the

Scot John Law and condoned by the Regent led to the first inflation of paper money, which reduced countless people to penury.

1724: Foundation of the Paris Bourse. The Quartier Saint-Honoré became the citadel of the financial aristocracy.

1732: Death in Paris of the cabinet-maker André Charles Boulle. In 1672 he had been named 'master-carpenter to the King' and had furnished Versailles, Fontainebleau and the Louvre.

1745: Jeanne Antoinette Poisson became the official mistress of Louis XV and received the title Marquise de Pompadour.

1751: Appearance of the first volume of Diderot and d'Alembert's 'Encyclopédie', including work by the leading figures of French Enlightenment: Buffon, Condillac, Duclos, Dumarsais, Holbach, Marmontel, Montesquieu, Morellet, Rousseau, Voltaire etc.

1752: This year saw the beginning of intense building activity by Louis XV, who had held back until then. It produced the Ecole Militaire on the Champ de Mars, the palaces on the Place Louis XV (now Place de la Concorde, the Mint (Hôtel des Monnaies) etc. The best-known architect of the period was Jacques Germain Soufflot (church of Sainte-Geneviève, now Panthéon).

1757: Oil-fired street lighting introduced in the city.

1774: Death of Louis XV. He was succeeded by Louis XVI, husband of Marie Antoinette, the daughter of the Austrian Empress Maria Theresa.

1782: First pavements built.

1783: A royal decree determined that streets must be at least 33 ft. wide and houses not more than 60 ft. high. On 15 October the physicist Jean-François Pilâtre de Rozier undertook the first manned air journey in a balloon. The brothers Etienne Jacques and Michel Joseph de Montgolfier had released the first unmanned hot air balloon from the market place in Annolay; it reached a height of almost 6,000 ft.

1784: Erection of the Parisian customs walls.

1789: The Revolution overthrew the

Dôme des Invalides, façade

Dôme des Invalides, sarcophagus of Napoleon I

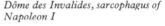

Ancien Régime. The storming of the Bastille on July 14 marked the actual beginning of the Revolution, and the date was declared a French national holiday in 1880.

1791: France became a hereditary constitutional monarchy. From this point the king was called 'King of the French' ('Roi des Français') rather than 'King of France'.

1792: Proclamation of the First Republic after the deposition of King Louis XVI.

1793: Robespierre overthrew the Republic. The reign of terror of the 'Committee of Public Safety' began; Louis XVI and Marie Antoinette were executed on the guillotine.

1794: Robespierre himself died on the guillotine. This was the beginning of the final phase of the Revolution, in which the bourgeoisie won through.

1795: Proclamation of the bourgeois constitution (Directoire).

1797: The Directoire was overthrown by a coup d'état on 18 Fructidor, with the assistance of General Napoleon Bonaparte among others; the Directoire continued to rule as a dictatorship, however.

1799: Napoleon Bonaparte finally overthrew the Directoire in the coup d'état of 18 Brumaire and established a consular constitution according to which he, as First Consul, had executive power and rights of legislation. Shortly afterwards he declared the Revolution concluded.

1800: Napoleon founded the Légion d'Honneur, the most important French order, and had himself declared consul for life by plebiscite. During the reign of Napoleon, who lived in the Tuileries, the Arc de Triomphe and the triumphal arch at the Tuileries palace were built, the Louvre was turned into a museum, the Rue de Rivoli came into being, high quays were erected in the Cité after severe flooding, and the Pont des Arts, Pont de la Cité, Pont d'Austerlitz and Pont d'Iéna built. Any treasures Napoleon acquired in the course of his conquests were brought back to Paris.

1804: Napoleon Bonaparte had himself crowned hereditary Emperor of the French ('Empereur des Français') in the cathedral of Notre-Dame, after being anointed by Pope Pius VII. The

View of the façade of the Eglise de la Madeleine

Civil Code, introduced in the same year, influenced legislation throughout Europe, and is to a large extent still valid.

1806: Sixteen Western German Estates of the Empire united under the protectorate of Napoleon in the Rhine Alliance and seceded from the Holy Roman Empire. A little later Franz II relinquished the imperial crown and declared the Empire void.

1810: After his divorce from Joséphine Beauharnais, Napoleon married Marie Louise, daughter of the Austrian Emperor Franz I.

1814: Entry of the allied troops of Prussia, Austria, Russia and Great Britain into Paris. Napoleon declared the new French régime under Talleyrand void, and made the Bourbon Louis XVIII, the brother of the guillotined Louis XVI, king. Napoleon abdicated, and was presented the island of Elba as his residence, as sovereign with imperial title.

1815 Napoleon tried to seize power once more. The adventure of the Hundred Days ended in defeat by England and Prussia at the Battle of Waterloo (Belle-Alliance).

1830: Renewed uprising of the bourgeoisie against the monarchy. Charles X was overthrown in the July Revolution, Duke Louis Philippe was chosen as king ('citizens' king'). In the following centuries Paris became a centre for political emigrants from Germany (Heinrich Heine, Ludwig Börne, Karl Marx etc.).

1832: 200,000 people fell victim to a cholera epidemic.

1835: Unsuccessful attempt on the life of King Louis Philippe, who reacted with a series of measures to quell the liberal opposition; the freedom of the press was restricted, sanctions against affray were strengthened. Paris became a centre for various revolutionary movements: liberals, republicans, socialists, communists etc.

1837: First railway between Paris and Pecq.

1841: The outline of Paris was finally defined by 36 kilometres of fortifications, enclosing numerous suburbs.

1842: Numerous stations were built as a result of the concession for a railway network centred on Paris.

1847: The Parisian Republicans organized public 'banquettes', from which

Eglise de la Sorbonne, N. façade (l), tomb of Cardinal Richelieu (r)

they demanded extension of franchise: the first hint of further revolution.

1848: Abdication of the citizens' king, Louis-Philippe, after the February Revolution. Declaration of the Second Republic. A revolt by Parisian workers in June was bloodily suppressed. Presidential elections won by Prince Louis Napoleon Bonaparte, later Emperor Napoleon III.

1851: President Louis Napoleon had leading opposition politicians arrested, and dissolved the National Assembly (end of the Second Republic).

1852: Accession of Louis Napoleon to the imperial throne, with the security of a plebiscite voting 99 per cent in favour. This marked the foundation of the Second Empire.

1855: Prefect Haussmann started to redesign Paris as the most beautiful and beautiful capital in Europe. People were driven out of the capital, the Baron's mechanical diggers tore down entire residential quarters in order to create dead-straight boulevards, monumental perspectives and uniform façades. Paris became a city of luxury and the upper middle class, and anyone who could not afford this luxury was banished to the suburbs, the banlieue. Modern Paris is essentially the city planned and rebuilt by Baron Haussmann.

1867: The Second Empire presented itself at the height of its power at the Paris World Fair.

1870: Napoleon III declared war on Prussia. The French army capitulated after the decisive German victory at the Battle of Sedan, Napoleon was taken prisoner by the Prussians and abdicated. A little later the Third Republic was proclaimed in Paris. The new 'Government of National Defence' organized a 'people's war' against the Germans.

1871: King Wilhelm I of Prussia declared German Emperor in the Salle des Glâces in Versailles. Ten days later Paris capitulated to the Germans. In May the Commune

uprising took place in the city. This republican-revolutionary uprising, directed against asocial home policies and the Franco-Prussian armistice, was suppressed by government troops.

1873: Marshall Macmahon became President of the Republic. He had put down the revolt of the Paris Commune in 1871 and was considered a symbol of conservative order. The seat of government moved from Paris to Versailles once more.

1879: After the resignation of Marshall Macmahon the Republican Jules Grévy was elected president. This meant that figures associated with constitutional monarchy were finally replaced by the Republican coalition of the industrial bourgeoisie and the rising middle classes. Government returned to Paris. A year later 14 July, the anniversary of the Storming of the Bastille (1789), was declared a national holiday.

1883: The Orient Express started to run between Paris and the European part of the Ottoman Empire.

1889: Mass demonstrations in Paris of the anti-German Boulangistes, supporters of the former revanchist war minister Georges Boulanger, who was finally accused of an attempted coup d'état. The World Fair took place in Paris in the same year. The Eiffel Tower, built for the Fair, was considered to have paved the way for modern architecture.

1890: Heavy industry began to establish itself around the outskirts.

1894: The Jewish officer Albert Dreyfus was stripped of rank and condemned to deportation to Devil's Island for life, ostensibly for spying, but on the basis of forged documents and proceedings which were judicially untenable. The Dreyfus affair led to an acute internal conflict between conservative circles in the army, nobility, clergy and the upper middle classes, and intellectuals insisting on

St-Etienne-du-Mont, mystical wine-pressing ▷

democracy and human rights. In 1898 Emile Zola brought about a retrial, resulting in the rehabilitation of Dreyfus and the parties of the left.

1895: The first performance of a film, by the brothers Lumières, took place in Paris. The Lumières established the art of the documentary film, in which almost all shots are unposed. Paris became the centre of the film industry.

1900: The Second Summer Olympics took place in Paris as part of the World Fair. Inauguration of the first Métro service between Porte Maillot and Vincennes.

1914: After the outbreak of the First World War the French government moved to Bordeaux, as Paris was under threat from the Germans.

1918: Marshall Ferdinand Foch and the German Reichstag deputy Matthias Erzberger signed the Armistice in the forest of Compiègne.

1919: The Paris peace conference accepted the constitution of the League of Nations. On 28 June the Peace Treaty with the German Empire was signed in the Galerie des Glaces in Versailles, and the treaty with Austria was signed in Saint-Germain-en-Laye on 10 September.

1924: Seventh Summer Olympics took place in Paris. Breton published his 'Surrealist Manifesto'.

1932: Creation of the Région Parisienne, corresponding roughly to the present Ile de France.

1936: An election victory by the popular alliance of Communists, Socialists and Radical Socialists led to the formation of the first popular front government under Prime Minister Léon Blum.

1940: German troops occupied Paris without fighting. A few days later General Charles de Gaulle appealed from London for continuation of the war against the Germans and declared himself the legitimate representative of France. On 2 July the Armistice was signed between Hitler's Germany and the French government of Marshall Philippe Pétain in the forest of Compiègne, in the same railway carriage in which the armistice conditions had been presented in 1918 at the end of the First World War. On 1 July Pétain transferred the seat of government to Vichy.

1944: On 25 August US troops and the French troops of de Gaulle, head of the French government in exile, marched into Paris.

1945: De Gaulle elected head of government.

1951: France, the Federal Republic of Germany, Italy and the Benelux States signed the treaty establishing the European Coal and Steel Community in Paris.

1952: The Council of NATO decided to make Paris its headquarters. In the same year the treaty forming the European Defence Community (EDC), which provided for the deployment of national armed forces under a common supreme command, was concluded in Paris.

1958: Constitution of the Fifth Republic accepted by referendum.

1960: Paris summit conference between the USA and the USSR collapsed because of the U2 incident (Moscow shot down a US spy plane).

1961: First EEC summit conference in Paris.

1962: Protection of ancient monuments brought in line with contemporary thinking by the 'Malraux Law'.

1963: De Gaulle and Chancellor Konrad Adenauer signed the Franco-German friendship treaty in Paris (Elysée treaty).

1966: France withdrew military, but not political, support from NATO.

1968: Student demonstrations led to disturbances almost on the level of civil war, wild-cat strikes and the occupation of factories.

1975: Representatives of the Western industrialized countries, West Germany, France, Great Britain, Italy, Japan and the USA met in the

Sainte-Chapelle, upper chapel, window▷

Rambouillet Palace for the first world economic conference.

1984: Paris was plagued with strikes (car workers) and demonstrations (against new school laws), some of which were bloody (Talbot). The concept of 'new poverty' was coined.

1985: Renewed strikes against cuts by the socialist government.

Churches and Ecclesiastical Buildings

Chapelle expiatoire (Rue Pasquier, 8.Arr.): This expiatory church was commissioned by Louis XVIII in 1826 on the site of the cemetery in which the victims of the revolutionary guillotine, including Louis XVI (executed 21 January 1973) and his wife Marie Antoinette (executed 16 October 1793), were buried. It is a two-storeyed chapel with a temple-like portico and arcades running right round the building. *Relief* above the entrance showing the transport of the royal pair to Saint-Denis. Monument to the two rulers within. The former burial place is marked by an altar in the form of a sarcophagus in the lower chapel.

Chapelle des Petits-Augustins (Rue Bonaparte, 6.Arr.): This church attached to the monastery of the Barefoot Augustines, later taken over by the Petits-Augustins, was built from 1608. The monastery buildings now accommodate the *Ecole des Beaux-Arts*. The hall church has a straight apse, Doric columns and pilasters and a fine marble floor, and is now used for exhibitions of sculpture.

Eglise de l'Assomption (262 Rue Saint-Honoré): This rotunda designed by C.Errart and consecrated in 1676 has a portico consisting of Corinthian columns with pediment and a squat dome and lantern. The interior, lit by high rectangular windows, is decorated with a *dome fresco* by de la Fosse ('Assumption of the Virgin', 1676); coffered ceiling.

There are also various pictures of the life of Our Lady.

Eglise du Dôme des Invalides (Place Vauban, 7.Arr.): This harmonious, coherent baroque masterpiece, reminiscent of St.Peter's in Rome and St.Paul's Cathedral in London, was built 1680–1706 by J.Hardouin-Mansart for Louis XIV, the Roi Soleil. It was intended as a chapel royal for the soldiers' church of Saint-Louis des Invalides (q.v.) and as a brilliant focal point for the S. side of the Hôtel des Invalides (q.v.); Greek cross plan, with a circular chapel at each corner. In the N. is the sanctuary with a circular sacristy at each side. Since 1840 the Dôme des Invalides has housed the tomb of Napoleon I.

The elegant façade on the Place de Vauban has two storeys and five bays with a protruding three-bayed central section; the imposing *drum dome* is over 300 ft. high.

The *interior* is dominated by the massive rotunda, to which all other design elements are subordinated. The corners are marked by four round pilasters. The architrave spanning the arms of the cross is supported by pairs of Corinthian columns, and pilasters. The relatively low entrances to the corner chapels are framed with round arches and decorated with reliefs. In the tympanums between the arms of the cross are impressive *portraits of the Evangelists* by de la Fosse (1705). On the base from which the dome springs are twelve medallions portraying French kings. Corinthian double pilasters divide the windows. Between the bands of the first bowl of the dome are the Twelve Apostles painted by J.Jouvenet. Above that is the second bowl of the dome with de la Fosse's *fresco* (1706), striking in its tonality and artistic expressiveness; it portrays St.Louis with angels, dedicating his weapons to Christ and the

Jeu de Paume, 'La Femme Cafétière' by Cézanne ▷

Mother of God. Above this is the third bowl of the dome.

The fine sculptures in the entrance are to the side, viewed from the S. of the building. Straight ahead is Visconti's baldacchino altar, with twisted columns (1852) and cross. Above the chapel entrances are reliefs, in the sanctuary pictures of scenes from the life of St.Louis. The four corner chapels are dedicated to the church fathers, the Lady Chapel is in the W. arm of the cross, the chapel of St.Theresa in the E.

Eglise de la Madeleine (Place de la Madeleine): If you walk up the Rue Royale from the Place de la Concorde you are confronted with the impressive façade, like an ancient temple, of 'La Madeleine', as the Parisians call the church. Napoleon commissioned the building from P.Vignon in 1806, as a hall of fame for his Grande Armée. It was not completed until 1842, by J.J.M.Huvé under the citizens' king, Louis Philippe. A portico with a total of fifty-two fluted Corinthian columns almost fifty ft. high runs round the entire building, which

Eglise de la Trinité, cross

is impressive not just in its lucid, neoclassical plainness but also in its size: 354 ft. long and 141 ft. wide.

Access to the *interior* is through H.de Triqueti's massive bronze door (1837), with reliefs of the Ten Commandments. The vestibule leads to a long nave with three bays and three domes, concluding in a semicircular apse. The whole of the long interior, more like an ancient hall of fame than a church, is surrounded by galleries on Ionic columns; the walls are decorated with marble inlay work. There are single-aisled chapels at the side. The most striking feature is the *high altar*, surrounded by a wrought-iron grille and standing on a small flight of steps; the *marble statues* are the work of Marochetti (1837): the angels receive Mary Magdalene in Heaven. Ziegler's great apse painting shows Christ encircled by individuals significant in Western Christianity, from the Emperor Constantine via Frederick Barbarossa and Joan of Arc to Napoleon I and Pius VII. Under this is a mosaic of Christ and Saints by Gilbert-Martin. In the vault spandrels are Apostle statues by Prachier, Rude and Toyatier, and the walled-up lunettes have painted scenes from the life of the church patron.

Eglise de la Sorbonne (Rue de la Sorbonne, 5.Arr.): The foundation stone of the present church in the courtyard of the Sorbonne (q.v. under Secular Buildings) was laid by Cardinal Richelieu in 1635, and the church completed at the end of the century. The magnificent *façade* on the courtyard side has a portico with Corinthian columns and allegorical figures. The two-tiered façade on the street side has Corinthian columns and pilasters, and also statues. The entire building is dominated by the tambour, surrounded by decorative turrets, articulated with Corinthian pilasters and with guardian angels in the lower section; above it are the dome and lantern. The interior is plain and elegant, with Corinthian pilasters, and rectangular chapels at the four corners. The Richelieu coat of arms is seen in the area near the windows, and in the spandrels of the interestingly painted drum dome are medallions of the church fathers.

Eglise de la Trinité (Place d'Estienne d'Orves): T.Ballu built this church in neo-Renaissance style in 1863–7; it has a two-tiered façade, porch and tower. Fine marble sculptures in front of the church, allegories of chastity and innocence by Gumery on the side portals.

Notre-Dame des Blancs Manteaux (21 Rue des Blancs Manteaux, 4.Arr.): The White Augustines founded a church and monastery here in the mid 13C, later taken over by the Guillaumites, who lived by the Benedictine Rule. The present church was built in the late 17C and extended in 1863. The façade was also added at that time; it came from a Barnabite church built in 1704 and was rebuilt here. The design is simple: the lower storey has a portal with Doric columns and two side portals, above then

a frieze with vessels and foliage. The upper storey is vaulted at the sides, and has inverted scrolls at each end; it is articulated with pilasters, and has a pediment with Christ in Glory and Cherubim. The interior also gives an impression of simplicity: the choir is semicircular, and the nave has narrow side ambulatories. The cornices are supported by Corinthian pilasters and depict scenes from the Old and New Testaments. The finest and most valuable feature of the furnishings is the *rococo pulpit*, dating from 1748&9; it was brought here from Belgium in 1864, and in its design, decoration and detail is reminiscent of works of art of the type found in Franconia. At its foot are statues of the Evangelists, the sounding board has a figure of St.Michael, the dragon-slayer. The pewter and ivory decorations, some of them gilded, show the imagination and craftsmanship of the master. The medallions on the banister and body of the pulpit show scenes from the Gospels, the rear section is decorated with a fine Annunciation: as well as Mary and the Archangel it shows God the Father with sceptre on the world

Notre-Dame, rose window

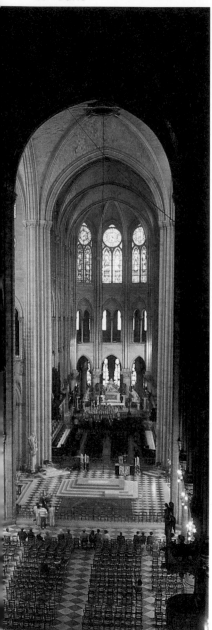

globe, with Isaiah and Solomon, both of whom had prophesied the coming of the Redeemer. Above is the Holy Spirit in the form of a dove.

Notre-Dame de Bonne Nouvelle (25 Rue de la Lune, 2.Arr.): The existing, austerely neoclassical building was built 1823–30 on the site of a 17C building pulled down after the Revolution. Anne of Austria prayed to the Mother of God for years in this church for the birth of an heir. Her wish was fulfilled on 9 September 1638, when Louis XIV, later the Roi Soleil, was born. Numerous interesting sculptures and paintings in the interior.

Notre-Dame de Lorette (18 Rue de Châteaudun, 9.Arr.): This church, reminiscent of an ancient Christian columned basilica, with delicate bell tower, was built 1823–36 by H.Lebas on the site of an earlier building destroyed during the Revolution. The façade is a portico with Corinthian columns, pediment relief (Adoration of the Virgin) and free-standing allegorical figures. The vestibule has two side chapels and leads to the nave with narrow aisles divided up almost like chapels; the square choir has a semicircular apse with fine grille. The furnishings are contemporary with thet building, and round it off in a pleasing fashion. Fine *paintings* in the style of the early Renaissance in the baptismal, communion and Lady chapels, and in the chapel of the dead.

Notre-Dame de Paris (Ile de la Cité): The cathedral in the heart of the city, the 'historic parish of France', offers eloquent testimony the the nobility and beauty of Gothic architecture. It took almost two centuries to complete. In the long years for which it has stood it has seen significant and moving events such as the coronation of Henry VI of England at the age of nine (1431), and

of the unhappy Mary Stewart as
Queen of France (1559), the trial of
Joan of Arc (1455), services for the
victories and death of Napoleon I, and
his enthronement; he placed the
imperial crown on his own head, in
the presence of Pope Pius VII on 2
December 1804. The cathedral has
also suffered from architectural mal-
practice, decay and destruction.
During the Revolution (1789–99) it
was not only badly damaged and
plundered and declared 'Temple de la
Raison', but was even threatened with
demolition. In 1841 the publication of
Victor Hugo's novel 'Notre-Dame de
Paris' stimulated such interest in the
cathedral that the great restorer Viollet-le-Duc was commissioned to res-
tore to its former beauty for posterity.
The parvis of Notre-Dame is dominated by the majestic three-storeyed
façade, with two squat rectangular
towers. Their squatness is alleviated
by tall louvres with lavish mouldings,
and they are topped with a pierced
balustrade; they house the church
bells, famous not just for the exploits
of the unhappy Quasimodo. There is
a fine view of Paris from the left-hand
tower. There are three portals; the
central one is the *Porte du Jugement*
(1220–30), defaced in 1771 and res
tored by Viollet-le-Duc. In the
tympanum Christ as Judge of the
World with angels bearing emblems
of suffering, St.John and the Mother
of God. On the lintel St.Michael as
Weigher of Souls with the Saved and
the Damned, below this the Awaken-
ing of the Dead. In the arch reveals
heads of angels, patriarchs and
prophets. At the foot Heaven and
Hell. On the jambs, Apostles by Viollet-le-Duc with typical attributes. On
both jamb shafts the Wise and Foolish
Virgins, on the central pier Christ as
teacher. The medallions on the lower
door frame show vices and virtues. To
the right is the *Porte de Sainte-Anne*.
In the tympanum Mary Enthroned

*Notre-Dame, chapel of the Seven
Sorrows* ▷

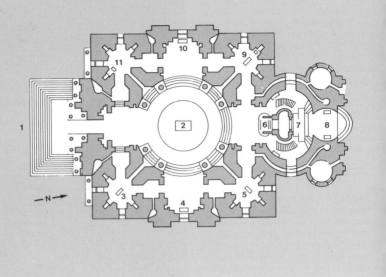

Paris, Eglise du Dôme des Invalides 1 Entrance **2** Tambour, crypt with tomb of Napoleon beneath **3** Augustine chapel with tomb of Joseph Bonaparte (1766–1844), elder brother of Napoleon and former King of Spain **4** Theresa chapel with tomb of S.Vauban (1633–1707), Louis XIV's fortress architect **5** Ambrose chapel with tomb of Marshall F.Foch (d.1929) **6** High altar by Visconti **7** Entrance to crypt **8** Tombs of Generals Duroc (d.1813) and Bertrand (d.1844) **9** Gregory chapel with tomb of Marshall Lyautey and urn containing the heart of the Grenadier de la Tour d'Auvergne **10** Lady chapel with tomb of the Vicomte de Turenne (d.1675) **11** Jerome chapel with tomb of Jérôme Bonaparte (1784–1860), youngest brother of Napoleon and former 'merry king' of Westphalia

with the Christ Child and angels, and a king and a bishop, possibly representing the individuals for whom the church was first built. In the lintel scenes from the life of St.Anne and in the arch reveals the heavenly host. The jambs show figures from the Old and New Testaments. On the left is the *Porte de la Vierge*. In the tympanum Entombment and Assumption of the Virgin, underneath prophets and kings. In the portal jambs saints, in the arch reveals the Heavenly Host, on the door jamb Virgin and Child and signs of the zodiac. Both portals have doors with fine old furniture. Above the portals is the *Gallery of the Kings* with twenty-eight figures (all replacements). The originals were taken down during the revolution, as it was not clear whether they were French or Biblical rulers. A balustrade with statues of Mary and angels and Adam and Eve forms a link with the level of the *rose window*; the side windows are set in fine tracery. The storey is topped with tall, plain tracery arches, and a gallery with the famous gargoyles.

The sides of the nave and choir have elegant flying buttresses, particularly striking in the area of the choir (14C,

Notre-Dame, choir screen, Massacre of the Innocents

by J.Ravy). Tall, slender Gothic tower with spire over the crossing; typical ornament and lavish statuary, largely restored.

The N. façade of the transept was completed *c*. 1250. It contains the *Portal du Cloître*, which formerly led to the cloister; it is lavishly articulated in the Gothic manner, has a large pediment and is flanked by two smaller portals. Old and New Testament scenes in the tympanum. On the jamb is a graceful and dignified late-13C statue of the Virgin; it is slightly damaged, but still the original. Above the portal, arches and a gigantic *rose window*, and a pediment with side turrets and another small rose. A little further to the E. is the little *Porte Rouge*, so-called because of the colour of the doors, with delicate, elaborate Gothic ornamentation and reliefs (scenes from the life of the Virgin). It is reserved for the cathedral chapter.

The S. transept façade was completed ten years later, and is similar in design.

The *interior* has a nave and four aisles and shows the simple dignity associated with Gothic cathedrals. Two aisles form an ambulatory around the entire nave and choir, separated by seventy-five round piers with lavish capitals and pointed arches. On the outer sides are twenty-nine chapels between the buttresses. This is where the so-called *May gifts* are kept: paintings presented on 1 May by the goldsmiths of the town between 1630 and 1707. The galleries have arches in pairs, or in threes on the choir side. In the clerestory, double lancet windows with rose and largely modern glass. The play of light in the very fine *stained glass* in the great transept roses is most striking when seen from the crossing. The *choir screen* still gives an impression of the ornate medieval furnishings; it was started in 1300 by P.de Chelles, continued from 1310 by J.Ravy and completed in 1351 by J.le Boutellier; it has fine tracery, and shows scenes from the Life of Christ.

The finest of the numerous works of art in the nave, aisles, transepts and chapels are the miraculous image of 'Notre-Dame de Paris', a gracious statue of the Queen of Heaven with the Christ Child (14C) on the SE pier of the crossing; the beautifully executed 18C choir stalls with scenes from the life of Mary. Behind the modern high altar is an impressive white marble Pietà (1733 by N.Coustou), flanked by dark angels and Kings Louis XII (on the right, by Coustou) and Louis XIV (on the right, 1715 by Coysevox). They are all that remains of an altar endowed by the Roi Soleil to redeem a promise made by his father on the occasion of his birth. The pulpit is also worth seeing, a masterpiece of mid-19C wood carving, and the organ.

The *treasury* is accommodated in the new sacristy, and has valuable cult vessels, gold, manuscripts and relics on display.

Notre-Dame des Victoires (Place des Petits Pères, 2. arr.): In 1629 Louis XIII laid the foundation stone of a church for the Augustinians, intended to commemorate the taking of the Protestant citadel of La Rochelle two years previously. The present building was not completed until 1740. The two-storey Renaissance façade articulated with Ionic and Corinthian pilasters is cool and austere. The interior also makes an austere impression. The walls of the deep choir are panelled in wood, some of it gilded, and decorated with symbols of the Augustinian Order. The painting above the *high altar*, which is decorated with a gilded bronze relief of the Entombment, and other pictures showing scenes from the life of St.Augustine, are by C.van Loo (1746–55). The painting over the altar shows Louis XIII and Cardinal Richelieu committing themselves and their forces into the hands of the Mother of God before the Battle of La Rochelle, and vowing to endow a church should they be granted victory. In the window above, the King is once more to be seen, with his con-

Notre-Dame, façade

sort, dedicating the symbols of his power, and with them his country, to the Mother of God. On the left-hand side altar is a good 19C stucco figure of St.Augustine. The aedicule on the *altar of Mary* is a worthy frame for the *miraculous image* of unknown origin set up here in the early 19C, a fine Queen of Heaven in stucco, with the Child, also wearing a crown; the figure is still an object of pilgrimage. The remains of the tomb of Lully, clearly once a splendid affair, are also still of interest; he was court composer to the Roi Soleil, and the tomb features a good portrait bust.

Sacré-Coeur/Basilica of the Sacred Heart (Parvis du Sacré-Coeur, 23. Arr.): After their defeat in the Franco Prussian War and the Commune revolt of 1871 the faithful patriots of the city decided to build an expiatory church; work started in 1876, to plans by P.Abadie, and was finished in 1919.

Thus the basilica in light stone, which has become one of the emblems of Paris, stands on Montmartre; it is built in the Romanesque-Byzantine style, often disrespectfully known as the 'pastrycook' style. The façade is tripartite, with domed side towers and a protruding portal section, framed with a squat aedicule and topped with a statue of the Sacred Heart in a similarly organized frame. Above this is the main dome on a tambour with round and triple arches; the two side domes follow a similar pattern. There is a fine view over Paris. Near the church is a massive free-standing campanile dating from 1912. The square interior has a choir with ambulatory and radiating chapels. It contains a striking *mosaic* showing Christ with flaming heart, surrounded by the Trinity, St.Michael, Joan of Arc, the family of Louis XIV, allegories and other figures and scenes.

Saint-Alexandre Nevski (Rue Darn, 8.Arr.): Russian Orthodox church built 1859–61 in the Russian ecclesiastical style with painted iconostasis, icons, pictures and sculptures.

Saint-Augustin (Place Saint-Augustin, 8.Arr.): V.Baltard, who

Church of Sacré-Coeur on Montmartre

*Saint-Denis du Saint-Sacrément, Descent from the Cross (1),
St.Etienne-du-Mont (r)*

was also responsible for the old market halls, built this formally interesting building 1860–70; the nave broadens into a square centrally-planned building with choir chapel. The façade has twin towers and dome with side towers in a mixture of styles.

Saint-Denis du Saint-Sacrément (Rue du Turenne, 3.Arr.): Plain church completed in 1835 in the style of an ancient Christian basilica. In the Chapel of Sainte-Geneviève is a Pietà painted by Delacroix (1844).

Saint-Esprit (Ave. Daumesnil, 12.Arr.): Modern church building dating from the first quarter of the 20C. Lavish interior with mosaics and frescos showing the works of the Holy Spirit.

Saint-Étienne du Mont (Place Sainte-Geneviève, 5.Arr.): Building began in 1492 but the church, which is a mixture of Gothic and Renaissance elements, was not completed until the early 17C. L.Guèrin's over-lavish façade combines various design approaches. In the centre is the temple-like portal, decorated with lavish frescos and carving, and above it an imaginative rosette framed with a squat aedicule, with split gable and frieze and statue niches at the sides. Above this is a pointed pediment with pilaster aedicule framing an oval oeil-de-boeuf. Behind this is the square tower with lantern. The nave has slender plain circular pillars separating it from the high aisles. There is a charming contrast between the compressed Renaissance design here and the pointed Gothic design of the choir. The crossing vault is particularly fine, with a pendant keystone

Saint-Esprit

like a drop of liquid. The spacious, slightly playful effect is emphasized by the balustrade running along the pillars in the nave and choir. The shallow-arched *rood screen* with recumbent angels separating nave and choir is an outstanding piece of 16C work. The spiral staircases at the sides, coiling around columns, repeat the pierced pattern of the balustrade on the screen. The finest features of the *furnishings* are Lestocart's pulpit (*c.* 1650), supported by a figure of Samson and crowned with a vigorously designed, lavishly decorated sounding board with trumpeting angels; the baroque organ with Christ Triumphant and angels and a 16C Entombment. There are also numerous paintings, mostly dating from the 17C, and some of the stained glass dates back to the time when the church was built. In the chapel of St.Geneviève is a reliquary of the

patron saint of Paris under a carved and partially gilded neo-Gothic baladacchino, which still attracts numerous pilgrims.

Saint-Eugène (Rue Saint-Cecile, 9.Arr.): Neo-Gothic church built 1854&5 in stone and iron to plans by L.A.Boileau. This combination of materials is particularly striking in the interior, the coherence of which is further emphasized by the furnishings, which are contemporary with the building.

Saint-Eustache (Rue du Jour, 1.Arr.): This splendid parish church in the Les Halles district has no tower, and is an attractive combination of late Gothic and Renaissance elements; it is considered to be one of the most beautiful churches in Paris. Building lasted from 1532–1640. The *façade* has a portico rising through

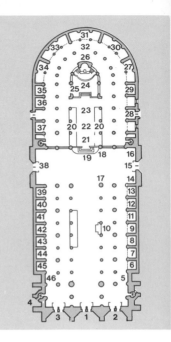

Saint-Etienne du Mont, interior

two storeys, pediment and adjacent tower stump, and makes a rather heavy impression; the façade of the S. transept seems like a simplified version of that of Notre-Dame de Paris. Nave and aisles and radiating chapels are topped with balustrades, and lightened by the use of flying buttresses.

The *interior* is also reminiscent of Notre-Dame; Gothic organization of space and Renaissance decoration (Corinthian and Ionic pilasters combined with high Gothic piers) give the church a charm of its own, further strengthened by the lavish net vaulting with pendant keystones in crossing and choir. The *stained glass* in the choir with church fathers, Apostles and saints dates from 1631. There are remains of old frescos in the chapels, though most of the painting is of more recent date. The 19C organ is famous for its tone, and the church

Paris, Notre-Dame de Paris 1 Porte du Jugement **2** Porte de Ste-Anne **3** Porte de la Vierge **4** Tower entrance **5** Calvary **6** Eligius chapel with Lebrun's Stoning of Stephen (1651) **7** Francis Xavier chapel with Lebrun's Martyrdom of St.Andrew **8** Genevieve chapel **9** Joseph chapel **10** Mirgon's pulpit (1868) with Apostles, symols of the Evangelists and angels **11** Peter chapel with fine 14C wooden figures of saints **12** St.Anne chapel **13** Sacré-Coeur chapel **14** Statue of Joan of Arc **15** Porte Sainte-Etienne, S. rose above **16** Statue of St.Theresa **17** Memorial for soldiers of the British Empire killed in the First World War **18** Notre-Dame de Paris, 14C statue **19** Statue of Dionysos by Coustou (1722) **20** Choir stalls **21** Access to Cardinals' vault **22** Lecterns **23** 17C marble floor **24** High altar (1866) **25** Angels bearing Instruments of Suffering **26** Pietà by Coustou **27** Dubois monument **28** Dionysos chapel **29** Magdalene chapel **30** George chapel **31** Chapel of the Seven Sorrows of the Virgin **32** Tomb of Bishop de Bucy (d.1809) **33** Pope Marcellus chapel **34** Louis chapel **35** Germanus chapel **36** Ferdinand chapel **37** Martin chapel **38** Porte du Cloître, N. rose above **39** Clotilde chapel **40** Saint-Landry chapel **41** Notre-Dame-de-Guadelupe chapel **42** Saint-Vincent-de-Paul chapel **43** Childhood chapel **44** Charles chapel **45** Baptismal chapel **46** Virgin by A.Vassé (1722)

Saint-Eustache, Ecstasy of the Magdalene

generally for its music: in 1855 the first performance of Berlioz' 'Te Deum' took place here, and in 1866 the 'Grand Festival Mass' by Franz Liszt.

A fine feature of the furnishings is the *tomb of J.-B.Colbert*, Louis XIV's finance minister. It was created by Coysevox to plans by Lebrun, and is considered one of his masterpieces: an expressive, beautifully modelled statue of the minister kneels on the sarcophagus, flanked by allegorical figures of women. Also worth mentioning: a painting of the Supper at Emmaus, attributed to Rubens, though this is much disputed, the 'Ecstasy of the Magdalene' by R.Manetti and 'Tobias and the Angel' by Santi di Tito. R.Mason's sculpture entitled 'The Departure of Fruit and Flowers' commemorates the demolition of the old market of Les Halles in 1971.

Saint-François-Xavier (Boulevard des Invalides, 7.Arr.): Church with twin-towered façade, in a combination of styles, started in 1861 and consecrated in 1875.

Saint-Germain-l'Auxerrois (Place du Louvre, 1.Arr.): This Gothic church dedicated to Saint-Germain, the 5C Bishop of Auxerre, was under construction for over two hundred years: choir, right-hand side chapel and central portal date from the 13C, the nave and aisles from the 14C, vestibule, transept and aisle chapels from the 15C. The 16C additions are in Renaissance style: choir portal and parts of the choir chapels. The late Gothic *façade* is picturesque in appearance; its lower storey contains the entrance to a vestibule with pointed arches. Inside are three portals lavishly famed with figures and ornament, above them a balustrade and the great rose window flanked with two slender towers; there is a smaller version of the rose in the pediment. In the large bell tower, which is similar to the two smaller towers, hangs 'La Marie', the bell which proclaimed the horror of St.Bartholomew's Eve in August 1572.

The *interior* with nave and four aisles is spacious and plain; it has a deep choir and low aisles. The choir screen (18C) is very fine, and so are the stalls by Mercier to designs by Lebrun (1684), once reserved for the royal family. Also 'La Vierge à l'oiseau', a fine statue of the Virgin on the lavish portal of the SE choir chapel, a wooden altar with scenes from the Passion (16C) and a fine statue of the Virgin and Child (14C) on the neo-Gothic altar of the Lady Chapel, St.Maria Aegyptiaca (16C), a graceful stone statue, and also wooden statues by Dubois (Descent from the Cross and the Risen Christ). The Renaissance retable dating from the time of Francis I is at present in the sacristy.

Saint-Germain-des-Prés (Place Saint-Germain-des-Prés, 6.Arr.): The heavy, sturdy bell tower with its upper storey with round arches and a stumpy spire dominates the rooftops of the area. There was a church here as early as the 6C; it was the burial place of three Merovingian kings and was dedicated to the Parisian Bishop Germanicus after his canonization in 754. After severe damage by the Normans on various occasions, the present building was built in the 11&12C; it has a late Romanesque nave and aisles and early Gothic choir (consecrated in 1163) with radiating chapels around the choir, and flying buttresses. Damage during the Revolution and later neglect necessitated radical restoration in the early 19C. Striking features of the nave and choir are the highly-decorated capitals of the piers and columns. The wall paintings in the nave (*c.* 1850 by H.Flandrin) juxtapose scenes from the Old and New Testaments. Also worth mentioning: fine marble statue of the Virgin and Child (*c.* 1340), the opulent tomb of the Polish King John I Casimir (d.1672), tomb slabs of the scholars Mabillon and Montfaucon (early 18C), the philosopher Des-

Saint-Eustache

cartes (d.1650) and the memorial tablet for the poet N.Boileau (d.1711) and the tombs of Douglas and Castellan. Also 17&18C paintings.

Saint-Gervais-Saint-Protais (Rue François Miron, 4.Arr.): Work started in 1494 on the present church; the nave has late Gothic flying buttresses and chapels with pointed roofs, and the massive tower is topped with a balustrade. The foundation stone of the magnificent façade with three bays and three storeys was laid in 1616 (work completed 1621), the first of its kind in France: above the lower storey, articulated with pairs of Doric columns and a portal with pediment in the central section is the first upper storey, articulated by the same order of Ionic columns with statue niches and a window echoing the portal design. Above this is the upper storey, set back and rather like a temple, with two pairs of Corinthian columns, portal-like window behind a balustrade, lavish segment gable and statues at the side.

In stark contrast with this lavish design is the plain, soaring late Gothic *interior*, with stellar vaulting in the nave. The *high altar* is flanked with wooden statues of the church patrons; it has a fine crucifix and good candelabra by Soufflot.

The organ is elegantly placed above a gallery supported by Corinthian columns, decorated with angels and cartouches. On the NE crossing pier is a statue of the Virgin (13&14C), and opposite an expressive crucifix by Perault (1840). Also worth seeing: tomb of H. le Tellier (d.1685), Louis XIV's chancellor, by Mazeline and Hurtrelle; a skilfully executed and unusual keystone in the Lady Chapel, (1517); stone relief of the Death of Mary (13C), forming the antependium in the Chapelle de la Madeleine; Chapelle Dorée (early 17C), with wooden panelling decorated with scenes from the Passion, and ornaments; *stained glass*, largely original, with scenes from the Old and New Testaments: outstanding are the Judgement of Solomon (1531 by Pinceignier) and the Condemnation of the Church Patrons. There are also fine paintings of the Passion (Flemish, 16C), and the Beheading of John the Baptist by C.Vignon.

Saint-Jacques-du-Haut-Pas (Rue Saint-Jacques, 5 Arr.): 17C church, simple inside and out. Some good paintings in the interior, also the tomb of Jean Duvergier, who introduced the concepts of Jansenism, which originated in Belgium, to France in the 17C. There has been an institution for the deaf and dumb in the adjacent former Augustinian monastery buildings since the 18C.

Saint-Jean l'Evangeliste (Rue des Abbesses, 18 Arr.): This reinforced concrete building dating from 1894–1904 with two low towers, high façade and open belfry is interesting not only for the possibilities afforded to the architect by the building technique, but also for the effect made by the division of the interior.

Saint-Germain-l'Auxerrois, pews

Saint-Jean-Saint-François (Rue de Perche, 3.Arr.): This church built in the 18C and extended in the 19C contains numerous paintings and a statue of St.Francis of Assisi with Stigmata by G.Pilon, and a good statue of St.Denis by J.Sarazin.

Saint-Joseph-des-Carmes (Rue de Vaugirard, 7.Arr.): This single-aisled church belonging to the convent of the Reformed Carmelites dates from 1613–25. It has a drum dome over a cruciform interior with four chapel niches built on to the nave. The broad interior has retained the style of the period in which it was built, both in design and decoration. The finest feature of the largely 17C furnishings is the monumental *Lady Chapel altar*, designed by Bernini. The church played a tragic role in the revolutionary year 1792; during the so-called 'September Massacres' over 100 clergymen, some of them high ranking, were murdered here. They are commemorated in the crypt.

Saint-Julien-le-Pauvre (Quai de Montebello, 5.Arr.): This little Gothic basilica built 1170–1240 was much altered in the 17C and is now used by the Greek Orthodox congregation. For this reason the iconostasis was introduced in 1901 to separate the Holy of Holies from the body of the church; on the iconostasis are several items from the older furnishings as well as numerous more recent icons.

Saint-Laurent (Boulevard de Strasbourg, 10.Arr.): This is one of the oldest churches in Paris, although the existing building, some of which dates from the 15C, has been much modified and extended subsequently. The most recent and striking addition is the neo-Gothic *façade*, (*c.* 1860) with fine portal with statues and side towers. In the 17C the choir, which dates from 1429, was decorated in the

◁ *Saint-Germain l'Auxerrois, Descent from the Cross*

baroque style, and the monumental baroque high altar was added. The artists responsible were F.Blondel and A.Lepautre. Also remarkable are the low keystones with figures in the transept and the chapels containing paintings built on to the nave.

Saint-Leu-Saint-Gilles (Rue Saint-Denis, 1.Arr.): The foundation stone of this church dedicated to Saint-Gilles (Giles), a Provençal hermit, and St.Leu (Loup), a bishop of Sens, who share a name day on 1 September, took place in 1235. The nave dates from *c.* 1320, and the choir from 1611. When the Boulevard de Sébastapol was pierced *c.* 1857, Baltard undertook certain alterations to the exterior of the church. Since the 18&19C it has been the seat of the Knights of the Holy Sepulchre (crypt), who were responsible for bringing the relics of St.Helena stored in the high altar to the church.

Saint-Louis-en-l'Ile (Rue Saint-Louis-en-l'Ile, 4.Arr.): The foundation stone of the present church was laid in 1664, and Le Vau, Le Duc and J.Doucet were involved in the work until its completion in 1725. The ground plan is cruciform, and the church has two aisles, ambulatory and radiating chapels. The interior, decorated elegantly in gold and white, makes a particularly festive impression. The furnishings, which include some fine paintings, reliefs and sculptures, include items from the 15–18C, and were gradually reassembled after the Revolution.

Saint-Louis-des-Invalides (Esplanade des Invalides, 7.Arr.): On the S. side of the cour d'honneur of the Hôtel des Invalides (see under Secular Buildings) the simple church completed *c.* 1676, and probably designed by L.Bruant, forms part of the group of buildings. It is also

St-Germain-l'Auxerrois, Virgin of the Bird ▷

Paris, Saint-Eustache 1 Nave **2** Aisles, in the N. Martyrdom of Saint-Eustache by Vouet and John the Baptist by Lemoyne **3** Transept **4** Choir with Baltard's baldacchino altar and Apostles, also Church Teachers in the windows **5** Ambulatory **6** Chapelle de la Vierge with frescos by Manet's teacher T.Couture (1856) and the Virgin of Pigalle on the altar (1748) **7–18** Baptismal chapel with copy of Rubens 'Adoration' **10** Joseph chapel with R.Mason's 'Departure of Fruit and Vegetables from the Heart of Paris' **14** Sainte-Geneviève chapel with Santi di Tito's 'Tobias and the Angel' **15** Saint-Vincent-de-Paul chapel with wall paintings from the Vouet studio **16** Madeleine chapel with Manetti's 'Ecstasy of the Madeleine' **17** Saint-Pierre-l'Exorciste chapel with Rubens' Supper at Emmaus **18** Saint-Louis chapel with tomb of Colbert **19–30** S. side chapels. Notable features: **21** Cecilia chapel with bust and memorial tablet to the composer Rameau and memorial plaque for the funeral of Mozart's mother **22** Chapel of the Innocents with Triqueti's 'Marriage of the Virgin'. **25** Agnes chapel with 'Entombment' by Giordano **27** Angel chapel with fine 17C paintings **28** Andrew chapel with Louis XV's confessional **31** Sacristy

known as Eglise des Soldats. The interior is spacious and broad, with aisles and gallery. Lovers of organ music rate the tone of the large 17C

baroque instrument very highly. The flags in the nave commemorate the victories and battles in which the French army was involved in the late 19 and early 20C (e.g. Crimean War, Mexico, Far East). Older trophies, largely from the period of Louis XIV and Napoleon I were destroyed so that they should not fall into the hands of the victorious Allied troops as they entered Paris. The *Chapelle Napoléon* (right aisle) contains memorabilia of the death and transportation of the corpse of Napoleon, including a death mask and the tomb slab from St.Helena.

Saint-Martin-des-Champs (Rue Saint-Martin, 3.Arr.): This church dating from the 11–13C once belonged to the massively fortified and powerful abbey of the monks of Cluny. Today the buildings house the Musée National des Techniques (see under Museums), which uses the former church as one of its exhibition galleries. The choir with double ambulatory and radiating chapels is still of particular interest.

Saint-Médard (Rue Mouffetard, 5.Arr.): The charm of this small, outwardly simple and unassuming church, built in various phases from the 15–late-18C, is the interior, where the dark, austere, late Gothic nave with aisles opens into the bright choir, built and decorated in Renaissance style. Remarkable features are the fine *baroque organ* (*c.* 1644), the *pulpit* (early 18C) and the 17&18C paintings distributed around the chapels. The church made history because of the tomb of the Jansenist Abbé Paris (d.1727), which was in the cemetery, no longer in existence, until the early 19C. As numerous sick, disabled and bedridden people claimed they had been miraculously healed by him, it became a place of pilgrimage for countless people in search of help. They were, however, soon joined by numerous charlatans and other sinister figures, who behaved so shamelessly and involved themselves in practices so little befitting the dignity of their surroundings that in 1732 troops drove out the 'Convulsion-naires', as these pilgrims were called, and were compelled to close the cemetery.

Saint-Merry (Rue Saint-Martin, 4.Arr.): This church, 16C but still in the late Gothic style, was built on the site of several earlier buildings; it was extended and the interior altered in the 18C, to plans by G.Bouffard and M.-A.Slodtz. The façade, which runs the gamut of late Gothic ornament, (although the statues are 19C), is part of the surrounding row of houses. This church also has an interior dominated by contrasts: the nave is still locked into the late Gothic

Saint-Germain-l'Auxerrois, Maria Aegyptica ▷

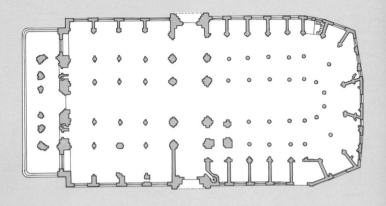

Paris, **Saint-Germain-l'Auxerrois** Spacious church with piered nave and four aisles, four bays in the nave, single-aisled, non-protruding transept, and choir with five aisles. Radiating chapels around the whole church. Fine late Gothic narthex in front of the entrance façade

period, with arches decorated with foliate carving and figures, the clerestory has tracery windows and unusual keystones. The choir on the other hand is lavishly decorated in the style of the 18C. The present *high altar* (second half of the 19C) has a massive marble crucifix with angels by J.-Ch.Dubois, with a a splendid gloriole above it, all that remains of the original high altar. The opulent and festive pulpit is the work of the Slodtz brothers. The *stained glass*, of which much is original, i.e. late Gothic or Renaissance, depicts scenes from the Bible and the lives of the saints. There are numerous 17&18C paintings in the church, outstanding among them two works by van Loo on

the choir piers: Carlo Borromeo Pleading for Milan and a picture of the Virgin.

Saint-Nicolas-des-Champs (Rue Saint-Martin, 3.Arr.): This church was also built over a considerable period. A place of worship on this site was mentioned in the 11&12C; this was later pulled down. The present façade with three axes, raised central section and pediment, seven bays of the nave and the massive cubic Gothic-style tower date from 1420–80. In the mid to late 16C the two aisles and a further section of the nave were added, in the early 17C two bays of the choir, the ambulatory and the chapels. It is impossible to overlook the transition from Gothic to Renaissance. 1581 is the date given for P.Delorme's magnificent, beautifully executed Renaissance S. portal. In the interior too there is an effective con-

Saint-Germain-des-Prés, capital (Musée de Cluny) (l), tower (r)

trast between Renaissance and Gothic styles in the various sections of the church. The massive two-tiered *high altar*, topped with four baroque angels, is a worthy framework for the altar panel, which covers both tiers; it was painted by S.Vouet in 1629 and shows an expressive and sympathetically painted Assumption. The 18C paschal candelabrum is also magnificent. The massive *organ* is considered to be one of the finest of its kind in Paris; it dates from the early to mid 17C, and is supported by powerful caryatids, decorated with figures of angels and birds, and topped with a statue of the church patron.
There are numerous 17–19C paintings in the chapels.

Saint-Nicolas du Chardonnet (Boulevard Saint-Germain, 5.Arr.): Although this is another church in which building lasted from the early

17C until beyond the mid 18C, uniformity of appearance has been maintained in its nave and two aisles, with transept incorporated in the radiating chapels. The interior seems plain, and the furnishings have no outstanding features. The painter and decorator Lebrun (Le Brun) acquired the choir chapel, dedicated to Carlo Borromeo, and created the altar painting himself; it depicts the saint at prayer. he was also responsible for the angels in the vault. J.Collignon executed Lebrun's designs for his mother's *tomb* in a masterly fashion in 1668: the dead woman (Julienne Le Bé) is awakened by the trumpet of the Angel of the Last Judgement, and leaves her grave with face transfigured. A.Coysevox created the tomb of Lebrun, who died in 1690, and his wife: the tomb slab is flanked with allegories of religion and painting; the face of the latter is particularly

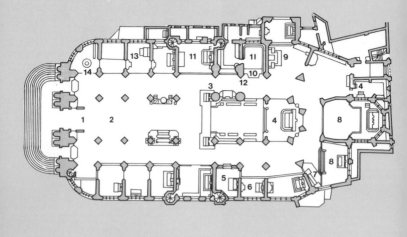

expressive of sorrow for the artist's death. Above this is a lifelike bust of Lebrun set in front of an obelisk in the shape of a pyramid. In the *Chapel of St.Francis de Sales* is the monumental tomb of J.Bignon (d.1665), who had started to arrange the Bibliothèque Nationale; the tomb is built of various components and sections, and has a bust of the dead man by F.Girardon. The church also has numerous 16–18C paintings, outstanding among which is the Martyrdom of St.John the Evangelist (right aisle), a lively early work by Lebrun.

Saint-Paul-Saint-Louis (Rue Saint-Antoine, 4.Arr.): The foundation stone of this Jesuit church, clearly reminiscent of Italian churches of the Order, was laid by King Louis XIII in 1627. Work on the magnificent, lavish, three-tiered *façade*, which certainly does not conform to the rules of the Order, started in 1629. The foundation stone is presumed to have been laid by Richelieu, and it is certain that the not entirely uncontroversial design was the work of P.F.Derrand: all three tiers are powerfully articulated with Corinthian columns, and a lavishly carved pediment is set above the main portal. In the first tier the pedimented side

Saint-Gervais-Saint-Protais, façade (l), interior (r)

portals are replaced with round-arched niches containing statues of saints. The topmost storey, like a temple, is balustraded and inset; it has a magnificently framed statue of the church patron, and the arms of France and Navarre in an equally lavish frame. The crossing dome has an open octagonal lantern, and the apse has tall round-arched windows and a pointed roof.

The interior is brightly coloured and gives an impression of space and breadth; the single-aisled chapels are interconnected and open into the aisles; the transept is short, and the apse semicircular. The entire church is surrounded by galleries with squat arches and a balustrade, and the walls are articulated with Corinthian pilasters. The drum of the dome has alternating tall round-arched windows and figure niches with Corinthian double pilasters and ornamental strips, and

draws the eye upwards into the spacious, open dome.

Notable features of the *furnishings* are the bronze, gilded antependium relief of the Supper at Emmaus by F.Anguier (17C) and the two shell-shaped stoups endowed by Victor Hugo right of the entrance. In the Chapel of the Sacred Heart (right aisle) is a picture from the studio of S.Vouet (*c.* 1640) 'St.Louis Receiving the Crown of Thorns from Christ' and a Christ on the Mount of Olives by Delacroix (1826). The chapel opposite is dedicated to the Blessed Virgin Mary and contains a statue of the Madonna with Child standing on a globe (1828 by A.Leonard), and two more paintings of scenes from the life of the church patron: 'King Louis XIII Presenting the Model of the Church to St.Louis' (studio of Vouet, *c.* 1650) and 'Death of St.Louis' (1668 by J.de Lestin). There are also two good sculptures alluding to the earlier patron of the church, the missionary St.Francis Xavier: 'Religion Teaching a Red Indian' by N.Adam and 'The Angel of Religion Destroying the Cult of Idolatry' by Vinache. The chapel dedicated to the Seven Sorrows of the Virgin has decorative symbols of the Virgin in its vaults, and houses a sensitive marble statue of the Mater Dolorosa by G.Pilon (1586), moving because of the facial expression and gestures.

Saint-Philippe du Roule (Avenue d'Antin, 8.Arr.): This plain church in the style of an early Christian basilica was built 1774–8 to a design by Chalgrin. Two sacristies, two chapels and the ambulatory were added in the mid 19C by important architects like Godde and Baltard. There are paintings by various 16–19C masters, and the Descent from the Cross in the apse, completed in 1855 by T.Chassériau, is particularly notable.

Saint-Pierre du Gros-Caillou (Rue Saint-Dominique, 7.Arr.): Godde built this church, reminiscent of an early Christian basilica, in the first two decades of the 19C; the style reflected current trends.

Saint - Pierre - de - Montmartre (Rue du Mont Cenis, 18.Arr.): Excavations have shown that there was a Roman temple on this site. Black marble columns incorporated in the present building are a reminder of a 7C Merovingian church, the existence of which has been confirmed. The early Gothic church, then part of a Benedictine monastery which used to be here, was dedicated in 1147 in the presence of St.Bernard of Clairvaux. The very plain façade dates from the 18C, and a radical restoration followed at a later date. There are 27 modern *stained glass windows* dating from 1956, depicting scenes from the life of St.Peter, a Crucifixion and Saints. Also two 17C paintings; a Descent from the Cross and Peter's Denial.

Saint-Roch (Rue Saint-Honoré, 1.Arr.): The Roi Soleil, Louis XIV, laid the foundation stone of this church designed by J.Lemercier in

Saint-Laurent, God the Father in the N. portal

1633; it was not completed until 1740. The pedimented façade, plain in comparison with many of its kind in Paris, was built in 1736 to plans by R.de Cotte. The lower storey with three round-arched portals and two statues of saints is articulated with Doric, and the curved upper storey with Corinthian, columns. There are also statues in the latter case, and two sets of sculpture on the sides. The open staircase leading to this façade was the scene of the collapse of a royal counter-revolution on 13 Vendémaire of the IV Year of the Revolution (5 October 1795): Napoleon Bonaparte had members of the opposing party, who had entrenched themselves in the church, summarily shot. The interior of this building, with nave and two aisles and side radiating chapels, gives an impression of light and breadth; the transept hardly protrudes at all, and the apse is semicircular.

The decorations, in bright colours and gold, date, like the ceiling painting (Christ Triumphant, angels, Apostles, and saints), from the 19C. Notable features of the *furnishings* are a series of tombs or monuments, or what remains of them (many were removed and demolished in the Revolution): memorial plaques for the writer Corneille (d.1684), the landscape gardener Le Nôtre (d.1700); the tomb of the scientist Maupertius (d.1759) consists of an inscribed tablet with a mourning guardian angel and another angel leaning on it, above this is a medallion relief of the dead man; the tomb of Cardinal Dubois (d.1729) has a statue of the cardinal in prayer by G.Coustou, and the bust of Marshall F.de Créqui (d.1687) is the work of Coysevox. There are also numerous fine statues and sculptures, of which the following are particularly notable: a moving seated figure of Christ on the Mount of Olives, deeply involved in his thoughts and fears (1757, by Falconet); a life-size marble group of the Baptism of Christ (1731) by J.-B.Lemoyne and his nephew of the same name, and the statue of St.Augustine (1765) by J.B.d'Huez.

Particularly noteworthy among the chapels are: *Calvary chapel* (behind the choir), restored to its original design in the 19C, with marble crucifix (1686 by M.Anguier), Mourning

Saint-Merry, tympanum of the W. portal

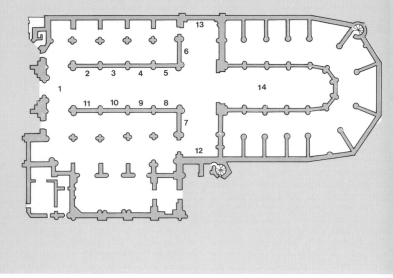

Paris, Saint-Merry 1 Nave in late Gothic style with splendid stained glass: 2 Life of Mary Magdalene 3 Miracles of Christ 4 Life of St.John the Baptist 5 Life of St.Thomas 6 Transfiguration of Christ 7 Annunciation to the Shepherds 8 Scenes from the life of the Virgin 9 Life of St.Francis of Assisi, death of a martyr 10 Life of St.Agnes 11 Life of St.Nicholas 12 S. rose: Madonna with Holy Ghost and Angels 13 N. rose: radiant sun 14 Choir in the style of the 18C. The stained glass depicts the story of Joseph, the life of St.Peter and Apostles

Madonna (1856 by Bogino) and good sculptures of the Crucifixion (Duseignier) and Entombment (Deseine, both first half of the 19C) and two paintings by de Vien (18C): 'Waking of Lazarus' and 'Christ and the Children'. *Lady chapel* with dome painting by J.-B. Pierre (Assumption) and an expressive sculpture of the Birth of Christ (1665) by M.Anguier on the altar. Above this is a gloriole by Falconet, all that remains of the Annunciation by this master which used to be here.

Saint-Séverin (Rue des Prêtres-Saint-Séverin, 5.Arr.): This church has a nave and four aisles and a fine tower, and is considered to be one of the most beautiful Gothic buildings in Paris. Work started in the 13C, but the church was destroyed, presumably by fire, and was rebuilt from 1450 in its present form, and extended in the 16&17C. There is a fine Gothic window in the W. façade. The portal probably came from another church, and was added in the 19C. The S. side of the building shows the entire range and inexhaustible richness of late Gothic ornamentation and carving. The apse is also worth seeing for the imaginative gables on the radiating chapels.

The *interior* shows marked contrasts: the first three bays of the nave are of simple, somewhat squat and compressed 13C design, while from the fourth bay the style of the 15C begins

Saint-Merry, nave and choir (l), relief on tabernacle (r)

to make itself felt, emphasizing the vertical and adding imaginatively treated capitals and keystones. The pairs of figures in the S. aisle are designed with particular love. The double *ambulatory* with its skilfully interweaving network of vaulting is a jewel of Gothic architecture. The *stained glass* windows are also notable: those showing Apostles in the first three bays of the nave are from St-Germain-des-Prés and date from the 14C. The remaining windows in the nave and choir, showing saints, date from the 15C. The three windows in the choir ambulatory are the work of J.Bazaine, *c.* 1966. The lavishly decorated *organ* is an 18C masterpiece.

Saint-Sulpice (Place Saint-Sulpice, 6.Arr.): The foundation stone of this remarkable church was laid in 1646, but it was not completed until over

100 years later, in 1756. The spacious church square was designed in its present form in the 19C; the fountain with figures of four well-known French preachers is a work of the Italian Visconti. The two-storey *façade* is simple and undecorated in design; the lower storeys of the towers are incorporated in the façade; their lower storey are closed, the upper ones have round arches. The portico in the lower storey is made up of Doric columns, standing singly on the inside and in pairs on the outer edges. The same pattern is followed in the upper storey, but here the columns are Corinthian. Only the N. tower was completed by J.F.Chalgrin in the late 18C: its third storey is like an ancient temple, with Corinthian pilasters and triangular pediment, and the fourth storey is in the style of a pavilion, decorated with sculptures and Corinthian columns, and topped with

Saint-Nicolas-des-Champs, interior

a balustrade. The vestibule is decorated with allegorical reliefs, and at the sides of the main portal are statues of the Apostles Peter and Paul. The transept façades are also in the form of temples, Ionic and Doric in the S. and Corinthian in the N. The statues here date from the 18C. There is a low dome on the apse.

The impression of spaciousness in the interior, with round-arched windows, fluted Corinthian pilasters and plain beams, is created by the light streaming in through the large arches of the windows. Only the transept has lavish and imaginative beam decoration. The simple altar with retable relief (19C) is surrounded by twelve statues on the choir piers of Apostles, Christ and Mary, created in 1735 by E.Bouchardon. The *pulpit*, lavishly decorated with foliage and acanthus work, seems to hover between the balustrades of the two flights of steps leading to it; the bases of the steps are decorated with allegorical figures of women. The sounding board is topped with a Madonna with Child and angel. In the transept is an unusual kind of *sundial*: a dark obelisk is struck by the light in such a way as to cast a shadow on a meridian line on the floor, making it possible to establish the exact moment of the winter solstice. The lavish *organ front*, articulated with Corinthian columns and decorated with statues dates from the 18C, and is also worth looking at. The two shell-shaped stoups are from Venice, and came to Paris as a present for Francis I; they are placed in front of an unusual background of imitation rocks in marble.

Other interesting features are the good *frescos* by E.Delacroix (completed two years before his death) in the Angelus chapel: Jacob's Fight with the Angel, Michael Killing the Dragon and Heliodorus Driven from the Temple. The Lady Chapel is magnificent if over-decorated; the altarpiece, consisting of marble columns supporting a round-arched section decorated with angels and garlands of fruit, is an appropriate framework for the graceful *statue of the Madonna*, who seems to hover with her haloed Child above the clouds and indeed the world. The walls are decorated with medallions and four paintings by van Loo, all depicting scenes from the life of the Virgin. On the ceiling is a picture of the Assumption.

Saint-Thomas d'Acquin (Place Saint-Thomas d'Acquin, 7. Arr.): This church with two-storeyed façade, articulated with Doric and Ionic columns with pediment with allegorical figures, dates from the 17&18C. The most striking feature of the interior is the lavish and imaginative decoration of the Corinthian capitals, also the curtain-like decoration of the choir arch. The altar in the Lady Chapel, two wooden reliefs of scenes from the Life of Christ (all

Saint-Nicolas du Chardonnet, exterior

Saint-Nicolas du Chardonnet, Martyrdom of St John the Evangelist

Saint-Paul-Saint-Louis, façade (l), view of dome (r)

18C), are notable; there are also some fine 17–19C paintings by various masters.

Saint-Vincent de Paul (Place la Fayette, 10.Arr.): This church, the most important ecclesiastical building commissioned by the Citizen King Louis Philippe, was completed in 1844, under the Cologne-born architect J.I.Hittorff. It is a skilful mixture of ancient temple and early Christian basilica. A broad flight of steps leads to the *façade*, in front of which is a massive portico with Ionic columns. The triangular pediment contains a relief by C.F.Leboeuf-Nanteuil of the church patron, with allegories of religion and mercy surrounded by people seeking help. St.Vincent de Paul (d.1660), also called the 'Apostle of Charity', dedicated his whole life to caring for the sick, the disabled and the despised. The façade, which has a

central balustrade with statues of the Evangelists, is surmounted by the two slender towers, articulated with fluted pilasters and topped with balustrades. In their second storey, which is incorporated in the façade, they have niches containing statues of the Apostles Peter and Paul.

The interior is a rather dim columned basilica with nave and four aisles. In the nave the architrave is supported by powerful Doric columns, decorated by a frieze by H.Flandrin which is one of his masterpieces. Above this is a row of Corinthian columns separating the galleries from the nave. The triumphal arch is decorated with angels and medallions of the Church Fathers and provides a view of F.E.-Picot's apse fresco, depicting Christ Enthroned with archangels, prophets and saints. Under this pictures of the sacraments. The round-arched *altar baldacchino*, surmounted by a triangu-

Saint-Paul-Saint-Louis, Christ on the Mount of Olives by Delacroix

Paris, Saint-Paul-Saint-Louis 1 Main entrance, organ above **2** Stoup, endowed by Victor Hugo **3** Single-aisled, five-bayed nave with chapels instead of aisles **4** Altar, in front of it Supper at Emmaus by F.Anguier **5** Chapelle de la Vierge **6** Chapelle du Sacré-Coeur **7** Chapelle du Saint-Sacrément with emblems of the Blessed Virgin **8** Chapelle Notre-Dame-des-Sept-Douleurs **9** Choir **10** Presbytery

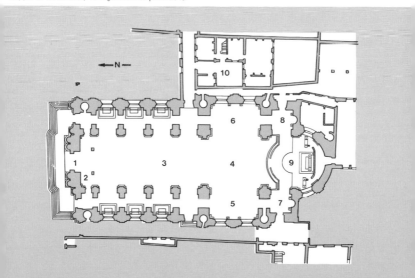

Saint-Pierre de Montmartre, interior (l), exterior (r)

lar pediment topped with the Dove of the Holy Spirit and supported by Corinthian columns with angels on top of them, frames a Crucifixion by F.Rude (mid 19C). Antependium with Last Supper by Bosio. Also notable are the pulpit carved with relief scenes by Duseigneur, the lavish font with Christ Triumphant and the stained glass windows, based on designs by the architect. The outer aisles are divided into chapels by means of grilles. The *Lady Chapel* was designed in the 19C, with eight pictures of scenes from the life of the Virgin by Bourquereau (1881–9). There are two plaster sculptures (Anne and the Virgin, Joseph with the Boy Jesus) and on the altar the sculpture by Carrier-Belleuse known as 'The Messiah': the seated Madonna holds up her child for all to see.

Sainte-Chapelle (Boulevard du Palais, 1.Arr.): This former palace chapel, small in its dimensions, but in its decoration and effect a grandiose jewel of High Gothic, is now almost swamped by the buildings of the Palais de Justice. All that is really visible is the delicate, tall, pointed roof turret with crockets and gables. King Louis IX, the Saint, acquired Christ's Crown of Thorns for a not inconsiderable sum of money from the Emperor of Byzantium in 1239, and later other items associated with the death of the Saviour. This wonderful shrine was built in three years to house Louis' precious relics of Christendom. The plain base rises through three storeys; at the level of the windows the chapel is articulated with flying buttresses decorated with delicate tracery turrets; the windows themselves are set in pointed arches. One the W. side is the façade with central rose window, behind the vesti-

MIGNARD

Saint-Roch, detail of ceiling (l), bust of Mignard (r)

bule (19C), which has two storeys, articulated with similar buttresses and topped with a balustrade. Above is another balustrade and the triangular pediment with small rose window and trefoil windows; the entire pediment is framed with crocketed turrets.

The interior of the chapel has two storeys. The *lower chapel* is crypt-like: low, with three aisles and five bays; there are some old tombs of clergymen in the floor. The deep ribs of the vaulting are supported on piers with lavish bud, foliate and tendril capitals. This decoration is repeated on the pilasters, which support pointed trefoil arches, and contain pictures of the Apostles. Recurring motifs in the distinguished decoration are the Bourbon lily and the triple-battlemented tower from the arms of Castile.

The actual Sainte-Chapelle is the single-aisled *upper chapel*, originally reserved for court nobility, and there-fore accessible from the palace. The visitor's attention is drawn first of all to the quality and play of the light streaming down in the many colours of the high windows. It is hard to escape the impression of being contained in a gigantic glass ball. However, once the eye is accustomed to the play of colour and light, it is possible to grasp the brilliant way in which the space is articulated. The base is relatively low, and has slender columns with an almost inexhaustible wealth of animal and plant motifs supporting pointed blind arches with pictures of martyrs in their quatrefoils. The spandrels are filled with delicate ornamentation and angels. In the bases of the slender, beautifully painted composite piers, soaring vertically to dissolve in the tight vault ribs, are statues of the Twelve Apostles under tracery baldacchinos. They are contemporary with the building,

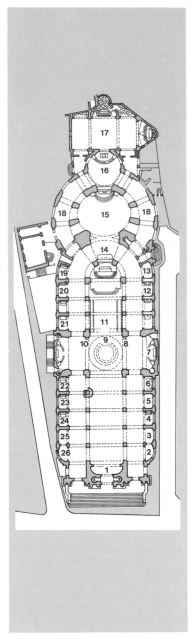

Saint-Séverin, interior

Paris, Saint-Roch 1 Main entrance, organ front above **2** Bust of F. de Créquis by Coysevox **3** Statue of Cardinal Dubois, Maupertius monument, Resurrection of Christ with Angels and Women at the Tomb **4** De Créquis' monument for Mazeline and Hurtrelle, scenes from the life of Saint-Etienne **5** Chapelle des Ames du Purgatoire **6** Sacré-Coeur chapel **7** Painting by de Doyen (Miracles of Ardens) and statues of Gregory the Great and Francis de Sales **8** Statue of the church patron **9** Painting 'Christus triumphans' **10** Statue of Christ on the Mount of Olives **11** Choir **12** Chapelle Sainte-Cathérine **13** Chapelle Sainte-Marie-Madeleine **14** High altar **15** Chapelle de la Vierge **16** Communion chapel **17** Calvary chapel **18** Ambulatory with numerous paintings **19** Charles Borromeo chapel **20** Francis de Sales chapel **21** Saint-Vincent-de-Paul chapel **22** Susan chapel with Epée monument **23** Chapel of the Sorrows of Christ **24** Nicholas chapel with monument to the painter Mignard **15** Chapel dedicated to John the Baptist with Baptism of Christ **26** Baptismal chapel

but are not all in their original places. The others are in the Musée de Cluny. Above this 'wall area' rise the tall, slender tracery windows, in four and some in two sections, with double

Saint-Séverin, apse gables

arches, trefoils and quatrefoils and roses in their pointed upper parts.

The *stained glass* is partially original and partially restored, and depicts more than a thousand scenes from the Old and New Testaments. The late Gothic rose window in the façade wall is almost entirely original (last decade of the 15C). The panes are set in orna tely twisting tracery and depict scenes of the Apocalypse.

The remains of the former stand for the reliquaries are in the apse. Two flights of wooden stairs lead to the beautifully carved wooden baldacchino with Gothic turrets. The side niches were intended for the Royal family.

Sainte-Clotilde (Rue las-Cases, 7.Arr.): This neo-Gothic building with two towers and three lavish portals with figures in the façade was built in the mid 19C to plans by F.C.Gau of Cologne. The interior with nave and two aisles, transept, ambulatory and radiating chapels makes a solemn, plain impression. Interesting features are the *wall paintings*, on which Pradier worked, e.g. reliefs of the Passion, and Bourgueveau's scenes from the life of St.Louis in the chapel dedicated to that saint; the 'Baptism of Clovis' and 'Benevolence of St.Clotilda'. The choir screen is decorated with reliefs of the life of the patroness of the church.

Sainte-Elisabeth (Rue du Temple, 3 Arr.): Marie de'Medici laid the foundation stone of this church of the Franciscan nuns in 1628; work was completed *c.* 1645. The two-storey façade is massive but plain; it has Doric and Ionic pilasters, statue niches and a segment gable decorated with garlands. Notable features of the plain interior are the friezes of the

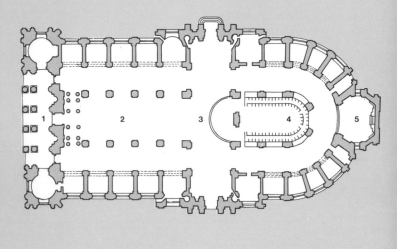

Doric pilasters with Christian symbols, and the wooden reliefs in the panelling of the ambulatory with Old Testament scenes.

Sainte-Marguerite (Rue Saint-Bernard, 11. Arr.): This outwardly plain building with an austere façade articulated with tall Corinthian pilasters and topped with a triangular pediment dates from 1712. The two pediment reliefs, a Madonna Enthroned (S. transept) and the Supper at Emmaus (N. transept) are the work of J.-B. Goy. The interior with pierced nave and two aisles is also plain and austere. Notable features are the plain *pulpit*, with reliefs of biblical scenes contemporary with the building, and numerous *paintings*, e.g. 'Descent

from the Cross' by F.Rossi, known as Salvati (16C) and the 'Massacre of the Innocents' by L.Giordano (17C) next to the main portal. There are three pictures with scenes from the life of St.Vincent de Paul (17&18C) in the Lady Chapel and 'St.Francis de Sales appoints St.Vincent de Paul as Superior of the Visitand Order' (1732) by Reston in the Chapel of Sainte-Marguerite. The chapel dedicated to the Souls in Purgatory is also worth seeing: it was designed in 1794 by V.Louis, and has trompe-l'oeil wall paintings by Brunetti, a picture by Gabriel (1761) depicting the Ascent of the Poor Souls into Heaven, and sculptures of the Virtues.

Temple de l'Oratoire (Rue Saint-Honoré, 1 Arr.): The church was built 1621–30, but not completed until the mid 18C by the addition of P.Casqué's façade; the church was

Saint-Sulpice, façade with towers (l), Visconti fountain in front of the church (r)

formerly the possession of the Congrégation de l'Oratoire de France, a fraternity devoted to religious instruction and the art of preaching. The massive monument to G.de Coligny (1519–72) on the façade on the Rue de Rivoli side was built in 1889 by S.de Gisors. Coligny was the leader of the French Hugucnots, murdered on St.Bartholomew's Eve, and the monument consists of a large figure of the Admiral, a mourning knight and a woman. The interior is in the style of an oratory, with Corinthian piers and ·pilasters, radiating rectangular chapels and low galleries.

Temple de Sainte-Marie (Rue Saint-Antoine, 4.Arr.): The little domed church with massive protruding façade was built in the early 17C to plans by F.Mansart. It belonged at first to the Visitands, who lived according to the Rule of St.Augus-

tine, and devoted themselves principally to caring for the sick, and education. The circular interior is articulated with Corinthian pilasters; the articulation of the walls and sculptural decoration are lavish, and extend all the way up to the dome, which is topped by a lantern.

Temple du Pentemont (Rue de Grenelle, 7.Arr.): Bernardine monastery built in the mid 18C. It now houses the Ministère des Anciens Combatants, and a small chapel with Ionic columned portal, plain both inside and out.

Val-de-Grâce (Rue Saint-Jacques, 5.Arr.): Anne of Austria redeemed an oath by laying the foundation stone of this baroque church, formerly part of a Benedictine Nunnery, in 1645. She had remained childless through 23 years of marriage, and promised to endow a church for the nunnery if she were to bear an heir to the throne. Her wish was fulfilled in 1638 by the birth of the future Roi Soleil, Louis XIV. The church was built by Lemercier and Leduc to plans by Mansart, following the design of St.Peter's in Rome, and completed in 1667. A flight of steps leads to the two-storey façade. The portal porch, supported by Corinthian columns and topped with a triangular pediment, is the central feature of the lower storey with lateral statue niches. A balustrade separates the lower from the upper storey; the latter is set back, and resembles the façade of a temple, framed with inverted scrolls, and also featuring Corinthians pilasters and columns, triangular pediment and aedicule with segment arches. Behind this is the tambour, surrounded by four delicate bell turrets, and articulated with Corinthian pilasters with guardian angels.

In the *interior* there are chapels in the three bays of the nave. The choir is immediately adjacent, centrally planned with four corner chapels. The walls are articulated with pilasters with lavish Corinthian capitals. Above the round arches are reliefs with allegories of the Virtues, and the ceiling vault has reliefs of the ancestors of Christ. M.Anguier's statues of the Evangelists in the spandrels of the dome are individual and lively in their execution. The dome painting, completed by P.Mignard in 1665, shows God the Father surrounded by the blessed, saints and martyrs. The choir, which has a fine coloured marble floor, concludes in Le Duc's mighty baldacchino altar. The chapels around the choir still largely have their old paintings and reliefs, and are therefore worth some attention.

Cemeteries

Cimetière de Montmartre/Montmartre Cemetery (Avenue Rachel, 18.Arr): Many celebrities, particularly in the field of literature, are buried in this spacious cemetery, and commemorated with monuments both elaborate and plain; it was laid out in the late 18C and significantly extended in the 19C. The tombs

Saint-Vincent de Paul

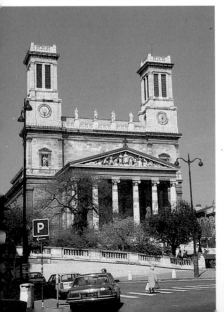

Sainte-Chapelle

include those of: the German poet and writer *Heinrich Heine* (1797–1856), who emigrated to Paris in 1831; the novelist *Henri Beyle* (1783–1842), better known under his pseudonym *Stendhal*; the writer *Alexandre Dumas Fils* (1824–95), who in his novel 'La Dame aux Camélias' immortalized the Parisian courtesan *Alphonsine Plessis* (d.1847), with whom he had a short-lived affair; this story forms the basis of Verdi's 'La Traviata' and a Garbo film, and Dumas himself is buried in a tomb decorated with red porcelain camelias. The mortal remains of *Emile Zola* (1840–1902) have been removed to the Panthéon. The composers *Jacques Offenbach* (1819–80) and Hector Berlioz (1803–69) are buried here.

Cimetière de Montparnasse/ Montparnasse Cemetery (Boul-

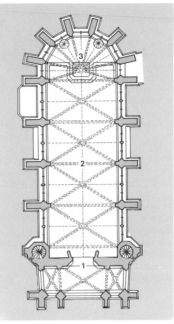

Paris, Sainte-Chapelle Upper chapels **1** W. façade with rose dating from the reign of Charles VIII with scenes from the Apocalypse **2** Nave. The stained glass depicts scenes from the Old Testament prophesying the redemption of the world by the Saviour. An exception is the window in the S. by the entrance. It depicts the legend of the Cross of Christ, the acquistion of the relics once stored here by Louis IX and the consecration of the chapel. **3** Choir with remains of the reliquary. The windows depict the Sufferings of Christ

Gargoyle on the Sainte-Chapelle

evard E.Quinet, 14.Arr.): The cemetery was laid out in 1824, and those buried here include: the sculptor *François Rude* (1774–1855), the author *Guy de Maupassant* (1850–93) and the poet *Charles Baudelaire* (1821–67). The monument to the composer *César Franck* (1822–90) is decorated with a medallion by Rodin.

Cimetière de Passy/Passy Cemetery (Avenue Henri Martin, 16.Arr.): This little cemetery has existed since the early 19C and contains the graves of the composer *Claude Debussy* (1862–1918) and the painter *Edouard Manet* (1832–83).

Cimetière du Père Lachaise/Père Lachaise Cemetery (Boulevard de Ménilmontant, 20.Arr.): This large, park-like cemetery has been in existence since *c.* 1804; it was laid out by Brougniart, who is also buried here, and was later much extended. It is named after the Jesuit priest F.de La Chaise, Louis XIV's confessor, who once owned a country house on the site of the present chapel. There is a

splendid view of Paris from the cemetery.

There are many tombs, some of which are beautiful, and the list of famous people buried here is very long. We shall restrict ourselves to mentioning: the composers *Luigi Cherubini* (1760–1842), *Frédéric Chopin* (1810–49) and *Georges Bizet* (1838–75); poets and writers *Honoré de Balzac* (1799–1850), *La Fontaine* (1621–95), *Molière* (1622–73), *Guillaume Apollinaire* (1880–1918), *Alphonse Daudet* (1840–97), *Marcel Proust* (1871–1922), *Oscar Wilde* (1854–1900) and *Sidonie-Gabrielle Colette* (1873–1954); the architect *Louis Visconti* (1791–1853) and the painter *Eugène Delacroix* (1798–1863); the great actress *Sarah Bernhardt* (1844–1923), the 'Paris sparrow', singer *Edith Piaf* (1915–63) and the American rock star *Jim Morrison*, who died in Paris in 1971. Also worth mentioning are the Monument for the Dead, built *c.* 1900, and the memorial to the unhappy 12C lovers Abelard and Héloïse. A plan identifying the position of all the tombs is available at the entrance.

Sainte-Chapelle, upper chapel, Angels with the Crown of Thorns

Cimetière de Picups (Rue de Picups, 12.Arr.): This little cemetery, now on the site of the mass graves of the victims of the revolutionary guillotine, is reserved exclusively for their families, and for this reason has developed into a cemetery for the nobility. An important feature is the tomb of the *Marquis de Lafayette* (1757–1834), who was also involved in the American War of Independence, and his wife.

Secular Buildings

Academies: See Institut de France.

Amphithéâtre anatomique (5 Rue de l'Ecole-de-Médecine, 4.Arr.): This building by Charles and Louis Joubert (1691–5) was originally the anatomy lecture theatre of the School of Surgery, and has kept its old name, although it is now used for lectures by the faculty of letters. From 1777–1933 it accommodated a free school of drawing, attended by Auguste Rodin. The building next door, No. 4, was the birthplace of the world-famous actress *Sarah Bernhardt*, whose real name was Rosalie Bernard; she was born on 22 October 1844, and is commemorated with a plaque. The novelist Emile Zola also had a flat in the Rue de l'Ecole-de-Medécine until he moved to 10 Rue de Vaugirard in 1862.

Arc de Triomphe de l'Etoile (Place Charles-de-Gaulle): The Arc de Triomphe, probably the most famous building in Paris after the Eiffel Tower and the Louvre, is in the centre of the former Place de l'Etoile, renamed Place Charles-de-Gaulle on 15 December 1970 in honour of the first President of the Fifth Republic, Charles de Gaulle, who died in 1969. The original name of the square, Etoile, dated from 1730, and referred to the five avenues which used to radiate from it like a star. Since Baron Haussmann's rebuilding, twelve avenues meet here, including the magnificent *Champs-Elysées* (see under Districts, Streets, Squares, Parks, Gardens); to the NE are Montmartre and the Sacré-Coeur; to the

Sainte-Chapelle, lower chapel, pilasters

Sainte-Chapelle, upper chapel, window

SE the Eiffel Tower, Dôme des Invalides and the Maine-Montparnasse skyscraper; to the W. the Défense skyscrapers.

Until 1860 Etoile was the city boundary of Paris. After his victory over the allied Austrians and Russians in the Battle of the Three Emperors at Austerlitz on 2 December 1805, Napoleon ordered the building of two triumphal arches in Paris, to be dedicated to the glory of the imperial armies: they were the Arc de Triomphe de l'Etoile and the Arc de Triomphe du Carrousel, near the Louvre. The architect Jean François Thérèse Chalgrin submitted successful plans for the Arc de Triomphe de l'Etoile; he attempted to increase the monumental impact of the building by restricting decoration to a minimum. Napoleon did not sur-

◁ *Sainte-Chapelle, upper chapel, Apostle*

vive to see the completion of the monument, 164 ft. high and 148 ft. wide (1836). The Arc de Triomphe was never officially inaugurated, as the Citizen King feared that this could lead to demonstrations by elements sympathetic to Napoleon.

The four reliefs represent: on the city side on the right the 'Departure of the Army in 1792' (also called 'La Marseillaise'); artist, François Rude) and on the left the 'Triumph of Napoleon in 1810' (Jean-Pierre Cortot). On the W. side are the 'Resistance of 1814' and the 'Peace of 1815' (Antoine Etex). On the inside walls are the names of 600 imperial generals. The name of Victor Hugo's father, who served as a general under Napoleon, is missing. Because of this, Victor Hugo, a year after the monument was completed, wrote the poem 'A l'Arc de Triomphe', with a dedication to his father: 'For Joseph Sigisbert Count Hugo, General in the King's Army, born 1774 volunteer in 1791, Colonel 1805, Brigadier 1809, Provincial Governor 1810, General 1825, died 1828—not listed on the Arc de Triomphe' In 1885 Victor Hugo himself lay in state under the Arc de Triomphe before he was moved to the Panthéon.

Victor Hugo's lying in state under the arch was not the only event there which led to a political demonstration: in 1840 the coffin containing Napoleon's mortal remains was placed on display under the arch; in 1852 Napoleon III received the freedom of the city and its homage here; in 1919 the allied parade after the Peace of Versailles took place here; in 1940 the Germans entered Paris through the Arc de Triomphe; in 1944 the people greeted the allied troops, led by de Gaulle, under the arch. Thus the Arc de Triomphe is not only a symbol of the city of Paris, but also a national political emblem.

Pierre Tombale du Soldat Inconnu (Tomb of the Unknown Soldier): The notion of a nameless victim of war, honoured as the symbolic representa-

Temple de l'Oratoire

tive of all the nation's soldiers who died, was first established in France after the First World War. On 11 November 1920, the anniversary of the Compiègne armistice, the body of an Unknown Soldier was buried under the Arc de Triomphe in Paris and simultaneously in Westminster Abbey, an example subsequently followed in many countries. There is a small ceremony each evening at 6.30, and on the 11 November the dead of the two World Wars are remembered.

Musée de l'Arc de Triomphe: The little museum in the upper storey houses a collection on the history of the building to the present day, memorabilia of Napoleon etc.

Arc de Triomphe du Carrousel (Place du Carrousel, 1.Arr.): The Arc de Triomphe du Carrousel was built 1806–8, for the same reason as the Arc de Triomphe de l'Etoile. The design, by Charles Percier and Pierre François-Léonard Fontaine, is based on the triumphal arch of the Roman Emperor Septimius Severus (AD 203): the quadriga on the top, with the Goddess of peace in a chariot, is the work of Bosio le Jeune (1828). The Arc de Triomphe was planned as an entrance to the Tuileries Palace courtyard; since the palace was pulled down it has been deprived of its function, and looks rather lost. The reliefs are scenes from Napoleon's German and Austrian campaigns.

Arènes de Lutèce (Amphitheatre; Rue des Arènes, 5.Arr.): This late-Roman amphitheatre dates from *c*. AD 200; it was attached to the settlement of Lutetia (the Roman name for Paris), seated about 17,000 spectators, and is only slightly smaller than the Colosseum in Rome: the arena is 184 ft. long and 157 ft. wide. It was used for theatrical and circus performances, abandoned in the late 3C AD and used as a quarry, then rediscovered in 1869. Restoration work was undertaken in the 20C.

Arsenal (former powder factory, now library; 1–3 Rue de Sully, 4.Arr.): A weapon and powder factory was built under Henri IV in 1594 by the Minister Maximilien de Béthune, Duc de Sully, and since 1797 has housed the valuable Bibliothèque de l'Arsenal (founded by the bibliophile René d'Argenson, Marquis de Paulny; it is the most important French library after the Bibliothèque Nationale); only a few of the rooms have remained unaltered since they were built (the names of the architects are not known with certainty). One of the famous directors of this library (1824–44) was the poet Charles Nodier, who lived in the Arsenal, and kept open house for the great names of Romanticism every Sunday (Hugo, Vigny, de Musset, Lamartine, Dumas among others); this group was known as the 'Cénacle'.

Barrière d'Enfer (former customs house; Place Denfert-Rochereau, 14.Arr.): The two customs houses, built 1784–7 by Claude-Nicolas Ledoux, were strikingly christened 'hell barrier'. Ledoux built 42 such checkpoints, known as 'barrières' and protected with barriers and guardhouses, in the streets leading out of the city and at the city walls; a transit toll was collected here. The majority of these 'barrières' were destroyed shortly after they were built, at the outbreak of the Revolution, as symbols of the Ancien Régime. Opera lovers will know the Barrière d'Enfer from Puccini's 'La Bohème'.

Bastille: See Place de la Bastille.

Bibliothèque Sainte-Geneviève (library; 8–10 Place du Panthéon, 5.Arr.): The library of Sainte-Geneviève was founded by Cardinal La Rochefoucauld in 1624, nationalized in 1790; the present long neo-Renaissance building was built 1844–50 by Henri Labrouste; 23 blind arches on the long and E. narrow sides contain the names of 30 famous writers of all nations. The cast- and wrought-iron-work in the interior were considered highly original at the time. Since 1929 the *Bibliothèque Doucet* has been attached to the main library; it possesses manuscripts by important writers from Baudelaire onwards into the 20C, and arranges readings by poets.

Bourse (Stock Exchange; Place de la Bourse, 2.Arr.): This imposing building was commissioned by Napoleon in 1809 and built in the form of an ancient temple with a single aisle. This temple of stocks and shares was designed by Alexandre Théodore Brongiart and Eloi de Labarre, and not completed until 1829. The building was extended in the shape of a cross in 1902&3.

Bourse du Commerce (Stock Exchange; Rue de Viarmes, 1.Arr.):

Cimetière de Montmartre, tomb of Emile Zola (l), tomb of Heinrich Heine (r)

This circular building on the edge of the former Halles was built in 1887 by Paul Blondel, on the site of the former Corn Exchange. The iron and glass dome is one of the most important constructions of its kind in Paris.

Catacombes (Cemetery; 2 Place Denfert-Rochereau, 14.Arr.): This underground necropolis houses the bones of around six million dead, and was still in use in the 19C. The passages were originally quarries, and from 1765 bones from all the cemeteries within the walls of Paris were brought here; cemeteries in the town had been closed because of the constant fear of infection. It is assumed that the remains of numerous famous personalities were transferred here, even though their official burial place is in another cemetery (La Fontaine, Molière, Descartes, Boileau, Rabelais among others). Guided tours.

Céramique-Hôtel (34 Avenue de Wagram, 17.Arr.): Art nouveau building by Jules Aimé Lavirotte.

Châtelet: See Place du Châtelet.

Cirque d'Hiver (Circus; Place Pasdeloup, 11.Arr.): Circus building with 20 sides (diameter 157 ft., height 92 ft.), built in 1852 by Jacob Ignaz Hittorff.

Collège de France (Rue des Ecoles, 5.Arr.): The Collège de France was founded in 1530 by Francis I, with the name Collège du Roi, as an alternative to the University, which had a theological bias; it is one of the most important French educational institutions. This 'Scholars' Republic', subject to the Ministry of Education, has the following privileges vis-à-vis the University: the lectures and practical sessions are open to all; there are no fees; the lectures and practical sessions are not aimed at examinations; the nature of a chair is determined by the research field of the chosen professor; the appointment of a don is not based on degrees and qualifications, but exclusively on his or her academic performance. Teaching is in three departments: a) Mathematics, Physics, Natural Sciences, b) Philosophy, Sociology, c) Philology, Archaeology. The core of the complex, which has been extended by numerous buildings well into this century, dates from 1611, when the foundation stone was laid by Louis XIII.

Conciergerie (Museum/remand prison; Quai de l'Horloge, 1.Arr.): The Conciergerie is the only surviving section of the medieval Parisian royal palace, built 1299–1313 by Philip the Fair, and subsequently much damaged and replaced. The façade on the Seine side is articulated with three defensive towers and the *clock tower* (Tour de l'Horloge) built *c.* 1350; the first public clock in Paris was built here *c.* 1370 (restored in the 19C).

The building was used as royal castle and gaol, as a parliamentary prison, and later played a notorious role during the French Revolution as the 'antechamber to the guillotine'. During the Reign of Terror those condemned to death were taken to the dark vaults under the building, and on the next day to the scaffold. The dungeons in which Danton, Hébert, Chaumette and Robespierre passed their last night are still shown to the public, and not far from them is Queen Marie Antoinette's cell.

Ecole des Beaux Arts (between the Quai Malaquais and the Rue Bonaparte, 6.Arr.): see under Churches and Ecclesiastical Buildings, Chapelle des Petits-Augustins.

Ecole Militaire (43 Avenue de la Motte-Piquet, 7.Arr.): Work on this early neoclassical building, designed by Jacques-Ange Gabriel as a school for 500 officers, started in 1751, then continued 1768–82 (its most famous pupil was Napoleon Bonaparte); it now houses the French Military Academy (not open to the public).

Eiffel Tower at night

The *chapel*, also the work of Gabriel, is an outstanding example of Louis-Seize architecture (visits only by written permission of the Commandant of the Ecole Militaire).

Eiffel Tower: See Tour Eiffel.

Faculté de Médecine (12 Rue de l'Ecole de Médecine, 6.Arr.): Foundation stone laid in 1774 by Louis XVI, built by Jacques Gondoulin; extended in the late 19C.

Gare du Nord (Place de Roubaix, 10.Arr.): Built 1861–3 by Cologne architect Jacob Ignaz Hittorf with neoclassical façade almost 600 ft. long. The departure hall is an iron construction in three sections (2330 ft. wide, 656 ft. long). The Gare du Nord is the departure point for trains to northern France, North Germany, Belgium, Great Britain and the Netherlands.

Grand Palais (Exhibition Hall; Avenue Winston-Churchill, 8.Arr.): Neo-baroque building for the World Fair of 1900, built under the direction of Charles Girault. It now accommodates part of the University and the Palais de la Découverte, a natural science museum (see under Museums, Palais de la Découverte). In the same street is the Petit Palais (q.v.), also built by Girault for the World Fair of 1900; this now houses the Musée de Beaux Arts.

Halles (Quartier des Halles, 1.Arr.): This was the 'belly of Paris', where the fruit and vegetable dealers used to ply their wares; it was made world-famous by Zola in his novel of the same name. When the wholesale market moved to Rungis and the market halls built by Baltard were pulled down the area became a building site for years. It is one of the largest underground junctions in the Parisian transport network, and above this is the *Forum des Halles*, opened in 1979, with shops, cinemas, restaurants and theatres.

Hôtels: The numerous Hôtels are palace-like buildings, mostly built as residences for high state officials or rich aristocratic families; many were

La Bourse (Stock Exchange), portico

also public buildings. The characteristic architectural style was established in the 17C. The Hôtel is usually separated from the street by an iron railing, or by a gatehouse and the cour d'honneur. The servants' quarters and kitchens are alongside the courtyard. The main building (corps de logis) contains living rooms on the courtyard side and rooms for public occasions on the ground floor of the garden side.

Hôtel des Ambassadeurs de Hollande (47 Rue Vieille-du-Temple, 4.Arr.): Built by Pierre Cottard 1657–60, and one of the best-preserved mansions in the Marais. Madame de Staël is said to have been baptized here (1766). The playwright Caron de Beaumarchais rented the palace ten years later and wrote his highly successful play 'Le Mariage de Figaro' here.

Hôtel d'Aumont (7 Rue de Jouy, 4.Arr.): Built by Le Vau *c.* 1635, extended by Mansart before 1660; ceiling paintings by Simon Vouet and Charles Lebrun.

Collège de France

Hôtel de Beauharnais (German Embassy; 78 Rue de Lille, 7. Arr.): Built by Germain Boffrand in 1714.

Hôtel de Beauvais (Museum; 68 Rue François-Miron, 4. Arr.): The Museum of Musical Instruments is housed in the corps de logis of this palace, built 1858–60 by Antoine Lepautre for Pierre de Beauvais and his one-eyed daughter, lady-in-waiting and confidante to Queen Anne of Austria, who had initiated the young Louis XIV into the secrets of married life. When the Mozart family arrived in Paris in November 1763—little Amadeus was playing in Versailles for the Marquise de Pompadour—they stayed in the Hôtel de Beauvais.

Hôtel de Biron (Rodin Museum; 77 Rue de Varenne, 7.Arr.): This two-storeyed Hôtel with eleven axes now accommodates the Rodin Museum (see under Museums); it was built 1728–31 by Jean Aubert to plans by Jacques Gabriel for the financier Peyrenc de Moras, and occupied by a series of celebrities. It is named after the Duke of Biron, who acquired the Palace in the second half of the 18C, and entertained on a lavish scale. From 1820–1904 the building housed a boarding school for the daughters of the nobility, run by the ladies of the Sacred Heart of Jesus (neo-Gothic chapel dating from 1875). After this the rooms were made available to artists as flats and studios. The dancer Isadora Duncan lived here, and so did the painter Henri Matisse. Rodin was given permission by the state to live on the ground floor until his death (1917). Rainer Maria Rilke was his secretary from 1908–14. Jean Cocteau rented a wing in 1908&9.

Hôtel Bourbon-Condé (12 Rue Monsieur, 7.Arr.): Masterpiece of Alexandre-Théodore Brongniart, built in 1783 for Louise-Adelaide de Condé.

Hôtel de Cluny (Museum; 24 Rue

de Sommerard, 5.Arr.): This residential palace of the abbots of Cluny, in three sections and lavishly furnished, and the ruins of the former baths (see Thermes), now accommodates the Cluny Museum of Medieval Art and Culture (see under Museums, Cluny).

Hôtel d'Hallwyl (28 Rue Michel-le-Comte, 3.Arr.): This palace built in the early 18C was rented to the Necker & Co. bank in 1757. Jacques Necker, who was later to be Minister of Finance, and his wife lived here until 1766; this was the year of the birth of their daughter Germaine, who became world-famous as Madame de Staël.

Hôtel des Invalides (Museum; Esplanade des Invalides): The gigantic Hôtel des Invalides, occupying an area of about 127,000 square kilometres and borrowing various ideas from palace, monastery, church and barracks architecture, was the manifestation of one of the (few) great social schemes of the period of Absolutism. Louis XIV intended the 'Hospital Palace' to be used by the disabled from his numerous wars. Work started in 1671 under Libéral Bruant, (Hardouin-Mansart took over), and continued until the late 17C (for the churches in the building see under Churches and Ecclesiastical Buildings, Saint-Louis des Invalides and Eglise du Dôme des Invalides). The portal in the central porch is decorated with a bas-relief and leads to the large cour d'honneur, surrounded by almost identical buildings. About 200 pensioners are still accommodated here, and the rooms also house military offices and the Army Museum (see under Museums, Armée).

Hôtel Lambert (Privately owned, not open to the public; 2 Rue Saint-Louis-de-l'Ile, 4 Arr.): One of Le Vau's masterpieces, built in 1640 for Nicolas Lambert de Thorigny. Semi-circular cour d'honneur, symmetrical staircase in two sections, Galerie d'Hercule with reliefs from the Hercules myth and paintings by Lebrun.

Hôtel de Lamoignon or **d'Angoulême** (Library; 24 Rue Pavée): In the

La Conciergerie at night

Conciergerie, 'Salle des Gens d'Armes' (above), clock tower (r)

late 16C Diane de France, the natural and later legitimized daughter (Duchess of Angoulême) of Henri II, commissioned this town palace (corps de logis with side pavillions), Charles de Valois added two wings on the courtyard side; the S. wing was pulled down in the 19C. In 1658 Guillaume de Lamoignon, the first President of the French Parliament, rented the Hôtel and received the most important artists, philosophers and writers of his time: they included Madame de Sévigné, Racine, Boileau, Regnard and Bourdalue. In the middle of the 18C an occupant of the Palace bequeathed his valuable private library to the city (14,000 volumes, 2,000 manuscripts); they became the core of the *Bibliothèque Historique de la Ville de Paris*, now accommodated in the Hôtel de Lamoignon. Alphonse Daudet was a distinguished occupant of the Palace

from 1867; he always held open house on Wednesday evenings, when his guests included Turgenev, Flaubert, Zola, Edmond de Goncourt, Anatole France, and Sully Proud'homme.

Hôtel de Lauzun (State guest-house; entrance only with special permission; 17 Quai d'Anjou, 4.Arr.): This Palace was built by Le Vau in 1656 and is impressive less for its plain exterior than for the magnificent *interior decoration* (panelling, carving, statues, ceiling paintings by Lebrun, Lesueur among others), an ideal setting for the 'Club des Haschichins', which used to meet here in the 19C in the gold-panelled rooms on the first floor. This group included Charles Baudelaire, who had been placed under a trustee because of his extravagance (he lived in a room facing the courtyard on the second floor), his fellow-poet and neighbour Théophile

Faculté de Médecine, X.Bichat ▷

Gautier, and also Alfred de Musset, Honoré de Balzac and Victor Hugo.

Hôtel de Matignon (Official residence of the Prime Minister; 57 Rue de Varenne, 7.Arr.): Built in 1721 by Jean Courtonne, later altered by Brongiart. One of the most important Hôtels in the Quartier des Invalides.

Hôtel de Mayenne (21 Rue Saint-Antoine, 4.Arr.): This Palace was built for Henri de Lorraine, Duke of Mayenne 1613–17 by Androuet du Cerceau, (altered in the early 18C), and one of the first Paris Hôtels 'entre cour et jardin': the corps de logis is set between the cour d'honneur on the street side and the garden behind. This design was later followed by many other Hôtels.

Hôtel de Rohan (Part of the Archives Nationales; 83 Rue Veille-

Gare du Nord, view of the neoclassical façade of the station, completed in 1863

The modern Forum des Halles, replacing the old market halls, with Saint-Eustache

du-Temple, 3.Arr.): Built in 1705 for Maximilien de Rohan, Prince Bishop of Strasbourg. Façade with seven axes, thirteen on the garden side; Cabinet des Singes with paintings by Christophe Huet (*c.* 1750). Above the portal of the former mews is a relief by Robert Le Lorrain of the Horses of Apollo.

Hôtel de Saint-Aignan (71 Rue du Temple, 3.Arr.): The remarkable feature of this palace, built by Pierre Le Muet for the Comte d'Avaux, is the magnificent *courtyard* with Corinthian pilasters in colossal order on three sides.

Hôtel Salé (Picasso-Museum: 5 Rue de Thorigny, 3.Arr.): The name 'Salé' is a reference to the fact that Pierre Aubert de Fontenay, who commissioned this impressive palace from Jean Bouiller de Bourges, who built it 1656–61, made huge profits from the salt tax. The building now houses the Picasso Museum (see under Museums, Picasso).

Hôtel de Salm (Chancellery of the Légion d'Honneur; 64 Rue de Lille, 7.Arr.). This magnificent mansion, built shortly before the Revolution by Pierre Rousseau, was the most important private Hôtel of the reign of Louis XVI. It was commissioned by Prince Frederick III of Salm-Kyrburg, who ruined himself completely by doing so; he ended up on the guillotine. The palace became the seat of the Légion d'Honneur in 1804.

Hôtel de Sens (1 Rue du Figier, 4.Arr.): Example of a late medieval hôtel, built 1475–1507 as the Paris residence of the archbishops of Sens. Renaissance garden.

Hôtel de Soubise (accommodates the Archives Nationales; 60 Rue des Francs-Bourgeois, 3.Arr.): One of the most lavish 18C hôtels, which also established a pattern for subsequent buildings of the type; it was built

Grand Palais, colonnade and statue of Peace

Portal of the Hôtel de Laffemas, one of the capital's fine old villas

Detail of the restored Hôtel de la Porte

1705–9 by Pierre-Alexis Delamair for the Prince of Soubise, François de Rohan. A colonnade of 24 double Corinthian columns surrounds the courtyard. The ground floor rooms are not open to the public. A brilliant feature of the interior is the *Salon Ovale* in the upper storey (ceiling painting with Psyche cycle by Charles Natoire).

Hôtel de Sully (houses the offices of the Monuments Historiques; 62 Rue Saint-Antoine, 4.Arr.): The most magnificent and lavish private palace of the reign of Louis XII, built 1624–30 to plans by Jean Androuet du Cerceau, acquired in 1634 by the Duke of Sully, a former minister of Henri IV. The courtyard is enclosed by the corps de logis with five axes and two wings with seven axes. The most striking feature is the lavish early baroque decoration on the façades.

Hôtel de Ville (Town Hall; Place de l'Hôtel de Ville, 4.Arr.): The Renaissance town hall, extended in the early 19C, originally built in the 16&17C to plans by the Italian architect Domenico da Cortona, known as Boccador, was burned down in 1871 at the end of the Commmune uprising; the new building dates from 1873, and is a copy of its predecessor, most accurately in the central section. The ostentatious interior is appropriate to the heavy exterior.

Hôtel de Villeroy (Ministry of Agriculture; 78 Rue de Varenne, 7.Arr.): This playful rococo palace was built 1720–4 by François Debias-Aubry for the actress Charlotte Desmares.

Institut de France - Collège et Chapelle des Quatre Nations (23 Quai de Conti, 6.Arr.): Since 1795–1806 the Institut de France has been

Hôtel de Beauvais, carving

the foremost official academic and artistic body art in France. It consists of five Academies: 1. Académie Française (language and literature), 2. Académie des Inscriptions et Belles-Lettres (inscriptions, literary history), 3. Académie des Sciences (natural sciences), 4. Académie des Beaux-Arts (painting, sculpture, architecture, graphics, music), 5. Académie des Sciences Morales et Politiques (philosophy, political science, jurisprudence, economics, history, geography). Members are admitted in the chapel of the Collège des Quatre-Nations, dissolved in 1793.

History of the Institut de France: Originally a private club for the promotion of the French language which met in the home of Valentin Conrart from 1629. On 2 January 1635 Cardi-

Hôtel de Cluny, portal ▷

Hôtel Biron

nal Richelieu expanded it into the Académie Française; this first met on 10 July 1637, and still has a constant membership of 40. In 1663 Colbert commissioned four of them to compose and edit inscriptions for public monuments. This commission, called the Petite Académie, was given the name Académie Royale des Inscriptions et Médailles in 1701, and a set of rules limiting its membership to 40 and extending its sphere of activity to the fields of history, archaeology and philology. A decree of the Regent on 4 January 1716 altered the former name to Académie Royale des Inscriptions et Belles-Lettres. The Académie des Sciences was added as the third by Colbert in 1666, reorganized in 1699 and extended in 1785. A Royal Academy of Sculpture and Painting (de Sculpture et Peinture) was established by Mazarin in 1648 and confirmed by Louis XIV in 1655. In 1671 Colbert founded an Academy of Architecture, and Louis XV declared himself its personal patron by open letter in 1717. The academies were dissolved as royal institutions by decree of the Convention of 8 August 1793, but reconstituted on 25 October 1795 as Institut National by the Directoire, and organized into three categories, to which Napoleon added a fourth in 1803. It has been known as the 'Institut de France' since 1806. In 1832 Guizot added the Académie des Sciences Morales at Politiques as the fifth academy; this had existed at the time of the Institut National, but was dissolved by Napoleon in 1803. Napoleon III created a sixth academy in 1855 (politics, administration and finance), but this was dissolved in 1866. The Academies are linked by numerous common practices. Vacancies are always filled by election, with confirmation by the head of state.

Hôtel des Invalides, cour d'honneur

Each Academy meets separately from the others; the whole membership meets once a year only, on 25 October (11 August, Napoleon Day, under Napoleon III). Prizes are announced on this occasion.

Building: The side sections are tall, square pavilions with Corinthian pilasters, and the beautifully decorated *façade* is a semicircle overlooking the Seine. In the centre of the arch is the *chapel* with portico and high drum dome and lantern. The festive interior contains the *tomb of Mazarin* (1602–61), completed by Coysevox in 1692.

Maison de l'O.R.T.F. (Radio and television building; 116 Avenue du Président Kennedy, 16.Arr.): Circular building with rectangular tower 230 ft. high, built 1952–63 by Henry Barnard. Until 1974 the Office de Radiodiffusion-Télévision Française (O.R.T.F.) was the state broadcasting company, responsible for all television and radio programmes in metropolitan France and overseas territories. Since 1 January 1975 it has been split into seven independent public institutions: public television sales company, audio-visual institute, radio company, first, second and third television channels and television production company.

Maison de l'UNESCO (Place de Fontenoy, 7.Arr.): UNESCO (United Nations Educational, Scientific and Cultural Organization) was founded in November 1945 in London as a special UN organization, and has been based in Paris since November 1946. (In 1983 the USA gave notice of withdrawal from UNESCO on 31 December 1984, for reasons of ostensible politicization of working topics, a hostile attitude to the freedom of the press and unrestrained expansion of

Hôtel de Salm, relief in the attica of the corner pavilion

the budget; the UK has since followed suit).

The three buildings—Secretariat (Y-shaped building in three sections), conference building and seat of the permanent delegations—came into being 1955–8 through international co-operation involving the most important artists of the fifties. The buildings were designed by Marcel Breuer (USA), Pier Luigi Nervi (Italy), and Bernard Zehrfuss (France) and were approved by a committee including famous architects Lucio Costa (Brazil), Walter Gropius (USA), Le Corbusier (France) and Ernesto Rogers (Italy), with final consultation of Eero Saarinen (USA). The *decoration* was also the responsibility of fine artists of the first rank: Pablo Picasso, Jean Arp, Henry Moore, Joan Miró, Jean Bazaine, Isamo Noguchi, Alexander Calder, Rufino Tamayo, Afro, Karel Appel, Burke Marx, Roberto Matta and others.

Maison Laroche (10 Square du Docteur-Blanche, 16.Arr.): First building in Paris by Le Corbusier (1923).

Monnaie (State Mint; 11 Quai de Conti, 6.Arr.): Built as the Royal Mint 1771–7 by Jacques Denis Antoine. The façade is 384 ft. long, and free of baroque excess (central section with five axes and wings with eleven axes).

Observatoire (Observatory; 61 Avenue de l'Observatoire, 16.Arr.): Built 1667–72 by Claude de Perrault as a block with façades facing the four points of the compass. Neither wood nor iron was used in the building, because of the risk of fire and effect on

Hôtel de Sully, cour d'honneur

compass needles. The famous 'speaking clock' is in the cellars, almost 90 ft. below ground level.

Palais - Bourbon - Assemblée Nationale (Seat of the National Assembly, interior open to the public only with written permission; Quai d'Orsay/Place du Palais-Bourbon, 7.Arr.): The Assemblée Nationale is the first chamber of the French Parliament under the constitution of the Fifth Republic (the second chamber, the Senate, meets in the Palais du Luxembourg). Comparison with the English Houses of Parliament cannot be made directly, as the Assemblée Nationale only has limited legislative competence and is severely restricted as an organ of control.
The Palais-Bourbon, built 1722–8 for Louis-François de Bourbon, was extended from 1765 for Louis Joseph de Bourbon, Prince de Condé, and

rebuilt as a Parliament building after confiscation in 1792. A remarkable feature of the Seine façade is the broad *peristyle* by Bernard Poyet (1806), a counterpart to the Madeleine.

Palais de la Bourse: See Bourse.

Palais de Chaillot (Museums; Place du Trocadéro, 16.Arr.): The palace was built in 1937 for the World Exhibition; it affords an impressive view of the Champ de Mars, and accommodates the following museums (see Museums): Cinéma, Ethnography, Shipping (Merchant and Naval) and Monuments Français (Architecture).

Palais de la Découverte: Scientific and Technological Museum (see under Museums) in the W. wing of the Grand Palais (Avenue Franklin D.Roosevelt, 8.Arr.).

Hôtel de Sens, courtyard

Palais de l'Elysée (Residence of the President of the Republic; 55 Rue du Faubourg-Saint-Honoré, 8.Arr.): Built in 1718 by Armand Claude Mollet, lavishly furnished by the Marquise de Pompadour, residence of the President of the Republic since 1873.

Palais de Justice (Boulevard du Palais, 1.Arr.): The kings of France lived here until 1358, the Parliament (Court) met here from the mid 15C, and sentences were passed here during the Reign of Terror at the time of the Revolution. It was rebuilt after the fire of 1871 to resemble the original building.

Palais du Luxembourg (Seat of the Senate; 15 Rue de Vaugirard, 6.Arr.): Queen Maria de'Medici commissioned this palace as a dower house from Salomon de Brosse; it was built 1615–31. After it became the meeting-place of the Senate in 1800 numerous alterations and extensions were carried out. The Jardin du Luxembourg is part of the palace. A notable feature is the *Fontaine de Médicis* between the palace and the Rue Médicis.

Palais-Royal (Official seat of the Conseil d'Etat and the Ministère des Affaires Culturelles; Place du Palais-Royal): Cardinal Richelieu commissioned this palace near the Louvre for himself, and bequeathed it to the King; it was built 1634–9 by Jacques Lemercier. Molière's company played in the part of the building, and it also accommodated the Cardinal's large collections of works of art. In 1643 Queen Anne of Austria moved into the palace with the young Louis XIV, and from then on it was known as the Palais-Royal. 1752–70 the corps de

Hôtel de Ville

Hôtel de Ville

logis was almost completely rebuilt by Pierre Contant d'Ivry, and the garden enclosed by three wings. After a period of neglect during the Revolution and under the First Empire (gambling dens, brothels), the building was restored 1818–30.

Palais de Tokyo (Museum; 13 Avenue du Président-Wilson, 16 Arr.): The Palais de Tokyo, the E. wing of the Palais de l'Art Moderne built for the World Fair of 1937, now houses the Musée d'Art et d'Essai (see under Museums, Art et Essai).

Panthéon (National memorial and burial place; Place du Panthéon, 5.Arr.): In classical antiquity the Greek word pantheon applied to a temple of all the gods, but also to buildings in honour of famous men. The Panthéon in Paris, originally intended as a church of St.Geneviève,

the patron saint of Paris, and decorated with pictures relating to her, was started in 1756 by Jacques-Germain Soufflot, completed in 1770 and just a year later transformed into a 'Panthéon Français' as the result of a decision by the Assemblé Nationale, to honour famous Frenchmen (the church windows were walled up to give the impression of a mausoleum). On 3 April 1791 the publicist and revolutionary politican Mirabeau ('we shall only yield to the might of the bayonet') was the first to be interred here, in the same year the mortal remains of Voltaire followed, and in 1794 those of Rousseau (the bones of Voltaire and Rousseau were stolen in 1814 by right-wing extremists and thrown on a rubbish tip by the Seine; they have still not been found). The building was used as a church under the Restoration (1822–30) and the Second Empire (1851–85), then

Palais Luxembourg, garden side

became a national burial place again when Victor Hugo was interred here in 1885. Sixty famous Frenchmen are buried here, including Emile Zola and Soufflot, the architect.

Parc des Princes (Stadium; 24 Avenue du Commandant-Guilbaud, 16.Arr.): Largest stadium in Paris, accommodating 50,000 (football, pop concerts and other large-scale events).

Petit Palais (Museum; Avenue Winston-Churchill, 8.Arr.): Built for the World Fair of 1900, the palace now accommodates the municipal art collections (see Petit Palais under Museums).

Porte Saint-Denis (Triumphal arch; 24 Boulevard Saint-Denis, 2/10 Arr.): Triumphal arch built by François Blondel on the pattern of the Arch of Titus in Rome (one arch) for

Louis XIV's victorious return from the Dutch campaign (1672).

Porte Saint-Martin (Triumphal arch; 33 Boulevard Saint-Martin, 3/10 Arr.): Triumphal arch built in 1674 by Pierre Bullet in honour of Louis XIV (three arches; reliefs with scenes from the king's campaigns).

Quartier Général de l'Armée de Salut (Headquarters of the Salvation Army; 12 Rue Cantagrel, 13.Arr.): This was one of the first residential buildings with sealed windows, ventilated by an air-conditioning system; it was designed by Le Corbusier 1932&3, and provides 'soap, soup and salvation'.

Rotonde de la Villette (former toll house; Place de Stalingrad, 10/19 Arr.):J Last building in a group of toll houses built by Ledoux in 1789 at this

Palais Royal, façade figure

junction (of the roads from Flanders and North Germany).

Sorbonne: See Quartiers, Streets, Squares, Parks, Gardens under Quartier Latin.

Thermes (Ancient baths; 24 Rue du Sommerard, 5.Arr.): On the site of the Musée de Cluny (Hôtel de Cluny) are ruins of Roman baths built *c.* AD 200. Significant sections of the frigidarium (cold baths), tepidarium (warm baths) and of the hot baths with under-floor heating have survived.

Tour Clovis (Place du Panthéon; 5.Arr.): Remaining section of a Gothic church dedicated to St.Genevieve, built in 1180 and pulled down in 1802.

Tour Eiffel (Quai Branly, 7.Arr.):

The emblem of Paris, built for the World Fair of 1889 by the engineer Gustave Eiffel, has undergone a complete overhaul in preparation for its hundredth anniversary. The tower is over 1,000 ft. high, is made of 12,000 steel sections and has three platforms, with restaurants in the two lower ones.

Tour de Jean Sans Peur (20 Rue Etienne-Marcel, 2.Arr.): Tower of the town palace of the dukes of Burgundy, built *c.* 1375.

Tour Maine-Montparnasse (Office tower block; Avenue du Maine): Highest office tower block in Europe; modern 'symbol' of the former Montparnasse artists' colonies. Good view from the 56th floor.

Tour Saint-Jacques (Avenue Victoria, 4.Arr.): Sole surviving section

Palais Royal, cour d'honneur

of the church of Saint-Jacques, pulled down in 1797.

Quartiers, Streets, Squares, Parks, Gardens

Bois de Boulogne: Its promenades and avenues, artificial lakes, artificial waterfall, folk museum (see under Museums, Arts et Traditions populaires), children's pleasure park, cafés, restaurants, cabarets, two racecourses (Hippodrome d'Auteuil, Hippodrome de Longchamp) make it the most popular recreation area within the city boundaries (850 hectares). In the Middle Ages it was a royal hunting ground, and it has been within the city boundaries since 1852. Bagatelle château and park in the NW.

Bois de Vincennes: See Vincennes.

Champ de Mars: This former parade ground at the W. end of the town between the N. bank of the Seine and the Ecole Militaire is now a park. World Fairs were held here from 1867. The site made history at the time of the Revolution: France's first constitution was solemnly sworn here on 14 July 1790. In 1794 the Feast of the Highest Being was held here, a notion which the revolutionary leader Robespierre instructed the French to believe in.

Champs-Elysées: This world-famous boulevard leads from the Place de la Concorde to the Arc de Triomphe. The W. section between the Arc de Triomphe and the Rond-Point is characterized by international brilliance (luxury shops, restaurants, cafés, theatres), the S. section is a park which developed from a pleasure grove laid out by Maria de'Medici and Louis XV. The Petit Palais and

Petit Palais, portal

the Grand Palais between the park and the Seine show the tastes of the turn of the century. The Elysée Palace opens symmetrically beyond the gardens on to the elegant Rue du Faubourg-Saint-Honoré with its luxury shops.

Faubourg Saint-Germain: In the 18C the Faubourg Saint-Germain was a residential area of distinction, cool, aristocratic and elegant, full of ministries and embassies. Most of the magnificently furnished and spaciously built palaces (hôtels) date from this period.

Les Galeries: These roofed shopping precincts are a typical feature of Paris; the Galerie Vero-Daudet is particularly fine. The Galeries Lafayette, a department store with a charming atmosphere, is also worth a visit.

Ile de le Cité: The island is rather like a ship—the towers and turrets of Notre-Dame give an impression of masts—and carries the massive Palais de Justice and the Préfecture de Police. Rebuilding in the 19C meant that the district lost many of its medieval characteristics as the core around which Paris grew (see History of the City).

Jardin du Luxembourg: See under Secular Buildings, Palais du Luxembourg.

Jardin des Plantes (Park; 57 Rue Cuvier, 5.Arr.): National Museum of Natural History (plants, minerals etc).

Jardin des Tuileries: See Louvre p. 130.

Marais: The Marais was rescued at

Petit Palais, façade

the last minute by restoration on a large scale, and is almost an open-air museum of secular architecture. The name refers to the marshy area which in the Middle Ages accommodated only a few ecclesiastical settlements. The Rue Saint-Antoine, following the line of a Roman road, cuts through the area; the Marais is bounded to the S. by the Seine, and is built around the former royal palace, the Hôtel Saint-Paul, stretching roughly from the Hôtel de Ville to the Place de la Bastille, from the Quais to the Boulevard Beaumarchais. Henri IV redeveloped the N. part of the area to a large extent; until then the Hôtel Carnavalet and the Hôtel Lamoignon were the only buildings on the site. He commissioned the Place Royale (now Place des Vosges) and planned the siting of the hôtels. In the 17C the quartier was still aristocratic and upper middle class, but lost this

cachet in the 18C, and fell into disrepair. It was not until the appropriate law was passed in 1962 that a basis was laid for the preservation of this historic and artistic heritage. The S. section, between the Rue Saint-Antoine and the Seine, has narrow streets clearly showing the medieval layout. Behind the Seine façade the little streets are lined with old *residences of the nobility*, altered to a greater or lesser extent. There are still some venerable *half-timbered houses* in the Rue François-Miron.

Montmartre: The 'Butte' ('Hill') of Montmartre, on which the Sacré-Coeur and the church of Saint-Pierre stand, is a highly individual district of the town, on the site of a village which was already 'very old' at the time of François Villon. At the foot of the Butte, in the *Place Blanche* and the *Place Pigalle* there is lively night life

in the bars and cabarets and in the streets. In the high season Montmartre is flooded with tourists, who cram the dense maze of narrow streets, steps and little squares, but it has retained its charm, and some wonderful views. The name derives from *Mons Mercurii* ('Hill of Mercury') or *Mons Martyrum* ('Martyrs' Hill'). It spread around a medieval shrine, and later around an abbey. In the 19C and early 20C numerous artists lived and worked here: Renoir, Utrillo, Emile Bernard, Gauguin, Dufy, Paulbot (who drew Montmartre street urchins), Othon Friesz, Juan Gris, Picasso, Van Dongen etc.

Parc Bagatelle: Bagatelle palace and park (18C) in the Bois de Boulogne.

Parc de Buttes-Chaumont (Place Armand-Carrel; 19.Arr.): Park laid out 1864–7 as a wild landscape in the English style, with waterfall, artificial grotto, lake.

Parc Monceau (35 Boulevard de Courcelles, 8.Arr.): Late-18C park redesigned under the Second Empire with arcades, a pyramid, ruins, an obelisk etc. Some old buildings overgrown with ivy.

Parc de Montsouris (22–8 Boulevard Jourdan, 14.Arr.): Park laid out 1867–78 as a wild landscape in the English style, with lake, cascade and pavilion.

Place de la Bastille: This circular square is on the site of the famous fortress prison, stormed and torn down at the outbreak of the Revolution on 14 July 1789 (the outline of the prison is marked on the paving stones). The July Column (Colonne de Juillet, q.v.) is in the centre of the square.

Porte Saint-Denis (l), Tour de Clovis (r)

Parc de la Villette, hemispherical cinema La Géode

Eiffel tower, bust of G.Eiffel (above),
Tour de Jean Sans Peur (below), Tour
Saint-Jacques (r)

Champs-Elysées, Palais de Glace

Jardin du Luxembourg, Fontaine de Medicis

Parvis de Notre-Dame (Ile de la Cité): The *Archaelogical Crypt* houses remains of the 6C Merovingian cathedral of St-Etienne, and of old houses.

Place Charles-de-Gaulle (formerly Etoile) see under Secular Buildings, Arc de Triomphe de l'Etoile.

Place du Châtelet: The square opposite the Cité is laid out around a 19C fountain and contains two theatres, the Châtelet and the Théâtre de la Ville.

Place de la Concorde: This magnificent square at the point of intersection of two streets was designed by Jacques Ange Gabriel under Louis XV. The great columned façades to the right and left of the Rue Royale were built 1760–5. At the beginning of the Champs-Elysées are the *Marly Horses*, by Coustou (brought here from Château Marly in 1795). Coysevox' statues of the *Goddess of Fame* and *Mercury* at the entrance to the Tuileries also came from Marly. In the middle of the square is the *Luxor obelisk* (see under Bridges, Fountains, Monuments). The Pont de la Concorde, widened and decorated with large statues under the Restoration, (see under Bridges, Fountains, Statues) was built by Perronet shortly before the Revolution.

Place Dauphine: Despite certain blemishes the square, laid out by Henri IV after the birth of the heir to the throne (Dauphin) Louis XIII (1601), has retained much of its charm. It was originally surrounded by three regular rows of houses with uniform façades, and the W. point of the triangle led the eye to the bastion of the Pont-Neuf.

Place Furstenberg: See Saint-Germain-des-Prés and Montparnasse.

Galerie Vero-Daudet, 1826 ▷

Galeries Lafayette, art nouveau dome

Montmartre, Place du Tertre, barrel-organist

Place de la Nation: The Rue Saint-Antoine leads from the Place de la Bastille to the Place de la Nation, where two columns and two pavilions mark the site of the former Paris toll house (remains of the rampart).

Place Pigalle: See Montmartre.

Place Vendôme: The harmony and balance of this square are a unique example in Europe. Louis XIV originally acquired the site for official buildings (library, academies) in 1685, but the plan came to nothing because of lack of funds. In 1698 the king presented the square to the city, with the condition that the façades were to be built to Hardouin-Mansart's designs; this did not apply to the buildings behind them. The equestrian statue of Louis XIV was destroyed in 1792, and on its site Napoleon commissioned the *Colonne de la Grande Armée* (1804–10), in imitation of Trajan's Column in Rome; the French version has neoclassical reliefs depicting scenes from the Napoleonic Wars. The statue of the Emperor on top of the column was used in 1814 to cast the equestrian statue of Henri IV on the Pont-Neuf, but the Citizens' King Louis-Philippe had the statue replaced in 1833. During the Commune uprising of 1871 the column was toppled, and the painter Gustave Courbet was found to have been responsible.

Place des Victoires: Statue of the 'Roi Soleil' Louis XIV dating from 1822.

Place des Vosges: This monumental square is the oldest in Paris; it was the centre of the Marais in the 17C. At this time it was the scene of various festivals, but also a place at which duels were fought.

Quartier Latin: The Boulevard Saint-Michel, laid out in the 19C, is the central axis of the Quartier Latin, which has been a student quarter for

Montmartre, Moulin de la Galette

centuries. It is the home of numerous schools and other academic institutions, of which the oldest is the university, the Sorbonne, named after Robert de Sorbon, who taught here at the time of Saint Louis.

Rue de Rivoli: Boulevard connecting the Place de la Concorde and the Madeleine, with restaurants ('Maxim's'), luxury shops etc.

Saint-Germain-des-Prés and Montparnasse: The quartier known as *Saint-Germain-des-Prés* is in the precinct of a former abbey, grouped around the former abbey church (see under Churches and Ecclesiastical Buildings, Saint-Germain-des-Prés). Despite widening and straightening of streets in the 19C many picturesque little streets have survived, including the *Rue de Furstenberg*, which broadens into a charming

Place du Châtelet with Tour Saint-Jacques and Théâtre Sarah Bernhardt

square containing Eugène Delacroix' studio, and also the narrow *Rues de l'Echaudé, Bernard-Palissy, du Sabot, du Dragon, Visconti.* There are particularly fine 17&18C hôtels in the *Rue Jacob* and the *Rue des Saints-Pères.* Saint-Germain was for a long time a peaceful middle-class area. The 'parish' became famous after the Liberation in the age of jazz and existentialism. A large number of discothèques and restaurants have come into being, and the ground floors of the former hôtels have been transformed by shop-window displays. The *Rue de Rennes* leads directly to the ultra-modern *Maine-Montparnasse* complex (1960s) and to the *Quartier Montparnasse,* which also has a very active night life. During the Belle Epoque and the Thirties it was a meeting-place for artists, writers and intellectuals: Modigliani, Kandinsky, Picasso, Klee, Matisse, Chagall, Rouault, Hemingway, Henry Miller etc.

Zoo de Paris: See Vincennes.

Bridges, Fountains, Monuments

Apollinaire (Monument; Square Laurent-Prache, 6.Arr.): By Picasso for the poet Guillaume Apollinaire, whose work fell between Symbolism and Surrealism (1880–1918); bronze female head.

Balzac (Monument; junction of Boulevard Raspal and Boulevard du Montparnasse, 6.Arr.): Monument to the writer Honoré de Balzac (1799–1850), author of the 'Comédie Humaine' cycle of novels, not erected until 1939; Auguste Rodin's suggested design was rejected in 1898.

Colonne de Juillet (Place de la Bas-

Place de la Concorde

ille, 4.Arr.): The July Column is both a monument to the July Uprising of 1830 and the tomb of the revolutionaries killed in that uprising. The names of those buried in the underground catacombs are listed on the shaft of the column.

Fontaine des Innocents (Square des Innocents, 1.Arr.): Loggias by Pierre Lescot with sculptures by Jean Goujon (relief with naiads), inaugurated 1549, rebuilt as a little temple by Quatremère de Quincy in 1786. Former site of the Cimetière des Innocents.

Fontaine de Mars (129–131 Rue Saint-Dominique, 7.Arr.): Neoclassical fountain *c.* 1806. Hygieia, the goddess of health, gives Mars, the god of war, a drink.

Fontaine des Quatre-Saisons (57–9 Rue de Grenelle, 7.Arr.): Built 1739–46 by Edmé Bouchardon in Louis-Quinze style, with a two-tiered façade. Statues of the four seasons and town goddess with Seine and Marne.

Fontaine Saint-Michel (Place Saint-Michel, 5/6.Arr.): This enormous fountain, like the façade of a building, was built 1858–60 by Gabriel Davioud.

Henri IV (Equestrian statue; on the bastion of the Pont-Neuf, 1.Arr.): Commissioned in 1604 in imitation of a model by Giovanni da Bologna, destroyed during the Revolution in 1792, recast in 1818 from the bronze of the Napoleon statue on the Vendôme column.

Lion de Belfort (Place Denfert-Rochereau, 14.Arr.): Small-scale copy of Alsatian sculptor Frédéric-

Auguste Bartholdy's Belfort memorial to Colonel Denfert-Rochereau, who successfully defended Belfort against the Germans in the Franco-Prussian War, only capitulating when he received permission from Paris.

Mémorial de la Déportation (Square de l'Ile-de-France): Built in 1962 as a memorial to the victims of deportations carried out by the German occupying forces in 1940–4.

Mémorial au Martyr Juif Inconnu (Jewish memorial; 17 Rue Geoffroy-l'Asnier, 4.Arr.): Built in 1956 for the unknown Jews who died under the Nazi terror. The names of concentration camps are listed on the bronze monument in the courtyard.

Musset (Memorial; corner of Cours la Reine/Avenue Franklin-Roosevelt, 8.Arr.): Created by Alphonse Emmanuel Moncel de Perrin in memory of the Romantic poet Alfred de Musset (1810–57).

Obelisk de Luxor (Place de la Concorde, 1/8.Arr.): This pink granite obelisk (almost 75 ft. high) dates from the 13C BC, and was presented to the Citizens' King Louis-Philippe by the ruler of Egypt in 1831.

Pont Alexandre III (Bridge; 8.Arr.): Built on the occasion of the World Fair of 1900.

Pont des Arts: Oldest iron bridge in France (1803); nine arches, each with a span of almost 60 ft. Connects Saint-Germain with the right bank of the Seine.

Pont au Change: Built in the early 18C between the Palais de Justice or Conciergerie and the N. bank of the Seine. It acquired the name 'Change' because money-changers used to operate here.

Pont de la Concorde (connects the Palais Bourbon and the Place de la

Place Vendôme, Colonne de la Grande

Place des Victoires, Louis XIV

Place de la Nation, bronze statue (l), Place des Vosges (r)

Concorde): After the Bastille was torn down, the stones from this symbol of despotic rule were used to build the Pont de la Concorde (1789–91) 'so that the people might tread them underfoot'.

Pont Marie (connects the Ile Saint-Louis and the N. bank of the Seine): Built 1614–35 under Louis XIII by Christophe Marie.

Pont-Neuf (connects the S. and N. banks of the Seine to the W. tip of the Ile de la Cité): The 'new bridge', built 1578–1607, is now the oldest bridge in Paris. It was the first bridge on which it was forbidden to build houses and which had separate pavements for pedestrians. Even in those days the lack of buildings opened up a splendid panorama. In September 1985 the Romanian artist Christo, now resident in the United States, wrapped up the entire bridge in plastic foil: a memorable and striking artistic event.

Pont Royal (connects the Louvre and the S. bank of the Seine): The name of the bridge, built 1685–9 by Jules Hardouin-Mansart, is a reminder of the fact that Louis XIV paid for it himself.

Soldat Inconnu: See under Secular Buildings, Arc de Triomphe de l'Etoile.

Statue of Liberty (Allée des Cygnes, 16.Arr.): Small-scale copy of the American Statue of Liberty, made in Paris by the Alsatian sculptor Frédéric-Auguste Bartholdy in 1886.

Theatres and Variety

Bouffes-Parisiennes: Operetta

Fontaine des Innocents

house in the Champs-Elysées, founded in 1827. It achieved world fame 1855–66 under the direction of Jacques Offenbach.

Folies-Bergères (32 Rue Richer, 9.Arr.): World-famous revue theatre. The Folies (the oldest of them was the Folies Dramatiques, founded in 1831) were originally small venues for opera and ballet, before the change to cabaretà was made.

Moulin Rouge: (Place Blanche, 18.Arr.): Dance cabaret.

Odéon—Théâtre Français (Place de l'Odéon, 6.Arr.): This theatre with surrounding arcades was built 1778–82 by Marie-Joseph Peyre and Charles de Wailly; it burned down in

Fontaine Saint-Michel ▷

Statue of Liberty with O.R.T.F building

1799, but was rebuilt from the original plans in 1807.

Opéra (Place de l'Opéra, 9.Arr.): Magnificent building in Second Empire style (opened in 1875), for a long time the largest theatre building in the world. The auditorium is decorated in shades of gold, with a ceiling painting by Chagall (1964).

Théâtre des Champs-Elysées: 15 Avenue Montaigne (8.Arr.).

Théâtre Français (Place du Théâtre Français, 1.Arr.): Home of the Comédie Française (Royal company from 1681). The core of the building dates from 1786–90 and it was partially rebuilt in 1863. Interior *c.* 1900.

Museums

Affiche (Musée de l'Affiche; 16 Rue du Paradis, 10.Arr.): Poster museum in a former sales hall of the Choisy ceramics company (turn of the century).

Armée (Musée de l'Armée; in the Hôtel des Invalides, 7.Arr.): Military museum with about 40,000 exhibits from the Middle Ages to the present day; armour, uniforms, weapons, figures, curiosities from all countries and periods; memorabilia of Napoleon I; plans of campaign; Renaissance craftsmanship, etc.

Art et Essai (Musée d'Art et d'Essai; in the Palais de Tokyo, Avenue du Président Wilson, 13/16.Arr.): Didactically arranged exhibition of works of art from the Louvre collections; temporary exhibitions of European avantgarde art; non-European modern art.

Art Juif (Musée d'Art Juif; 42 Rue

Pont des Arts, Institut de France

des Saules, 18.Arr.): Museum of Jewish art with various interesting exhibits.

Art Moderne (Musée d'Art Moderne de la Ville de Paris; 11 Avenue du Président Wilson, 16.Arr.): Special department of the art treasures owned by the city of Paris; it shows a collection of works exclusively by 20C artists, including major works by Fernand Léger, paintings by Robert Delaunay, Jacques Villon, Maurice Vlaminck, André Derain, Suzanne Valadon, Henri Matisse ('La Danseuse'), Marc Chagall, Kees van Dongen, 60 paintings and water colours by Georges Rouault, more than 100 paintings and drawings by Marcel Gromaire.

Also temporary exhibitions and

Cours la Reine, Quai de la Conférence ▷

Pont Alexandre III, Goddess of Fame (l), street lamp on bridge (r)

centre of Pierre Gaudibert's ARC ('Animation—Recherche—Confrontation'), founded in 1967.

Arts Africains et Océaniens (Musée national des Arts Africains et Océaniens; 296 Avenue Daumesnil, 12.Arr.): Collections of art and sculpture from Black Africa, North Africa and Oceania; aquarium and terrarium.

Arts Décoratifs (Musée d'Arts Décoratifs; 107 Rue de Rivoli, 1.Arr.): Museum of applied art in the N. wing of the Louvre, with around 50,000 items of furniture, tapestry, porcelain etc. from the Middle Ages to the Belle Epoque. The history of French, European, Mohammedan and oriental applied art is presented chronologically (furniture, wood carving, tapestries, ecclesiastical and secular work in gold, ceramics).

Important paintings include works by Lucas Cranach ('Venus and Cupid'), Monsù Desiderio, Jacques Louis David ('Paris and Helen'), Jean Auguste Dominique Ingres and 25 paintings and 150 drawings by Jean Dubuffet.

Arts et Traditions populaires (Musée des Arts et Traditions Populaires; 6 Route du Mahatma-Gandhi, Bois de Boulogne): Ethnographic museum; pre-industrial civilization; exhibits on agriculture, cattle breeding, craft techniques, domestic life, religious worship and customs; folk art, folk theatre, history of marionette theatre; posters. graphics, playing cards.

Baccarat (Musée de Baccarat; 30 Rue de Paradis, 10.Arr.): Crystal and glass. Items from the two-hundred-year-old Baccarat crystal business.

Pont Alexandre III

Balzac (Musée Balzac; 47 Rue Raynouard, 16.Arr.): Home of Honoré de Balzac 1840–7 with very full collection on the life and work of the creator of the 'Comédie Humaine'; library of first editions.

Bibliothèque Nationale (58 Rue de Richelieu, 2.Arr.): Its six million volumes make it the best-endowed library in the world; 130,000 manuscripts, of which more than 10,000 include valuable miniatures or drawings. The library puts on important exhibitions on the history of art and books.

Bourdelle (Musée Bourdelle; 16 Rue Antoine-Bourdelle, 15.Arr.): Ensemble of studios and courtyards in which the sculptor Bourdelle lived until his death in 1929. Drawings, gouaches, paintings, sculpture and plaster casts are evidence of the creative life of an artist who tried to connect the line of classical art with new styles introduced by Rodin.

Carnavalet (Musée Carnavalet and Musée de l'Histoire de Paris; 23 Rue de Sévigné, 3.Arr.): This museum is accommodated in one of Paris' finest Renaissance palaces, the Hôtel Carnavalet, built in the 16C by Pierre Lescaut and later rebuilt by François Mansart. The lavish collections illustrate the history of the city from Henri II to the present day (furniture, craft marks, documents, models, paintings, and engravings, François Gérard's 'Madame Récamier' etc).

Centre Beaubourg = Centre Pompidou = Centre National d'Art et de Culture Georges Pompidou (Plateau Beaubourg; 3.Arr.): This building was the result of an initiative by President Georges Pompidou; it was designed by architects Renzo Piano and Richard Rogers. The collections provide a unique view of the development of modern painting, with an emphasis on French painting, from the late 19C to the present day. The museum which opened in the new building in 1977 was formed by combining the Musée National d'Art Moderne and the Centre National d'Art Contemporain. The Nabis are very well represented by Maurice Denis, ('The Muses'), Edouard Vuillard, Pierre Bonnard ('The Toilet') and Paul Sérusier ('Bathers', 'The Green Valley'). The Fauves are also very well represented by Henri Matisse ('Odalisque', 'The Painter and his Model'), Albert Marquet, Raoul Dufy ('Three Bathers'), Charles Camoin, Kees van Dongen ('Madame Jenny'), André Derain ('Stranded Barques in Camaret') and Maurice de Vlaminck. Also the principal Cubists: Pablo Picasso ('Still Life witho Guitar', 'Fashion Salon', 'The Muse'), Georges Braque ('Billiard Table'), Fernand Léger ('Night', 'Homage to David'), Roger de la Fresnaye, Juan Gris, Jean Metzinger, Albert Gleizes, Jacques Villon. Abstract painting: Frank Kupka, Robert Delaunay, Wassily Kandinsky, Nathalie Goncharova, Mikhail Larionov, Jean Pougny. Dadaists and Surrealists: Francis Picabia, Giorgio de Chirico, Salvador Dalí, Max Ernst, Joan Miró, Yves Tanguy, André Masson. Also Op Art, New Realism, Pop Art and other movements in contemporary art. But the Centre Pompidou is more than a museum, it is a meeting place, and a place for cultural exchange. It contains a public library of audio-visual aids, the Institute of Acoustic and Musical Research directed by Pierre Boulez and the Centre of Industrial Design. There are also numerous temporary exhibitions.

Centre de la Mer et des Eaux (195 Rue Saint-Jacques, 5.Arr.): Museum of the sea; films of the work of the

The Pont Neuf

Moulin Rouge cabaret

Façade of the Opéra

Bibliothèque Nationale, Galerie Mazarin

marine explorer Jacques Yves Cousteau.

Cernuschi (Musée Cernuschi, Musée d'Art Chinois de la Ville de Paris; 7 Avenue Velasquez, 8.Arr.): This museum accommodated in its founder's palais traces the art of the Far East, particularly China, from the earliest times to the present day; tomb figures of the Han (3C BC) and T'ang dynasties (8C), Buddha figures, silk paintings; the famous T'ang dynasty painting 'Horses and Grooms', attributed to Han Kan.

Chasse (Musée de la Chasse et de la Nature; 60 Rue des Archives, 3.Arr.): Museum of hunting and weapons.

Cinéma (Musée du Cinéma/Cinémathèque Française; in the Palais de Chaillot, 16.Arr.): History of the development of film from the 'living pictures' of the Lumière brothers to the present day.

Clemenceau (Musée Georges Clemenceau; 8 Rue Franklin, 16.Arr.): Memorabilia and furniture of the man who was probably the most powerful and interesting political personality in the Third Republic (radical socialist; Prime Minister 1906–9 and 1917–20; d.1929).

Cluny (Musée de Cluny; 6 Place Paul Painlevé, 5.Arr.): The Gothic town house of the abbots of Cluny contains outstanding collections of medieval fine and applied art; sculpture, furniture, gold work, weaponry, wrought iron, ceramics, games etc. There are also enamels from the Maas, the Moselle and the Rhine, and from Limoges; woven carpet in six sections

Bibliothèque Nationale, ceiling in the map room (l), Carnavalet, statue of Victory (r)

'The Lady with the Unicorn'; woven carpet in twelve sections 'Legend of Stephen'.

Cognacq-Jay (Musée Cognacq-Jay; 25 Boulevard des Capucines, 2.Arr.): Furniture, porcelain, sculpture and other 18C works of art, and also a collection of important paintings including works by François Boucher, Jean-Honoré Fragonard, Jean-Baptiste Siméon Chardin, Hubert Robert, Jean-Marc Nattier, Nicolas de Largillière, Maurice Quentin de la Tour; twelve drawings by Antoine Watteau.

Delacroix (Musée Delacroix; 6 Place de Furstenberg, 6.Arr.): Painter Eugène Delacroix' studio, showing numerous important works.

Dix-Neuvième Siècle (Musée du 19.Siècle; Quai Anatole France, 6.Arr.): Museum of 19C culture housed in the former Gare d'Orsay (railway station).

Gobelins (Manufacture des Gobelins; 10 Boulevard Montmartre, 9.Arr.). State Gobelin factory, in which tapestries are still knotted using old techniques.

Grevin (Musée Grevin; 10 Boulevard Montmartre, 9.Arr.): Wax figures of historical personalities.

Guimet (Musée Guimet; 6 Place d'Iéna, 16.Arr.): Collection of far-Eastern art unique in the Western world, principally from India, Ceylon, Afghanistan, Central Asia, Tibet etc, and covering a range from the great statue of Buddha to jewellery, from porcelain to lacquer work;

Rue de la Reyne, 'Head Birth'

sections of frescos from Ajanta, Badami and Sigiriya.

Histoire Naturelle (Musée d'Histoire Naturelle; Jardin des Plantes, 5.Arr): Unique mineralogical, geological, anatomical and palaeontological collections; jewels, gems. valuable minerals.

Homme (Musée de l'Homme; in the W. wing of the Palais de Chaillot, Place du Trocadéro, 16.Arr.): Important museum of ethnography, anthropology, prehistory, ethnology.

Hugo (Maison Victor Hugo; 6 Place des Vosges, 4.Arr.): House occupied by the poet, painter and politician Victor Hugo from 1832–48; since 1903 it has been a museum with memorabilia, a didactically structured introduction to life and work, around 300 drawings.

Impressionisme (Musée de l'Impressionisme (Jeu de Paume); Jardin des Tuileries, Entrée Concorde; 1.Arr.): Special department of the Louvre with the most important collection of Impressionist painting in the world. Edouard Manet ('Olympia', 'The Balcony', 'Emile Zola'), Edgar Degas ('Absinthe', 'Les Repasseuses' etc.), Alfred Sisley, Camille Pissarro, several rooms with works by Claude Monet (see also under Marmottan Museum); Pierre Auguste Renoir ('Le Moulin de la Galette' etc.), Paul Cézanne ('The Hanged Man's House'), Paul Gauguin ('Tahitian Women' 'And the Gold of their Bodies') Vincent van Gogh ('Church at Auvers', 'Dr. Gachet' etc), Georges Seurat ('Circus'), Henri Toulouse-Lautrec ('Moulin Rouge', 'Jane Avril'), Henri Rousseau ('War', 'The Snake-Charmer'); see also Orangerie (Musée de l'Orangerie).

Centre Pompidou (l), Jeu de Paume 'L'Arlésienne' by van Gogh (r)

Jacquemart-André (Musée Jacquemart-André; 58 Boulevard Haussmann, 8.Arr.): Various works of art displayed in a magnificent 19C palais: paintings, sculpture, tapestries, furniture and small works of Renaissance and 18C art. Outstanding collection of paintings with works of the Italian Renaissance and French 18C painting; Rembrandt's 'Christ in Emmaus'; Tintoretto, Tiepolo, Botticelli, Carpaccio, Mantegna, Uccello, van Dyck, Rubens, Hubert Robert, Watteau.

Jeu de Paume: See Impressionisme (Musée de l'Impressionisme).

Louvre: The gigantic Louvre building, the largest palace in Europe, former Paris residence of the kings of France was declared the property of the nation during the French Revolution, together with the royal collection

of paintings, antiquities and applied art. The Louvre has long been one of the most famous museums in the world. This is not just because of the immeasurable wealth of its collections, but because the building is in itself a work of art.

The medieval Louvre: The name 'Louvre' (Lupera) dates back to the time when wolves were hunted (Lat. lupus = 'wolf'). King Philippe II Auguste commissioned a well-fortified building with a massive keep near the Seine crossing on the site of the SW precinct of the Cour Carrée in 1190; this castle was intended to protect the town against attacks from the N. The keep was completed in 1214. It was popularly known as the 'Tour de Paris', housed the state treasury, the archives and the royal storerooms, and also served as a prison. The Louvre declined in importance as a fortress when the town expanded

Jeu de Paume, 'Nature Morte à la Soupière' by Cézanne

rapidly in the second half of the 14C, and Charles IV had the palace extended in the N. and E. in 1360–70 (this first magnificent addition has not survived); this meant that the old keep was now entirely surrounded by buildings, and the Louvre was no longer the kings' residence: they lived in the Hôtel Saint-Pol in the E. of the town and then, until the early 16C, in the Loire valley.

The Renaissance building: In 1527 Francis I decided to make the Louvre his residence. The infamous defensive tower was pulled down, and in 1546 Francis commissioned Pierre Lescaut to rebuild the palace completely. The king's collection of paintings remained in the Palace of Fontainebleau until the mid 17C. Under Henri II Lescaut completed the Lescaut wing (1547–9; the S. part of the W. wing of the present Cour Carrée), which was decorated by the sculptor

Jean Goujon, and also the Pavillon du Roi with the royal apartments (on the site of the present Salle des Sept Cheminées). After the death of Henri II a second residential building was built from 1559 for the Queen on the bank of the Seine. This set of buildings, in the shape of a square, form the core of the present palace, the so-called Old Louvre.

Tuileries and Galeries: In 1563, after the early death of her husband, Queen Catherine de'Medici commissionèd Philibert de l'Orme to build a dower house for her on the site of a former tile factory ('les tuileries'), about 500 yards W. of the Louvre. Catherine then built the Petite Galerie (now Galerie d'Apollon) near the Pavillon du Roi, running down to the Seine at right angles, to form a link between the palaces, which were rather far apart. The Grande Galerie, which finally joined the Louvre and the Tui-

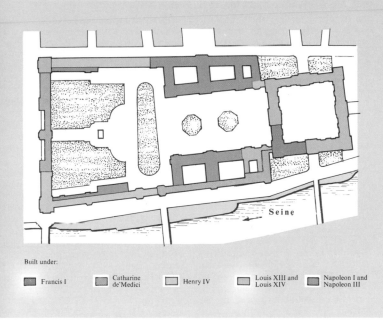

Built under:

▪ Francis I ▪ Catharine de'Medici □ Henry IV ▪ Louis XIII and Louis XIV ▪ Napoleon I and Napoleon III

leries, was built on the Seine 1595–1608 by Louis Métczeau (E. section) and Jacques II Androuet du Cerceau (W. section). The Pavillon de Flore joined the Galeries to the Tuileries.

Extensions and Colonnades: Louis XIII began to extend the Cour Carrée to its present dimensions. The length of the sides of the square courtyard was doubled, making the courtyard four times as big (the Gothic N. and E. wings of the old building were pulled down). The Pavillon de l'Horloge, which formed a connection with Lescaut's W. wing, was built by Jacques Lemercier from 1624; another residential wing was added to the latter, corresponding precisely with Lescaut's work. Nicolas Poussin painted the ceiling of the Grande Galerie with subjects from the legend of Herculcs in 1641&2, and Anne of Austria's rooms on the ground floor of the Petite Galerie were decorated by

Paris, Louvre The most important building phases from Philippe-Auguste to Napoleon III

the Italian artist Romanelli 1655–7. After the death of Lemercier in 1654, Louis le Vau assumed responsibility for the building; he completed the courtyard square in 1659–64 and, after the fire in the Galerie des Rois in 1661, built the Galerie d'Apollon on the first floor of the Petite Galerie. After completion of the courtyard square the question of a design for the E, façade arose, and a competition for this was announced. In 1667 Louis XIV chose the famous colonnade design, a joint project by Claude Perrault, Charles le Brun and Le Vau: a colonnade with central gable and corner projections, consisting of 28 double Corinthian columns.

Neglect: Building stopped in 1674, as the King's attention had turned exclusively to his new residence in

Versailles. The Louvre, to some extent still a roofless shell, began to fall into disrepair, artists established studios in the rooms, and some of the nobility even started living in the large rooms which had become vacant. In 1725 the exhibition of the Académie Royale de Peinture took place in the Salon Carré for the first time; this practice continued until 1848, and the exhibition was always known as a 'Salon'. The King's collection of paintings was organized on the lines of a museum, and from the beginning of Louis XIV's reign was housed in the Louvre and the adjacent Hôtel de Grammond; the collection started to be dispersed, however.

Transformation into a museum: Work on roofing and restoring those buildings open to the weather did not begin until 1755. Also in 1755 a public exhibition of selected paintings from the royal collection took place in the Palais de Luxembourg, and the old sections of the building which blocked both the way to and the view of the Cour Carrée were pulled down; this work was completed in 1774. Also in 1774 the Comte d'Angiviler was appointed superintendent of the royal buildings and submitted plans for the creation of a museum in the Grande Galerie. Henri de Robert was entrusted with preparatory work for equipping the museum in 1784. In 1789 top-lighting was installed in the Salon Carré, and the royal collections were nationalized in 1791&2. Works of art from churches, monasteries and emigrants' palaces were confiscated, and in 1793 the 'Musée Central des Arts' opened in the Louvre.

Napoleonic period: The Louvre collections increased enormously during the Napoleonic Wars with the addition of art treasures purloined from the Netherlands, Germany and Italy. In 1800 Napoleon took up residence in the Tuileries, in 1802 Vivant Denon became director of the museum, which in 1803 was renamed 'Musée Napoléon'. In 1805 Napoleon gave orders for the restoration of the Louvre, from 1806 Percier and Fontaine built the Arc de Triomphe du Carrousel, the monumental arch at the entrance to the Tuileries, and the N. wing on the Rue de Rivoli.

The Tuileries

19&20C: After the fall of Napoleon most of the stolen works of art were returned to their countries of origin, but an important number of them remained in the Louvre. In 1848 the Second Republic decided to extend the Louvre as a 'people's palace' of arts and science (opened in 1851 by Prince Regent Louis Napoléon, later Emperor Napoleon III). In 1852 Baron Haussmann had the old buildings between the Louvre and the Tuileries pulled down, and Louis-Tullius Visconti's and Hector Lefuel's New Louvre was built 1852–7: Louvre and Tuileries were connected in the N. by buildings which completed the square. New wings were built on the sides of the Cour Napoléon; their spacious courtyards made it easier to build large galleries with overhead lighting. The Pavillon de Flore was rebuilt 1861–70 (Lefuel, Jean-Baptiste Carpeaux), as was the E. wing of the Grande Galerie. Under the Commune, conservators of the museum included famous artists of the calibre of Gustave Courbet, Honoré Daumier and Félix Braquemond. The walls left standing after the fire in the Tuileries in 1871 were not removed until 1883.

Jardin des Tuileries: The present gardens were originally the work of Le Nôtre, who from 1664 created the broad avenue which forms the central axis, pools at the intersections and the sequence of symmetrical, geometrically arranged flowerbeds with adjacent tall bosquets. The urns and sculptures are 18C additions; Aristide Maillol's sculptures on the lawns of the Place du Carrousel were transferred to the Tuileries in 1964. The Arc de Triomphe du Carrousel (early 19C) is a free imitation of a Roman monument.

The Rue de Rivoli, running parallel to the gardens, is lined with majestic 19C buildings with arcades.

Musée Nationale du Louvre: The Louvre collections, unique in their quality and scope, give a complete insight into all aspects of fine art from the beginning of history to the 19C. Special departments of the Louvre are the Musée d'Impressionisme (see under Impressionisme) in the Jeu de Paume and the Musée de l'Orangerie (see under Orangerie), both with

Louvre, Venus de Milo

unique collections of Impressionist painting; also associated is the Cabinet des Dessins with 70,000 items (and 30,000 individual items in the collection of graphics endowed by Baron Rothschild), the most important collection of this kind after the Albertina in Vienna.

The Louvre has more than 200,000 exhibits in the following departments:
1. Greek and Roman antiquities
2. Egyptian antiquities
3. Oriental antiquities
4. Medieval, Renaissance and modern sculpture
5. Medieval, Renaissance and modern applied art
6. Paintings and drawings.

The present guide could not hope to include a thorough survey of the collections, for reasons of space. We simply mention some outstanding individual items.

Greek and Roman: Nike of Samothrace (3 or 2C BC, Venus de Milo (2C BC), fragment of the Parthenon frieze with Panathenaic procession (5C BC), fragments of the Temple of Zeus at Olympia (5C BC), replica of the larger-than-life-size cult statue of Athene by Phidias (5C BC), Barberini Suppliant (5C BC), Roman copies of lost works by Phidias, 5&4C works by contemporaries and successors of Phidias (Alkamenes, Kallimachos, Polykletes, Kresilas), works by Praxiteles (4C BC) and Lysippos (4C BC), idealized portraits of Greek poets, also Hellenistic sculptures, mosaics, frescos, tomb and votive reliefs, sarcophaguses, bronzes, vases etc.

Egyptian: Collections from the Thinite period (4th millennium BC), the Old, Middle and New Kingdoms and the Late Period; colossal granite statue of the sphinx, Mastaba, archaic monuments, columns, sarcophaguses, figure of the crouching scribe, statues of kings, silver find from Tod; also Coptic art.

Oriental: Excavations from Mesopotamia, the Sumerian and Semitic areas, small finds from Dura-Europos, Asia Minor, Cyprus and Syria and also fringe areas of the Mediterranean (Phoenicia); Codex of Hammurabi; statue of the royal overseer Ebihil; capital from the palace of Artaxerxes II; stele of King Naram-Sin, Gudea Statues, writings, sarcophaguses, roll seals, ceramics.

European sculpture: Romanesque and Gothic statues, mainly from churches and monasteries, outstanding Renaissance and Mannerist works. Michel Colombe, Jean Goujon, Michelangelo are well represented; also items by Benvenuto Cellini, Pierre Puget, Nino Pisano etc.

Applied art and furniture: Items from the Middle Ages to the 19C; furniture by Charles-André Boulle; objets d'art from monastery treasuries; 'Rain' diamond (137 carats), crown jewels in the Galerie d'Apollon (ceiling painting by Eugène Delacroix).

Paintings and drawings: First-class works of all European Schools from the earliest times to Impressionism, with the emphasis on painting of the French and Italian Schools. The collection is centred on the Grande Galerie, in which the paintings are arranged on a European basis, i.e. Italian masters and placed with French and Spanish paintings etc. The core of this collection is formed by Leonardo's 'Mona Lisa', Titian's 'Young Woman at her Toilet' and 'Portrait of Francis I', Raphael's 'Baldassare Castiglione' and 'Johanna of Aragón', and also Correggio's 'Mystic Marriage of St.Catharine'. Also works by Fra Angelico ('Coronation of the Virgin'), Leonardo ('Madonna of the Rocks', 'St.Anne with Virgin and Child'), Paolo Uccello ('Battle of San Romano'), Sandro Botticelli ('Virgin with Child and Five Angels'), Andrea Mantegna ('Crucifixion', 'Parnassus'), Antonello da Messina ('Condottiere'), Pisanello ('Princess d'Este'), Giorgione ('Rural Concert'), Domenico Ghirlandaio ('Old man with Grandson'), Tintoretto ('Bath of Susanna', 'Self-portrait'), Paolo Veronese ('Wedding at Cana'), Caravaggio ('Death of the Virgin'), Raphael

('Madonna Jardinière', 'St.Michael'), Vittore Carpaccio ('Sermon of St.Stephen before the Gates of Jerusalem'). Also Spanish masters including El Greco ('Crucifixion'), Francisco de Zurbarán ('Death of St.Bonaventure'), Bartolomé Esteban Murillo ('The Little Beggar'), and Diego Velazquez ('Marie-Anne of Austria'). Also French painters Philippe de Chamapigne ('Ex voto of 1662'), Georges de La Tour ('Mary Magdalene'), Claude Lorrain ('Harbour and Capitol'), Nicolas Poussin ('The Four Seasons'). Also Giotto ('Stigmatization of St.Francis'), Enguerrand Quarton ('Avignon Pietà'), works of the Fontainebleau School ('Diana the Huntress'), Jean Clouet ('Francis I'), François Clouet ('The Apothecary Pierre Quthe').

Outstanding painters of the Flemish School are Jan van Eyck ('Chancellor Rolin Madonna'), Anthonis van Dyck ('Charles I of England'), Jacob Jordaens ('The Four Evangelists'), Peter Paul Rubens (cycle of 'Scenes from the Life of Maria de'Medici'). Also Pieter Breughel ('The Cripples'), Jean and François Clouet, Rembrandt

('Uriah Lettres', self-portraits), Adriaen Brouwer, Jan Gossaert, Barend van Orley, Joos van Cleve, Jan Vermeer van Delft, Albrecht Dürer, Lucas Cranach the Elder, Hans Holbein the Younger, Frans Hals ('Gypsy'), Jacob van Ruisdael, Meindert Hobbema, Gerard van Honthorst.

Of the 18C painters the following should be mentioned: Jean-Baptiste Greuze ('Village Bride'), Hubert Robert ('Steps at the Palace of Caprarola'), Antoine Watteau ('Embarcation for Cythera'), Jean-Honoré Fragonard, François Boucher, Jean-Baptiste Siméon Chardin ('The Rochen'), Francisco de Goya, Francesco Guardi, Canaletto, Giovanni Battista Tiepolo.

The collection of 19C painting is also unique: Jacques Louis David ('The Oath of the Horatii'), Jean Auguste Dominique Ingres, Eugène Delacroix, Théodore Guéricault, Jean-Antoine Gros, Gustave Courbet, Jean-Baptiste Camille Corot, Honoré Daumier etc.

Marine (Musée de la Marine; Palais

Musée Rodin, Gate of Hell, detail

Musée Rodin, Gate of Hell (l), Techniques, portal (r)

de Chaillot, Place du Trocadéro, 16.Arr.): History of French naval and merchant shipping from the galley to the steamship; models, pictures, figureheads, maps. Important individual items are Christopher Columbus' 'Santa Maria', the 'Valmy' in ebony, ivory and silver, the 'La Gloire' (first armoured ship in the world) etc.

Marmottan (Musée Marmottan; 2 Rue Louis Boilly, 16.Arr.): 65 paintings by Claude Monet, including 'Impression, Soleil Levant', the painting which gave its name to Impressionism. Also furniture, paintings and Renaissance and Empire applied art.

Monnaie (Musée de la Monnaie; 11 Quai de Conti, 5.Arr.): Collection on the history of money, housed in the imposing Hôtel de la Monnaie (1770–7): coins, medals, dies, stamps, tools etc.

Montmartre (Musée du Vieux-Montmartre; 17 Rue Saint-Vincent, 18.Arr.): Museum of the 'Butte' Montmartre.

Monuments Français (Musée des Monuments Français; Palais de Chaillot, Place du Trocadéro, 16.Arr.): Detailed copies of important sculptures and architecture; established on an initiative by Viollet-le-Duc.

Moreau (Musée Gustave Moreau; 14 Rue de la Rochefoucauld, 9.Arr.): Unique collection of paintings, water colours and drawings by the Symbolist Moreau.

Nissim de Camondo (Musée Nissim de Camondo; 63 Rue de Monceaux, 17.Arr.): Rococo furniture and tapestries (18C); costume.

Orangerie (Musée de l'Orangerie; Place de la Concorde, Tuileries entrance, 1.Arr.): Temporary exhibitions. Sequence of pictures of water lilies which occupied the last seventeen years of Claude Monet's life. The room housing the Walter/Guillaume collection contains works by Henri Rousseau, Paul Cézanne, Pierre Auguste Renoir, André Derain, Henri Matisse, Pablo Picasso, Amedeo Modigliani, Chaim Soutine.

Palais de la Découverte (Avenue Franklin D.Rooosevelkt, 8.Arr.): Scientific or technical museum with experiments set up; planetarium for the World Fair of 1937.

Palais de Tokyo (13 Avenue du Président Wilson, 16.Arr.): The E. wing of the palais houses the Musée d'Art Moderne de la Ville de Paris (see under Art Moderne), and the W. wing the Musée d'Art et d'Essai (see under Art et Essai). Temporary exhibitions are devoted to European avant-garde art and non-European modern art.

Petit Palais (Musée du Petit Palais; Avenue Winston Churchill, 8.Arr.): Collection of art treasures in the possession of the city, including antiquities, tapestries, porcelain and paintings (with the exception of 20C painting, which is housed in the Musée d'Art Moderne de la Ville de Paris). Outstanding works by French painters: Alfred Sisley, Eugène Boudin, Claude Monet, Paul Gauguin, Edgar Degas, Henri de Toulouse-Lautrec, Paul Cézanne, Edouard Vuillard, Pierre Bonnard, Gustave Courbet, collection of works of Odilon Redon etc. Works by non-French painters: Lucas Cranach, Jacob van Ruisdael, Meindert Hobbema, Adrian van Ostade, Rembrandt, Peter Paul Rubens etc.

Picasso (Musée Picasso; in the Hôtel Salé, 5 Rue de Thorigny, 3.Arr.): Pablo Picasso's private collection of paintings with works by Cézanne, Corot, Degas, Gauguin, Matisse, Douanier Rousseau etc.

Poste (Musée de la Poste; 34 Boulevard de Vaugirard, 15.Arr.): History of post and philately.

Rodin (Musée Rodin; 77 Rue de Varenne, 7.Arr.): Home of the sculptor (Hôtel Biron, built 1728–31) with fine park; copies of world-famous sculptures by Rodin in park and museum.

Sculpture en Plein Air (Musée de Sculpture en Plein air; Quai Saint-Bernard, 5.Arr.): Open-air museum on the Quai Saint-Bernard which has been made into a park; sculpture by the most modern sculptors.

S.E.I.T.A. (Musée du S.E.I.T.A.; 2 Avenue Robert Schumann, 7.Arr.): Museum of tobacco and smoking run by the state tobacco company Service d'Exploitation Industriel des Tabacs et des Alumettes (S.E.I.T.A.).

Techniques (Musée National des Techniques; 292 Rue Saint-Martin, 3.Arr.) Technical museum with exhibits from all spheres of science and technology: old gearboxes, television technology, Pascal's calculating machines, flying, clocks, vending and games machines, vehicles, weaving, spinning, locomotives, printing technology, photography etc.

Zadkine (Musée Zadkine; 100 Rue d'Assas, 6.Arr.): Home and studio of the Russo-French sculptor Ossip Zadkine, who came to Paris in 1909, joined up with the Cubists and used their ideas of form in sculpture. Zadkine worked from 1928 to his death in 1967 in the museum which is now devoted to his work and which contains numerous pieces from his estate.

Île de France

Arcueil

94 Val-de-Marne   p.256□D 2

The town of Arcueil, in the Bièvre valley on the S. border of Paris and in the N. area of Cachan, is only important today as an industrial centre. The name 'Arcueil' indicates that the history of this Parisian suburb goes back to Roman times; it derives from the Latin *Arcus Julianus* ('Arch of Julian', after the aqueduct on the Cachan boundary).

In the 18C the chemist Claude Louis Berthollet and the mathematican and astronomer Pierre Simon Laplace founded the 'Société d'Arcueil' here; important members included scholars like the physicist and chemist Joseph Louis Gay-Lussac and the physicist Domenique François Jean Arago. In 1923 the composer Eric Satie, who lived in Arcueil, founded the group of composers known as the 'Ecole d'Arcueil', which included Henri Cliquet-Pleyel, Roger Désormière, Maxime Jacob and Henri Sauget.

Saint-Denis: This basilica with nave and two aisles, started in the 13C, was based to some extent on Notre-Dame de Paris; it was renovated in the 18C.

Aqueduct: Of the three aqueducts, only the one dating from the 19C has survived intact. The Roman aqueduct built in the 2C or 3C (fragments remain) is attributed to Julian the Apostate, who is said to have brought water from Rungis to the Roman camp near Paris on the S. bank of the Seine in the area which was to become the Quartier Latin. Julian was declared Emperor in Paris in 360.

The second aqueduct, famous in its time, had 28 arches up to almost 80 ft. high, and extended for over 400 yards through the Bièvre valley; it was commissioned from Louis Métezeau and the Florentine Tomaso Francini by Queen Maria de'Medici, and built 1614–24, to irrigate the gardens of her palace (Luxembourg). 1868–72 the third aqueduct was built on the instructions of Baron Haussmann to

Arcueil, aqueduct

take water into the city from the Vanne; it has seventy arches spanning the valley, and they are visible over a considerable distance.

Argenteuil
95 Val-d'Oise   p.256☐C 2

The industrial town of Argenteuil to the NW of Paris has interesting past associations with artists.

Argenteuil originated around a monastery founded in 656, transformed into a nunnery under Charlemagne, and it was here that the famous Héloïse took the veil after her lover and father of her child, the theologian and philosopher Peter Abelard, had been castrated by her uncle, Canon Fulbert. In 1129 the establishment became a monastery again, from which a restored church has survived. The principal relic is an ostensibly seamless robe belonging to Christ, said to have been bequeathed to Charlemagne by the Byzantine Empress Irene. During the Revolution it was torn to pieces by the Jacobins. The remains are preserved in a golden-bronze reliquary.

The Seine, its bridges and the traffic on the river are the subject of numerous works painted in Argenteuil by the leading Impressionists. Claude Monet was enabled by a legacy and his wife Camille's dowry to move into premises in Argenteuil in 1871 (Rue Porte Saint-Denis). This marked the beginning of one of his most creative periods, during which he established himself as the true leader of the Impressionist movement. The title of one of the pictures which he painted in Argenteuil gave its name to the new movement: 'Impression, Soleil Levant' (1872, Paris, Musée Marmottan). Monet's paintings 'Regatta at Argenteuil' (*c.* 1872) and 'Boats—Regatta at Argenteuil' (1874) are in the Louvre in Paris. In 1874 Alfred Sisley and Auguste Renoir also came to Argenteuil to work with Monet. They developed a new technique of juxtaposing tiny flecks of paint, thus causing forms to dissolve in shimmering light. Attracted by this approach, Edouard Manet also went to Argenteuil, where he tirelessly painted the Seine, its bridges, gardens, plains and hills, regattas and yachts, but also the snow-covered town in winter, from his so-called boat studio.

Environs: Gennevilliers: Directly to the W. on the other side of the Seine is Gennevilliers, one of the river ports of Greater Paris (12 quays). *Sainte-Marie-Madeleine* (16&17C).

Aubervilliers
93 Seine-Saint-Denis   p.256☐D 2

This important industrial centre to the N. of Paris (oil refinery, chemical, glass and steel industry) has a *pilgri-*

mage church (Notre-Dame-des-Vertus), which has been visited since the 14C; some 15&16C sections have survived (restored in the 19C). The town was first mentioned in 1060 as a possession of the monastery of Saint-Martin-des-Champs in Paris, and it passed later to the abbey of Saint-Denis. Aubervilliers was Henry IV's headquarters at the time of the siege of Paris.

Auvers-sur-Oise
95 Val-d'Oise   p.256☐C1

The little town of Auvers-sur-Oise became world-famous as the residence of numerous artists in the second half of the 19C. Cézanne, Corot, Daubigny, Daumier, Dupré, Guillemin, Harpignies, Morisot, Pissarro and others lived and painted here. *Notre-Dame* (12&13C, originally the chapel of a castle which has been destroyed) is known throughout the world from reproductions of the masterpiece which it inspired the great Flemish painter Vincent van Gogh to create.

Argenteuil, the Seine at Gennevilliers

Auvers was also the scene of the tragic struggle for life fought out by van Gogh in the months preceding his death in 1890. He had spent a year, from 8 May 1889 to 15 May 1890, in the lunatic asylum in Saint-Rémy; he had tried to commit suicide there on numerous occasions by eating poisonous oil paints. Finally he wanted to leave the institution, in order to seek a cure in the North. He wrote to his brother Theo: 'In my mental illness I think of many other artists who suffered in the same way, and tell myself that this condition does not prevent one from painting, and that things are as if nothing were wrong. I can see that the crisis is taking an absurd religious turn. I believe that this calls for a return to the North'. In the January 1890 number of the magazine 'Mercure de France' an article in praise of van Gogh appeared, and one of his oil paintings was sold at the Vingtiste exhibition in February 1890. Van Gogh was on the verge of an artistic breakthrough. On 17 May 1890 he left the asylum and travelled unaccompanied to Paris to stay with his brother Theo and his sister-in-law Jo. On 21 May he travelled to Auvers-sur-Oise where he was examined by Dr.Gachet. Gachet was described by Vincent as 'eccentric'; he painted himself, and counted the painters Paul Cézanne, Armand Guillaumin, Camille Pissarro, Alfred Sisley, Auguste Renoir, Claude Monet and others among his friends. Van Gogh moved into a café-restaurant and threw himself into his work. On 27 July he borrowed a revolver to use for hunting crows. Towards evening he injured himself severely with a shot in the chest, dragged himself to the inn with the bullet in his body, and when asked what had happened replied : 'Nothing, I've hurt myself'. Later the innkeeper found him bleeding in his room and alerted Dr.Gachet. Theo travelled to Auvers at once. On the morning of 29 July van Gogh died of his wound. Vincent and Theo van Gogh, who died shortly afterwards, are buried in the cemetery at Auvers. The *Van Gogh Memorial* in the municipal gardens near the school was created by the Franco-Russian sculptor Ossip Zadkine in 1961.

Auvers-sur-Oise, Notre-Dame (l), Vincent van Gogh monument (r)

Bagneux
92 Hauts-de-Seine   p.256☐D 2

Bagneux is a southern suburb of Paris, and is essentially a residential area, but has some industry (engines, machine tools, aluminium processing, tanneries).

Saint-Hermeland: The 12&13C church was rebuilt in the 19C.

Environs: Bourg-La-Reine (2 km. SE): In 1455 the poet François Villon found refuge with a barber in the town, which now has 19,000 inhabitants; he had mortally wounded the clergyman Philippe Sarmoise after a quarrel. Villon fled from Bourg-La-Reine to the monastery of Port-Royal. There is a memorial plaque to the writer Léon Bloy at No 7 Rue André-Theuriet; he died here on 3 November 1917.
Châtillon or **Châtillon-sur-Bagneux** (1 km. NW): *Saint-Philippe-et-Saint-Jacques* (14C, renovated in the 19C).
L'Hay-les-Roses (5 km. NE): Famous *rose garden*.

Beaumont-sur-Oise
95 Val-d'Oise   p.256☐D 1

Together with the nearby town of Persan (N; industry) and others the area around Beaumont has more than 20,000 inhabitants. In Beaumont is *Saint-Laurent* (12&13C) with Renaissance tower; remains of a 13C *castle*. The forest of Carnelle (ponds) extends to the S.

Beaumont-sur-Oise, window in Saint-Laurent

Bièvres
91 Essone   p.256☐C 2

The village of Bièvres in the valley of
the river with the same name on the
edge of the forest of Verrières is associated above all with memories of
France's prince of poets Victor Hugo,
who repeatedly refers to Bièvres in his
novels and poems, and devoted a
poem to the village church. He often
spent the summer here with his
family, while his mistress Juliette
Drouet was quartered in the nearby
hamlet of Les Metz, a few kilometres
to the W. (house in the Rue Victor
Hugo there, with plaque and some
lines by Victor Hugo; also in the
Auberge de l'Ecu-de-France). The
château between Les Metz and Les
Roches in the village of Vauboyen
once belonged to the journalist Louis-
François Bertin, who kept open house
for all the important Romantics.
Hugo and Juliette used an ancient
hollow chestnut tree at the 'Croix-
Rolland' junction between château
Les Roches and Les Metz as a letter-
box or met in the wood near the
'Homme-Mort' junction, while
Hugo's wife Adèle was visited by the
writer and critic Sainte-Beuve, who
was later to make the three-way
relationship between Hugo, Adèle
and Sainte-Beuve the basis of his
novel 'Volupté'.

Bobigny
93 Seine-Saint-Denis   p.256☐D 2

This industrial town in the E.
suburbs of Paris is the administrative
centre of the Saint-Denis Département. Modern Préfecture. Modern
housing estates. High-rise flats.

Environs: Aulnay-sous-Bois: The
industrial town of Aulnay-sous-Bois,
with 63,000 inhabitants, is adjacent to
the NE. 12&18C *church*.
Bagnolet: Further to the S. on the E.

border of Paris is the industrial town
of Bagnolet, with 35,000 inhabitants.
Drancy: Drancy is a commuter town
to the NW (70,000 inhabitants) and
was the site of a concentration camp
in 1941. The painter and poet Max
Jacob died here on 5 March 1944; he
had been arrested as a Jew shortly
before.
Sevran (8 km. NE): This town in the
NE suburbs of Paris on the Canal de
l'Ourcq has a 16C *Renaissance church*.
The *Parc Forestier de Sevran* is on
both sides of the canal.

Bondy
93 Seine-Saint-Denis   p.256☐D 2

The great forest of Bondy was
formerly considered a retreat of
bandits. Only a part of it remains
(Parc Forestier de Bondy) near the
residential suburb of Clichy-sous-
Bois to the E. of Bondy, with 16,000
inhabitants and the chapel of Notre-
Dame-des-Anges.

Boulogne-Billancourt
92 Hauts-de-Seine   p.256☐C 2

This SW suburb of Paris was created
in 1925 by joining two parishes to
form what has become the industrial
town of Boulogne-Billancourt, set in a
bend of the Seine and also known as
Boulogne-sur-Seine; it consists not
just of the industrial area in the S. of
the town but also of the elegant residential area in the N. adjacent to the
Bois de Boulogne (a royal hunting-
ground in the Middle Ages, part of
the city of Paris since 1852).
Three buildings by the Franco-Swiss
architect, town-planner, painter and
sculptor Le Corbusier are particularly
worth mentioning: the *Maison Lipchitz* (9 Allée des Pins), built by Le
Corbusier in 1924 for the Franco-
Polish sculptor Jacques Lipchitz, one
of the principal exponents of

Cubism. Lipchitz lived in the house (now privately owned) until he moved to the USA in 1941. Le Corbusier was also responsible for the neighbouring *Maison Miestchaninoff*, also built for a sculptor in 1924. Another building is the *Maison Cook*, which is built on stilts; it dates from 1926, is privately owned, and is at 6 Rue Denfert-Rochereau.

Boulogne was originally known as Menus-les-Saint-Cloud. In 1319 Parisians returning from a pilgrimage to Palestine and landing in Boulogne-sur-Mer founded, as they had sworn to do, a church in Menus (restored 1860–3), which they called Notre-Dame-de-Boulogne-sur-Seine.

Environs: Issy-les-Moulineaux: In the E. on the other side of the Seine is the industrial town of Issy, with 52,000 inhabitants. *Saint-Etienne* (17&18C). Theological college.

Vanves (on the Paris city boundary): *Saint-Rémy* (15&19C).

Champigny-sur-Marne
94 Val-de-Marne   p.256☐E 2

This residential and industrial suburb in the SE of Paris owes its sad fame to the bloody battles of 30 November and 2 December 1870 during the Franco-Prussian War: the Germans lost 220 officers and 5,082 men, and German reports claimed French losses as heavy as 10,000–12,000 men. *Saint-Saturnin* (12&13C).

Environs: Chennevières-sur-

Champs-sur-Marne, château from the garden

Marne (2 km. S.): 13C *Saint-Pierre*, rebuilt in the 18C.

Champs-sur-Marne

77 Seine-et-Marne · p.256□E2

Château: The château of Champs-sur-Marne was built in the early 18C and subsequently most beautifully furnished and decorated. The Marquise de Pompadour was one of the distinguished people who lived here, and in the 20C it has become the official guest house for foreign heads of state. It is unique in the Ile de France in the impression it gives of the domestic culture of the nobility in the final stages of the Ancien Régime, who rose so rapidly to power and honour, then lost them just as quickly.

Charles Renousard de la Touanne had made his fortune as paymaster to the forces and treasurer of the light cavalry, and it was he who commissioned the simple, restrained and distinguished building from Jean-Baptiste Bullet in 1699; he was, however, declared bankrupt in 1701, and died, it is said of over-excitement, on the steps of the incomplete building when his arrest was being attempted. The new owner was Paul Poisson de Bourvalais, a former lackey who had made his fortune as a supplier of goods to the army, and it was he who had the building completed and furnished. He also managed to arrange the award of a barony (free territory) to Champs-sur-Marne. In 1717, ten years after completion of the castle, Poisson de Bourvalais was arrested for embezzlement and imprisoned in the Bastille, where he died two years later. The new owner was the Princesse de Conti, a natural daughter of King Louis XIV and his mistress Louise de la Vallière, who left it to her nephew

Champs-sur-Marne, château, chinoiserie ▷

in 1739. He was the Duc de la Vallière, who commissioned important improvements to the château. The most striking features are the *gardens* designed by Claude Desgots and the *painting* (Chinoiserie) by Christophe Huet (*c.* 1740). The Marquise de Pompadour, who used the château as a country residence 1757–62, invested about a twenty times the purchase price in the improvement and embellishment of this 'delightful palais'.

The château fell into disrepair after the Revolution, and was not restored until the late 19C and early 20C; it was acquired by the French state in 1935.

Charenton-le-Pont
94 Val-de-Marne   p.256☐D 2

Charenton is on the SE border of Paris at the confluence of the Seine and the Marne, and was once famous for its Protestant church, built in the 16C to Jacques Debrosse's design. Officials of the Reformed Church held their Councils here until it was pulled down in 1686 after the repeal of the Edict of Nantes. The bridge after which Charenton-le-Pont is named is the seventeenth at this point since Romanesque times. The lunatic asylum in Charenton-Saint-Maurice is also famous; it was refurbished in 1847, and the Marquis de Sade died here in 1814. He is buried in the cemetery of the asylum.

Environs: Ivry-sur-Seine: The town of Ivry, with 62,000 inhabitants, is adjacent to the S; the name indicates its Gallo-Roman origins (*Ivriacum*). 13,16&17C *Saint-Pierre*. *Fort*.

Châtenay-Malabry
92 Hauts-de-Seine   p.256☐D 2

François-Marie Arouet is said to have

been born on 20 February 1694 in a country house in the Place Voltaire, which no longer exists (he did not adopt the pseudonym Voltaire until 1718). Research mistrusts this claim by Voltaire, who seems not to have been proud of being the son of a bourgeois household, and put around the idea that he was the child of one of his mother's noble lovers. It is now considered certain that he was born in Paris on 21 November 1694.

Near Saint-Germain l'Auxerrois (11–13C) is the house in which the first French winner of the Nobel Prize for Literature, Sully Prudhomme, died on 7 September 1907.

La Vallée-aux-Loups: The entrance to this little Empire château in the 'Valley of the Wolves' is at 87 Rue Chateaubriand in the part of the town known as Aulnay. François René Chateaubriand, the leader and most influential of the French early Romantics, lived here 1807–18, after he had left Paris for political reasons, and received most of the Romantic poets here. The Chateaubriand Society has established a *memorial collection* for the poet in the château. The *Auberge de la Vallée-aux-Loups* at 104 Rue de Chateaubriand is equally rich in literary memories; this is where the poet Henri de Latouche, who lived at No 108, accommodated his guests. Latouche died here in 1851, and his tomb is in the cemetery of Châtenay-Malabry.

Chevreuse
78 Yvelines   p.256☐C 3

Chevreuse is a summer resort in the Vallée de Chevreuse on the Yvette; it has a church with 12&14C sections and numerous old buildings. The *Château Madeleine* was pulled down in the 17C, and only impressive ruins remain. In 1661 the young Jean

Champs-sur-Marne, château, chinoiserie ▷

Châtenay-Malabry, Château 'La Vallée-aux-Loups', portal

Racine was an assistant director of this castle. The 'Chemin de Racine' is marked with milestones showing the poet's route from the Place des Halles to Port-Royal. The barony of Chevreuse was raised to a dukedom in 1545 and the peerage in 1612. The little town is known for the notorious Duchesse de Chevreuse (1600–79), who married the Constable of Lynnes at the age of 17, lost her husband four years later and married the Duc de Chevreuse. After her second marriage in particular she threw herself into the cauldron of intrigue and conspiracy which dominated the political world at the time. Richelieu had no more dangerous adversary than this woman, but he nevertheless succeeded, as the man who broke the power of the aristocracy, in rendering her harmless as well. She fled to England, where she remained until the death of Louis XIII. She did not reappear on the political scene until the Fronde uprising in 1650.

Choisy-le-Roi
94 Val-de-Marne   p.256☐D 2

The name of this little residential, commercial and industrial town on the Seine between Créteil and Orly in the S. suburbs of Paris is a reminder of the period in the 17C in which the château, built in the 17C by Jacques IV Gabriel and extended in the 18C, was one of Louis XV, the Much-Beloved's, preferred residences. It was destroyed in 1797, and little of it remains. Saint-Louis (18C) has become the cathedral.

Choisy was the last home of the poet Rouget de Lisle, author of the words of the 'Marseillaise'; he died here in complete poverty on 26 June 1836.

During the Franco-Prussian War of 1870&1 Choisy was the scene of violent fighting on the night of the 28 to 29 November 1870.

Environs: Thiais (4 km. NW): 13C *Saint-Leu-Saint-Gilles*, restored in the 19C. Large *cemetery*.
Villejuif (4 km. E.): 12,16&18C *Saint-Cir-Saint-Juliette*. *Théâtre Romain-Rolland*. The Gustave-Roussy Institute is one of the most important cancer research centres in Europe.
Vitry-sur-Seine (3 km. NW): 13&14C *Saint-Germain*.

Clamart
92 Hauts-de-Seine   p.256☐D 2

Jean de la Fontaine, the author of the 'Fables', passing through Clamart,] which is to the S. of Paris, on a journey into the Limousin in 1653, was enthusiastic about the lush meadows, and the fine butter which he was given ('Le Voyage en Limousin'). Today the only tenuous reminders of this idyll are the vegetables for which Clamart is known.

Environs: Plessis-Robinson, Le: Residential town (23,000 inhabitants), directly to the S. *Sainte-Madeleine* is modern with 13&18C sections.

Clichy
92 Hauts-de-Seine   p.256☐D 2

The 'Quiet Days in Clichy' of Henry Miller's novel exist only in literature. Clichy is an industrial centre with smelting works, hammer shops, foundries, and machine factories etc. The town arose near an old village where the Merovingians had a palace called *Clipiacus*, in which King Dagobert I

Clamart, Saint-Pierre-et-Saint-Paul, portal ▷

spent a great deal of time. A council was held here in 636.

Saint-Vincent-de-Paul: This church was built in the 17C; it is named after St.Vincent de Paul (d.1600), who served as a priest in Clichy.

Colombes
92 Hauts-de-Seine　　　　　　p.256□D 2

This town in the NW suburbs of Paris is essentially residential, but has some industry. The Yves-du-Manoir stadium, built for the 1924 Olympics, can seat 65,000 and is the largest building of its kind in Greater Paris.

Corbeil-Essonnes
91 Essonne　　　　　　　　p.256□D 3

Corbeil-Essonnes is at the confluence of the Essonne and the Seine, and is famous for its mills, particularly those which supplied Paris from

the 12C, set on the banks of the Seine. The town is the seat of a Catholic bishop and has two churches which are worth seeing, *Saint-Spire cathedral* (12–15C) and *Saint-Etienne* (12&13C). The history of Corbeil goes back to the Gallic period, when the town was called *Corboilum*. A castle was built here as a defence against the Normans in the 9C, by 960 it was the principal town of a county which was united with the Crown Demesne in 1112.

Environs: Sainte-Geneviève-des-Bois (11 km. W.): The *well* and *grotto* of Sainte-Geneviève-des-Bois have long been a place of pilgrimage. The keep of the 14C castle, rebuilt 17C, is all that has survived.

Coulommiers
77 Seine-et-Marne　　　　　　p.258□G2

The little town of Colommiers, 55 km. E. of Paris, on the Grand Morin, a tributary of the Marne, is one of the market centres of the dairy-producing area of Brie, which among other

Courances, view of the château

hings provides Paris with fresh milk; there is also some industry: as well as cheese and jam factories there are a sugar refinery, food factories, goldsmiths' studios, printing works, tree nurseries, basket factories etc. Coulommiers cheese, produced in the town and named after it, is a Brie made on a slightly smaller scale for ease of transport.

History: The village of Coulommiers, known as *Colombariae* under the Romans, developed around a medieval castle, and was granted a charter in 1231. The town was the property of the counts of Champagne and passed to the aristocratic Longueville family in the 16&17C. This dynasty was descended from one of the sons of Dunois, the Bastard of Orleans, who became Count of Longueville and died in 1491 as Governor of Normandy. His successors were granted the dukedom in 1505 for services rendered in war, and became Princes of the Blood in 1571. The Longuevilles played an outstanding role in the Fronde uprising (see under Paris, History of the City).

The most distinguished son of the town is the Franco-Italian painter Valentin de Boullongne (or de Boulogne or Moïse Valentin), who was born in Coulommiers in January 1594 ('The Soothsayer', one of his principal works, is in the Louvre in Paris).

Also worth seeing: *Saint-Denis* (13&16C)*Capucin church* (17C). The chapel houses a Museum of Archaeology and Local History (Musée d'Archéologie et d'Histoire Locale). A Commanderie des Templiers with Gothic chapel has survived among a group of modern buildings.

Courances
91 Essonne   p.256☐D 4

Château: The castle *park* was designed by landscape gardener André le Nôtre and with its canals, pools, paths and trees is considered one of the finest in the Ile de France. The château was built by Gilles le Breton *c.* 1550 and rebuilt *c.* 1662; the double steps in the façade are an

Créteil, modern tower blocks

imitation of the open-air staircase at Fontainebleau.

Courneuve, La
93 Seine-Saint-Denis   p.256☐D 2

This little town SE of Saint-Denis has a 16C church (Saint-Lucien), a large sports centre and a Parc Départemental.

Créteil
94 Val-de-Marne   p.256☐D 2

The new town of Créteil to the SE of Paris is the administrative headquarters of the Val-de-Marne Département. In 1906 a group of young writers calling themselves Unanimists, founded the Groupe de l'Abbaye, a literary association, at 69 Rue du Docteur Plichon; the group rented the house, which was known as the Abbey. The writers, whose number included Georges Duhamel, Jules Romains, Charles Vidrac and René

Ecouen, château

Arcos, wanted to print and bind their own works. Two Créteil streets are still named after Duhamel and Vidrac.

The thirteen-year-old Victor Hugo wrote the poems 'Pierre' and 'Choses Ecrites à Créteil' in the Auberge du Petit-Cochon-de-Lait at the mouth of the Morbras.

Dourdan
91 Essonne   p.256☐C 3

The little town of Dourdan, an important corn market since the Middle Ages is considered to be the birthplace of Hugo Capet, founder of the Capetian dynasty. The little town was involved in wars until the 17C, and has now become a centre of the tourist industry.

Saint-Germain: This church has been much rebuilt, but dates originally from the 14&15C; it has two different, slate-roofed towers. Behind the altar is the tombstone of the writer and dramatist Jean-François Régnard (1655–1709), who lived and died as an Epicurean at Château Grillon, his country seat not far from Dourdan.

Château: Built by Philippe Auguste *c.* 1220, the castle has an interesting *keep*. An *ethnographgic museum* is housed in the château.

Ecouen
95 Val-d'Oise   p.256□D 1

Château: A visit to the Renaissance
château of Ecouen with its new
Renaissance museum is essential for
anybody who wishes to be thoroughly
informed about architecture and fine
art in the Ile de France.
The château has four wings and was
built by Charles Billard from 1535
under Francis I and Constable Anne
de Montmorency. From 1556 work
continued under Jean Bullant, the
great master of French Renaissance
architecture, who borrowed the colossal column order from classical
models and applied it in Ecouen. Bullant died in Ecouen in 1578, and is
also presumed to have been born
there. Alongside Pierre Lescaut and
Philibert Delorme he was one of the
founders of neoclassical French architecture. Sculptor Jean Goujon's
workshop was responsible for the
interior decoration, and Jean Cousin
provided the windows. Until the
Revolution the château was owned by
the House of Condé. In 1806 Napoleon established a boarding school for
300 daughters of officers of the
Légion d'Honneur. After thorough
restoration the château was opened to
the public as a museum in 1962.
Musée de la Renaissance: Thanks to
the wonderful achievements of the
French custodians of ancient monuments, large parts of the original
interior have survived or have been
rediscovered. The collections exhi-
bited are largely drawn from the inexhaustible treasures of the Musée
Cluny in Paris: tapestries, sculpture,
paintings, furniture, goldsmiths'
work, jewellery etc.

Saint-Acceuil This church dates
from the 16&17C and has fine Renaissance windows. The façade is
modern.

Environs: Champlâtreux (13 km.
N.): The *château* was built *c.* 1760 for
Jean-Michel Chevotet as a country
home for court president Mathieu-
François Molé.
Luzarches 11 km. N.): This village
contains the ruins of the 13C *Château
de la Motte*, one of the oldest fortresses in the Ile de France. *Saint-
Côme et Saint-Damien* dates from the
12C (Romanesque origin still recognizable, particularly in the apse and
choir); the Renaissance façade dates
from the 16C.

Enghien-les-Bains
95 Val d'Oise   p.256□D 2

Thermal baths were established in
this town on Lake Enghien in 1821. It
was a popular place for 19C excursions (Casino, country houses); suf-
ferers from breathing difficulties, skin
diseases and rheumatism still visit the
eight sulphur springs.

Environs: Saint-Gratien (W. of
the lake): *Château Saint-Gratien* was
the summer residence of Princess
Mathilde Bonaparte, the daughter of
Jérôme Bonaparte, Napoleon's youngest brother. Under the Second
Empire she received important
artistic and literary figures here
(including Sainte-Beuve, Flaubert).
Sannois (3 km. NW): *Church* in
which the author Cyrano de Bergerac
(1619–55) was buried. *Sannois mill* at
a height of 532 ft.

Etampes

91 Essonne   p.256☐C 4

The town of Etampes has many historic buildings and is picturesquely sited in the valley of the Chalouette and the Juine. Badly damaged by Second World War air raids in 1940 and 1944. Etampes was the birthplace of the natural historian Etienne Geoffroy Saint-Hilaire (1772–1844).

History: The fate of modern Etampes was largely determined by the royal mistresses who ruled here as duchesses, but its history goes back to ancient times. Etampes, Roman *Stampae* in Pagus Stampensis, was the scene of the battle in 604 in which mayors of the palace Beroald of Burgundy and Lantherich of Neustria were killed. The town was plundered by the Normans in 886.

Etampes became a demesne of the royal crown under Hugo Capet, the founder of the Capetian dynasty. Queen Ingeborg, banished from the court, spent over ten years imprisoned here; she was the daughter of King Waldemar I of Denmark, and became the second wife of Philippe II Auguste here in 1193. The marriage was dissolved by the Archbishop of Rheims because the couple were said to be related, and Ingeborg was banished to the convent of Beaurepaire, while Philippe married Agnes of Merano in 1196. However, Pope Innocent III declared the divorce invalid, and when Philip refused to take Ingeborg back again Innocent laid France under an interdict in 1200. Philippe capitulated in November of the same year and separated from Agnes, but Ingeborg was not released from the dungeon in Etampes until 1213.

Charles IV made Etampes a county in 1327 and Francis I raised it to a duchy in 1536, which he then conferred on his mistress Anna de Pisselieu, whom he had married to Jean de Brosse, Count of Penthièvre. After the death of Francis I, Diane de Poitiers came into the duchy, but Charles IX returned it to Jean de Brosse. After his death it returned to the crown in

Sannois (Enghien-les-Bains), mill (l), Etampes, Saint-Basile, gargoyles, Notre-Dame (r)

1565, Henry IV presented it to his mistress Gabrielle d'Estrées in 1598, whose successors (the dukes of Vendôme) retained possession of Etampes until the death of Louis Joseph in 1712, when it once more passed to the crown. Numerous councils were held in Etampes (1092, 1130 and 1247).

Notre-Dame-du-Fort: Like all the churches in Etampes, Notre-Dame-du-Fort dates from the 12C, but has since been much rebuilt. It has a Romanesque crypt with choir above it (16C glass). The tower is one of the finest Romanesque bell towers in the Ile de France. The S. portal dates from the mid 12C and is reminiscent of Chartres. Notre-Dame-du-Fort became a fortress church in the 13C, with arrow slits and battlements.

Saint-Basile: Most of this church dates from the 15&16C. The W. portal, the central tower and the transept are Romanesque or early Gothic (restored).

Saint-Gilles: Founded by Louis VI (1123) and largely altered or rebuilt in the 15&16C. Façade and nave are Romanesque.

Saint-Martin: Choir from *c.* 1150, transitional period from Romanesque to Gothic; 16C leaning tower.

Other buildings: Early 16C *Hôtel. Tour Ginette*, the rectangular keep of the castle, built *c.* 1150–70, often used as a royal residence and destroyed by Henry IV. The tower, almost 90 ft. high and with walls up to 13 ft. thick, was used by Philippe II Auguste as a prison for his rejected consort Ingeborg.

Environs: Chamarande (10 km. N.): *Château* built by François Mansart in the 17C in the middle of a park through which the Juine flows; there is a network of canals.
Farcheville (11 km. E.): *Fortress* dating from the late 13C with ditches, ramparts, battlements etc (no public access to the interior). With the exception of the corps de logis (17C) the almost square fortress has retained its medieval character.
Méréville (16 km. S.): 17&18C *châ-*

Etampes, Saint-Basile, capitals on the W. portal

teau with atmospheric park (for a fuller description see main entry under Méréville).

Morigny (3 km. NE): The *parish church* was originally part of a former Benedictine abbey; 13C rectangular tower. *Prehistoric collection* in the *Palais des Abbés*.

Evry

91 Essonne   p.256☐D 3

The new town of Evry, administrative centre of the Essonne Département, still a village with barely 8,000 inhabitants in 1968, is intended by the planners to have 450,000 inhabitants. The town is designed roughly like a four-armed cross, and between these arms are tapering mountains of flats, flats like boxes, office blocks, giant shopping centres, administrative buildings (Agora, Palais de Justice, university) and parks.

Environs: Ris-Orangis (directly to the N.): 12C *church*. The *Town Hall* is housed in the former *Château Fromont* (17C).

La Ferté-Alais

91 Essonne   p.256☐D 4

'La Ferté' occurs in numerous French place names. 'Ferté' is an old form of the modern 'fermeté' ('strength, firmness') and is roughly equivalent to fortress. Thus La Ferté-Alais means 'Fortress Adélaïde', a reminder of the name of a former mistress of the castle. The castle which gave the place its name no longer exists, however.

Etampes, Saint-Basile, W. portal

Château de Fontainebleau

Fleury-en-Bière

77 Seine-et-Marne p.256☐E 4

Château: Cosme Clausse, secretary
to Henry II, commissioned this château close to Fontainebleau for himself from 1550, and its architect is
considered to have been the Renaissance architect Pierre Lescot (courtyard façade of the W. wing of the
Cour Carrée in the Louvre). The
building is surrounded by a sturdy
wall (no public access to the interior);
it has a regular façade and long side
wings arranged around an impressive
inner courtyard. It was modernized in
the 18C, but still shows what a mid-
16C aristocratic country seat with
park and canal was like.

Fontainebleau

77 Seine-et-Marne p.256☐E 4

Fontainebleau is 60 km. SE of Paris,
and its unique features are the
magnificent interior decoration and
furnishings in the style of the upper
Italian Renaissance. At no point
during the construction of this
gigantic château with five enclosed
courtyards, largely built in the 16C,
was any stress laid on unified and
clearly delineated buildings, or an
impressive exterior. The objective
was to provide interiors to house the
creations of the Italian artists summoned by Francis I from 1530; they
founded the epoch-making school of
Fontainebleau, which was to have
such an impact on courtly art in
France. According to tradition the
name Fontainebleau came from a
hound in the royal pack which got lost
in the forest. A more likely explana-
tion is that Fontainebleau is an abbre-
viation of 'Fontaine-Belle-Eau',
meaning 'spring of bright water'.

Fontainebleau town: The little
town of the same name in the forest of
Fontainebleau (see below under
Environs) is a residential and recreation area for the residents of Paris. Its
inhabitants are called 'Bellifontains'.
It economy is dependent on the
manufacture of Brie cheese and table
wine (Chasselas); there is also an iron

Fontainebleau, park

industry. Fontainebleau was the Headquarters of NATO until 1967.

Château de Fontainebleau

History: 998: The Capetian King Robert the Pious built a hunting lodge in the lonely depths of the forest of Fontainebleau. Robert's cultural activities were much more effective than the political aspects of his reign; he was considered the finest composer and writer of hymns of his period, best known for his composition 'Veni sancte spiritus'. He was a failure, however, in both politics and marriage: he had to be separated from his first wife, his cousin Bertha of Burgundy, in 1004 in order to avoid excommunication for marrying a relative; his second wife, Constance d'Arles, daughter of Count Guillaume Taillefer de Toulouse, embittered his life with her dominating behaviour and intrigues.

1169: King Louis VII rebuilt Robert the Pious' original hunting lodge. Louis is considered to have been the actual founder of the château at Fontainebleau, which subsequently became the preferred retreat of the kings of France.

1268: Birth of Philip the Fair in Fontainebleau. This important Capetian king also died here on 29 November 1314.

1527: Francis I had all the old hunting lodge pulled down, with the exception of the keep, and commissioned the Parisian architect Gilles Le Breton to build a new château on the foundations of the old one.

1530: Francis I sent for the Italian Rosso Fiorentino and entrusted him with the interior decoration. Francis was concerned to bring about a revival of French art of the kind that he had experienced in Italy. By 1517 he had brought Leonardo da Vinci to

Fontainebleau, Escalier du Roi (l), sculpture 'La Nature' by Le Tribolo (1528)

France and established him in the château de Cloux, near Amboise, but two years later Leonardo was dead. Rosso Fiorentino was responsible for the 12 bays of the Galerie François Premier.

1532: Francis I summoned the Italian Francesco Primaticcio, who himself sent for Niccolò dell'Abbate. Rosso and Primaticcio were the founders of the first School of Fontainebleau. Primaticcio's decorations for the Chambre du Roi and the Chambre de la Reine (both completed 1535) have not survived, but there are fragments of his frescos in the Salon de la Duchesse d'Estampes.

1540: Death of Rosso Fiorentino in Paris. After his death Primaticcio assumed responsibility for decorative work at Fontainebleau.

1544: The later King Francis II was born at Fontainebleau.

1545: The Upper Italian Mannerist Niccolò dell'Abbate also came to Fontainebleau. He became Primaticcio's right-hand man, and one of the central figures of the Fontainebleau School. He was responsible for the decoration of the ballroom and the Salle d'Ulysse, but these were pulled down in the reign of Louis XV in 1697. On 22 November 1545 the later Spanish Queen Elisabeth of Valois (wife of Philip II) was born in Fontainebleau as the daughter of Henry II and Catharine de' Medici.

1547: Death of Francis I. At this point only about three quarters of the work was complete. The new king was Henry II, who transferred architectural control to the Renaissance master Philibert Delorme (all that has survived of his work in Fontainebleau are the ceiling and monumental fireplace in the ballroom).

1551: Birth of Henry III at Fontainebleau.

1570: Primaticcio died at Fontainebleau. His death marked the end of the first School of Fontainebleau, where the pace of building and painting had slowed down considerably. A year later Niccolò dell'Abbate also died in Fontainebleau.

1594: The Bourbon King Henry IV came to the throne and decided to continue building Fontainebleau. Henri's 'Premier Peintre du Roi', Toussaint Dubreuil, (paintings and drawings in the Louvre) who painted the Legend of Hercules in the Pavillon des Poésies (destroyed in 1703) is considered the principal representative of the second School of Fontainebleau. In 1597 Dubreuil became director of carpet and tapestry manufacture. Antwerp Mannerism was introduced to France by the painters of the second School of Fontainebleau.

1601: Birth of the later King Louis XIII in Fontainebleau.

1603: Martin Fréminet, who had trained in Italy with Caravaggio and Parmigianino became 'Premier Peintre' in succession to Dubreuil, who had died in the previous year. His major work are the frescos in the Trinity Chapel (1608–10). At about the same time the Flemish painter Ambroise Dubois completed the paintings in the Diana gallery (destroyed); his frescos in the oval room with scenes from the story of Theagenes and Charicleia have survived. There is a panel from the Clorinde sequence in the Salon de la Reine in the Louvre ('Baptism of Clorinde').

1608: Birth of Gaston d'Orléans at Fontainebleau. This duke became a leader of the aristocracy opposed to the policies of Richelieu and Mazarin.

1620: A year after Fréminet's death, Queen Maria de'Medici summoned Peter Paul Rubens to Paris to decorate the Palais du Luxembourg. This marked the end of the second School of Fontainebleau.

Despite this, the School of Fontainebleau continued to influence art in France. Female nudes became prototypes for the presentation of naked women by the Mannerists. Interior designs were reproduced on tapestries and engravings and became known well beyond the borders of France. For this reason many of the originals can be reconstructed even though they were destroyed.

1631: During the Thirty Years War a defence agreement between France and Bavaria against Emperor Ferdinand II was signed at Fontainebleau.

1657: The former Queen Cristina of Sweden, who in the previous year had been converted to Catholicism, had her chief Master of the Horse, the Marquis Mondaldeschi, 'executed' by some of her followers with knives and daggers for alleged high treason, after she had held court proceedings.

1661: Birth of the dramatist Dancourt on 1 November at Fontainebleau. He wrote comedies of manners and farces ('Le Cavalier à la Mode', 'Fêtes de Village').

1685: Louis XIV proclaimed the Edict of Restitution at Fontainebleau, revoking the Edict of Nantes, which had guaranteed cultural freedom to the Huguenots. This resulted in a mass flight of Huguenots from France to Germany and Holland.

1812–14: Pope Pius VII held prisoner in Fontainebleau. On 25 January 1813 he concluded the French Concordat with Emperor Napoleon I.

1814: Napoleon abdicated as Emperor of the French in Fontainebleau and was given the island of Elba as his residence, as sovereign with the title of Emperor.

1832: Birth of the philosopher Jules Lachelier in Fontainebleau.

The château became the President's summer residence under the Third Republic.

Exterior: The château is surrounded by gardens and arranged around five courtyards. The main entrance in the Place du Général de Gaulle leads to

Fontainebleau, Salle de Bal, fireplace ▷

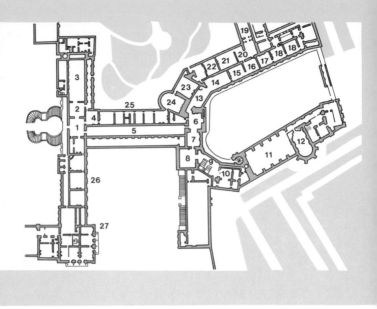

the *Cour du Cheval Blanc* or *Cour des Adieux*. The first name refers to a plaster cast of the equestrian statue of Marcus Aurelius which stood here for a long time. It was then associated with farewells because the Emperor Napoleon took leave of his guard here after his abdication. The courtyard is bordered on the left by the François Premier wing, and on the right by the Louis XV wing.

The *Cour de la Fontaine* leads to the carp pond in which some of the fish are said to be a hundred years old, and on to the park. The Cour de la Fontaine is bordered by the Galerie François Premier, the Queen Mother's wing and the Belle Cheminée wing.

The *Porte Dorée*, with the salamander emblem of Francis I in the tympanum, is set into one of the pavilions and leads to the *Cour Ovale*, with the royal chambers on the left and the ballroom on the right. To the N. of the château is the *Jardin de Diana*, below the windows of Napoleon I's Empire apartment. In the SW is the *English Garden*, redesigned in the 19C.

Interior (Musée National du Château): The château has been open as a museum since 1921, and its panelling, stucco and frescos give an impressive idea of the style of the so-called first

Fontainebleau, Empress' bedroom, ceiling

School of Fontainebleau, which established court style in France for subsequent centuries. The School consisted principally of Italian artists responsible for the interior of the château, led by the Bolognese painter and decorator Francesco Primaticcio, together with Rosso Fiorentino and Niccolò dell'Abbate.

Galerie François Premier: The decoration of the Galerie François Premier was the principal work of Rosso Fiorentino, who here, with the assistance of numerous stucco works, paid homage to the King with allegorical frescos depicting scenes based on Homer and Ovid (1531–40).

Other rooms: Francesco Primaticcio, Niccolò dell'Abbate, Jean Cousin the Elder and other Flemish, French and Italian masters decorated the walls and ceilings of the *Galerie Henry II*, the *ballroom* and the so-called *Escalier du Roi*. The mythological scenes (1540–50) in the *apartments of Catharine de'Medici* are by Antoine Caron. Outstanding works of the second School of Fontainebleau, dating from the reign of Henry IV, who also established a fine *library*, are Ambroise Dubois' cyle 'Theagenes and Chariclea' in the *Salon de la Reine Maria de'-Medici*, the painting in the *Galerie d'Ulysse* by Toussaint Dubreuil, and finally frescos of Scenes from the Old and New Testaments executed in the early 17C in the *Chapelle de la Sainte Trinité* by Martin Fréminet. The *Grands Appartements* of the Emperor Napoleon I have choice Empire decoration. The *museum* also houses an important collection of cartoons which formed the basis of Beauvais Gobelins, including the cycle of Louis XV hunting created 1733–45 by Jean-Baptiste Oudry. The *Chinese Museum* is worth seeing; it houses *objets d'art* brought back to France from China.

Environs: Barbizon: The little town of Barbizon on the W. edge of the Forest of Fontainebleau has about 2,000 inhabitants and is popular for summer excursions. It owes its importance to the so-called Barbizon School, a mid-19C school of painting which pointed the way to French Impressionism. Théodore Rousseau, already a convinced Republican, had painted in Barbizon for a time after his withdrawal from Paris 1832&3, and as a lover of painting in the open air had discovered the charm of subjects which had up till then not attracted attention, such as isolated groups of trees. However, his work did not appeal to the predominant taste for Romanticism, and was regularly rejected by the Paris Salon. He was so annoyed that he settled permanently in Barbizon in 1847 and realized his ideal of artists working close to nature, well away from urban culture; his associates, little known at the time, included Henri Harpignie, Charles-François Daubigny, Narcisse Diaz de la Peña, Jules Dupré and Constant Troyon. Camille Corot also painted for a short time in Barbizon.

Gif-sur-Yvette
91 Essonne   p.256□C 3

The C.N.R.S (Centre National de la Recherche Scientifique) has important research establishments run by the Ministry of Education in the château in this village on the Yvette. In 1973 Le Duc Tho and Henry Kissinger had important talks in Gif during the Vietnam War. 13,15&16C church. Former abbey.

Fontainebleau, 'Recumbent figure' in the Escalier du Roi

Gros-Bois, Château

93 Val-de-Marne   p.256☐E 3

The interior of Château Grosbois, built *c.* 1580 and altered in the 17C, is one of the most important examples of Empire style in the Ile de France. Marshall Berthier, who acquired the château in 1805, furnished the building in a most luxurious fashion; the *furniture* is from the workshop of the cabinet-maker François Honoré Jacob.

Berthier, the son of a sapper, entered the corps of engineers, then went with Lafayette to North America, where he fought against the English; after his return he became a colonel in the French General Staff and commanded the National Guard in Versailles in 1789. In 1795 he became Chief of the General Staff in the Italian Army with the rank of Brigadier, and entered into a friendly relationship with Napoleon, which continued until 1815. As supreme Italian commander he entered Rome in 1798 and proclaimed the Republic there. He was involved in the Egyptian campaign as Chief of the General Staff.

Berthier became Minister of War after Napoleon's coup d'état of 1799, and when Napoleon took the title of Emperor, Berthier became Imperial Marshall and Grand Officer of the Légion d'Honneur. He took part in the campaigns of 1805–7 as Chief of the General Staff and in 1807 became sovereign lord of the principalities of Neuchâtel and Valangin, Vice-Constable of the Empire and Imperial Prince. In 1808 he married Princess Marie Elisabeth Amalie, the daughter of Duke Wilhelm of Bavaria, of the Pfalz-Zweibrücken-Birkenfeld line. After the Battle of Wagram he became Prince of Wagram. When Napoleon fell he switched his allegiance to Louis XVIII, and on Napoleon's return from Elba in 1815 Berthier, uncertain what he should do, went to his father-in-law in Bamberg, where he suffered a complete mental breakdown, and threw himself from a balcony, agitated by a march-past of Russian troops, on 1 June 1815.

Environs: Bonneuil-sur-Marne (4

Château Gros-Bois

km. N.): A school is now housed in the former *château* of Rancy (18C).

Brie-Comte-Robert (8 km. SE): Little survives of the medieval *château* in this important market town on the Brie, former capital of Brie Française. The château was built *c.* 1120 by Robert, Count of Dreux and brother of King Louis VII. *Saint-Etienne* dates from the 12C and was restored in the 15&16C; the stained glass in the rose window in the apse is original.

Limeil-Brévannes (5 km. W.): 12–15C *church. Château* rebuilt in the 18C with French garden, now old people's home and sanatorium.

Villecresnes (3 km. S.): *Church* with some 12C sections. *Rose growing.*

Guermantes

77 Seine-et-Marne   p.256□E 2

Château: The château of Guermantes, built in the early 17C in Louis-Treize style, at the period of transition from Renaissance to baroque,(restored in the 20C), owes its world fame to Marcel Proust's novel 'A la Recherche du Temps Perdu' (1913 ff.), in which Proust describes the fall and dissolution of the aristocracy which so fascinated him, despite his awareness that at the beginning of the 20C this social class was merely an 'empire of nothing'. In the third part of the cycle, 'Du Côté de chez Guermantes' he describes the fictitious life of Duke Basile de Guermantes, his wife Oriane and the other aristocrats who live in the Château de Guermantes or who are connected with the family in some way. It must be pointed out, however, that Proust's Guermantes has nothing to do with the actual château: it was the plangency of the name 'Guermantes' which appealed to the author, and it was not until years after writing 'Du Côté de chez Guermantes' that he visited the château himself. The building was modernized by Robert de Cotte *c.* 1700 and a picture gallery was added. Cottes was also responsible for the design of the 90 ft. gallery known as 'La Belle Inutile' ('Beautiful and Useless'). The ceiling decoration was not added until 1852. André

Guermantes, château as seen from garden

le Nôtre landscaped the park. The magnificently decorated rooms contemporary with the building are the most interesting features of the château.

Environs: Ferrières-en-Brie (4 km. S.): This château in a spacious park, restored in the 19C by Baron Rothschild was used during the Franco-Prussian War by the Prussian Prime Minister Otto von Bismarck and the French negotiator. The *church* dates from the 13C.

Jossigny (6.5 km. E.): This *château* surrounded by a park was built in the mid 18C in Louis-Quinze style. It is a mixture of rococo and neoclassical design; the roofs are reminiscent of Chinese pagodas.

Houdan
78 Yvelines   p.256☐A 2

Houdan is best known for its poultry (Houdan chickens). The only surviving evidence of the former strategic importance of the village are the 12C *keep* and two 16C *towers*.

Church: Façade and nave (15&16C) in the Flamboyant style, the portal dates from the 17C, the apse is Renaissance. The interior vaulting is decorated with large keystones.

l'Isle-Adam
95 Val-d'Oise   p.256☐C 1

This town on the Oise is a popular resort (beach, forest). An Adam, lord of Villiers, built a castle on the Oise island in 1014, and thenceforth was known as Villiers de l'Isle Adam. The poet Auguste, Comte de Villiers de l'Isle Adam (1838–89), friend of Baudelaire and Mallarmé, was one of his descendants. Balzac stayed in Isle-

L'Isle-Adam, Saint-Martin, pulpit, (1560)

Adam on various occasions and described it in his novel 'Un Début de la Vie'.

Saint-Martin: 15&16C church with a remarkable portal.

Joinville-le-Pont
Val-de-Marne   p.256☐D 2

The town of Joinville, known among other things for its film studios, is sited on both sides of the Marne to the E. of the forest of Vincennes; there are attractive residential areas on the left bank of the Marne, while the old town is on the right. The town took its present name from the Prince of Joinville in 1831; he was the third son of Louis Philippe, the Citizens' King.

'Le Parango': The former country seat of the authoress Madame de La Fayette is close to the Marne bridge by the church; it is now used as a monastery school. Madame de la Fayette spent the summer months here, met her life-long friend La Rochefoucauld and wrote part of her world-famous novel 'La Princesse de Clèves'. At that time the area was part of nearby Saint-Maur-des-Fosses.

Jouarre
77 Seine-et-Marne   p.258☐G 2

The church in the little town of Jouarre has a crypt with important 8–13C sarcophaguses. The abbey is still occupied by Benedictines but apart from the 12C tower all the buildings are 18C (one of them houses offices of the Jouarre Hôtel de Ville).

Monastery: Founded *c.* 630 by Ado, to follow the Rule of St.Columba. Ado, along with his brothers Dado and Rado, also founded the monastery of Meaux, to follow a mixture of the Rule of St.Colomba and the Benedictine Rule. Jouarre later became a nunnery, with aristocratic abbesses.

Crypt (behind the parish church): This is really two chapels half sunk into the earth with remains of Merovingian masonry and the 7C church. The sarcophaguses of Ado, the

Jouarre, crypt, St.Paul chapel

founder of the monastery, Théochilde, the first abbess, her brother Agilbert, Bishop of Paris and the Irish saint Ozanne are in the Saint-Paul chapel. The chapel dedicated to St.Ebrégisile contains the sarcophagus of this saint (Bishop of Meaux) and his sister Aguilberte.

Parish church: Completely rebuilt in the 15C. The most striking features apart from the old and modern stained glass are the shrines (the oldest dating from the 12C) and the stone statue of Notre-Dame-de-Jouarre.

La Ferté-sur-Jouarre: This church has been rebuilt, but has a 14C tower.

Unfortunately work was broken off through lack of money, and so only the important *choir* was completed. The French national saint Joan of Arc is said to have raised a child from the dead behind the altar. The name Notre-Dame-des-Ardents is a reminder of the 'mal des ardents', a skin disease prevalent in France at the time when building began, presumed to have been caused by the use of poor-quality flour mixed with rye. The former Benedictine abbey (founded in the 7C) is now the town hall.

Also worth seeing: *Saint-Furcy* (15C): The church has a late Gothic façade. The *Place de la Fontaine* is surrounded by old houses.

Larchant
77 Seine-et-Marne   p.256☐E 4

The village of Larchant is considered to be the birthplace of St.Mathurin, born *c.* 250 and buried according to popular opinion in the chapel above

Lagny-sur-Marne, former abbey, tower

Lagny-sur-Marne
77 Seine-et-Marne   p.256☐E 2

Lagny, on the left bank of the Marne, was formerly a fortified market town; it is now part of Marne-La-Vallée. This new town on the E. edge of Paris, which formerly included 26 parishes and has a total area of 150 sq.km., was planned to relieve some of the pressure on the capital.

Former abbey: Building of the former abbey church of Notre-Dame-des-Ardents started in the 13C on the foundations of earlier buildings.

which *Saint-Mathurin* was built in the 12 (choir), 13 and 14C; it is dominated by a tower with porch and portal. The top of the tower collapsed in the 17C. The church contains statues and a 15C retable. Larchant has remained a popular place of pilgrimage. St.Mathurin is the patron saint of the mentally sick.

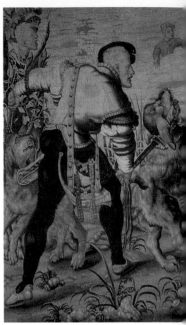

Maisons-Laffitte, château, Gobelin

Magny-en-Vexin
95 Val d'Oise   p.256☐B 1

This little town, a former mail staging post on the Paris-Rouen route, has numerous old buildings and palaces of the aristocracy. The mayor's office is housed in an Hôtel dating from the reign of Louis XVI.

Church: The church was originally 15C, but rebuilt in Renaissance style in the 16C. Inside are a *font* dating from 1534, a 16C *alabaster Madonna* above the altar and three fine *statues* decorating the tomb of a former feudal lord (17C, right transept).

Environs: Alincourt (4 km. N.): Picturesque, lonely 15C *castle* much rebuilt until the 17C.
Ambleville (7 km. W.): Modern *church* with a painting attributed to the Spaniard Jusepe de Ribera. Opposite is the *Renaissance château*

with ornate façade and restored gardens.

Maisons-Laffitte
78 Yvelines   p.256☐C 2

At the edge of the Forest of Saint-Germain, on the left bank of the Seine in the NW suburbs of Paris is Maisons-Laffitte with its château, one of the earliest of the neoclassical period and a masterpiece by François Mansart. The little town which grew up around the château is largely residential (villas, holiday homes). It also has a famous racecourse.

Château: The building was commissioned by Robert de Longueil, president of the Parisian Parliament and Governor of Versailles and Saint-Germain-en-Laye, and later Minister

Maisons-Laffitte, château, exterior

of Finance, in 1642. The building was completed in 1646, the decoration by 1650, and de Longueil received his first guests in 1651: the Queen Mother, Anne of Austria and the thirteen-year-old King Louis XIII. A little later Longueil lost the post of Minister of Finance, but the château, now with accommodation for the King, continued to receive the highest in the realm.

In the late 18C the Count of Artois, brother of Louis XVI and later king himself 1824–30, acquired the château. He had some rooms restored and commissioned the racecourse. In 1818 the château passed to the rich opposition politician Jacques Laffitte, Governor of the Bank of France, and in the early stages of the July Revolution was the Antiroyalist faction's base: La Fayette, Benjamin Constant, Thiers, Arago among others. Laffitte more or less financed the July Revolu-

tion from his private funds. After the Revolution he became Prime Minister and Finance Minister, but was forced to resign in 1831, and compelled by his creditors to sell his possessions. The park in front of the château was split up, and villas were built on much of it.

In 1905 Maisons-Laffitte was acquired by the French State. After the Second World War it was restored, and rooms which had been altered, including the *King's apartment*, were returned to their original condition. Parts of the *park* were landscaped to Mansart's original plans.

Exterior: François Mansart had a free hand in the building of the château and was able to realize his own ideas, to the extent that a wing was pulled down because the architect did not like it, which also gives an idea of the wealth of the man who commissioned the work: he had to pay for the demolition and rebuilding. The core of the axially aligned building (kitchens and mews etc. have not survived) with three courtyards and a park is the corps de logis, with two storeys except in the protruding central section, which has three; the wings are short, with corner pavilions. The façades are lavishly articulated with Doric and Ionic pilasters, supplemented by columns in the central section. Maisons-Laffitte stands at the point of transition from Renaissance to baroque, and is considered the first significant neoclassical building, but the steep roofs with tall chimneys on the wings are still in the 16C tradition.

The carved decoration is largely the work of Jacques Sarrazin and colleagues.

Malmaison, Château
92 Hauts-de-Seine   p.256□C 2

The name of Château Malmaison, in the W. suburbs of Paris, and in which the Empress Josephine lived after her

divorce from Napoleon I until her death, goes back to a leper house ('mala mansio') run here by the abbey of Saint-Denis in the Middle Ages.

The building, of no great distinction, was commissioned by the Parliamentarian Christophe Perrot in Louis-Treize style in 1622; it is now a museum, housing one of the most important Empire collections (furniture, porcelain, paintings, sculpture, silver etc.). The possessions were confiscated during the French Revolution, Josephine acquired them in 1799, Bonaparte's wife from 1796, and she had the château extended and restored by Charles Percier and Pierre François Léonard Fontaine, the leading Empire architects.

Josephine was born in 1763 in Martinique as daughter of the royal harbour master Joseph Tascher de la Pagerie. She came to France at the age of fifteen and married her fellow-countryman, Vicomte Alexandre de Beauharnais, in 1779. The children of this marriage were Eugène, later Duke of Leuchtenberg, and Hortense, later consort to King Louis Bonaparte of Holland. After the execution of her

Malmaison, château

husband in 1794, Josephine was herself arrested, but released after the fall of Robespierre; some of her confiscated goods were returned. In the house of her friend and protector Barras she met General Napoleon Bonaparte, whom she married out of ambition in 1796. She followed him to Milan for a time, and otherwise led a luxurious and adventurous life at Malmaison. When Napoleon returned she was able to attract members of the Royalist party to her little court, with which she moved to the Tuileries in 1800, but she at the same time acquired an excessive taste for luxury, which caused her acute financial embarrassment. Despite her own extravagant conduct she was unwilling to tolerate Napoleon's little escapades; their relationship was always rather tense. When he was attempting to gain the imperial crown she did everything in her power to prevent him from doing this, as she foresaw that the foundation of a Napoleonic dynasty would lead to the dissolution of her childless marriage. When Napoleon crowned himself Emperor on 2 December 1804 she had to accept her fate. She was not, however, prepared to accede to Napoleon's wish that she should herself ask for a divorce, and resisted the separation vigorously until it was pronounced legal in 1809. After the separation she lived with imperial title and splendour first in Navarre, then in Malmaison. Napoleon's fall broke her spiritually and physically, although the Allies treated her with great consideration when they visited her in Malmaison in 1814. She was denied her wish to accompany Napoleon to Elba. She caught a cold during a boat trip on the occasion of a visit by Tsar Alexander I and died in Malmaison on 29 May 1814. About a year later, after the collapse of his rule of a Hundred Days, Napoleon took leave of the members of his family in Malmaison.

In the 19C Malmaison passed through the hands of a number of owners. Emperor Napoleon III bought it back and established a memorial museum for Napoleon and Josephine in 1867; it was dissolved after the Franco-Prussian War and the proclamation of the Third

Malmaison, Empress Josephine's bed (l), Napoleon's bed (r)

Republic. The château passed to the banker Daniel Ilffa Osiris, who left it to the state in 1904. Malmaison has been open to the public as a museum since 1906.

Museum: Malmaison's original furnishings were lost during the 19C, but its half-private, half-public character has been restored by the acquisition of objects and furniture from other former Napoleonic residences. The public rooms are on the ground floor, the private ones on the first floor.

Ground floor: The vestibule, reached via a tent-like porch, contains archaistic marble busts of members of Napoleon's family. Dining room with chairs by the Jacob brothers and a gold dinner service by the goldsmith Henri Auguste, presented to the imperial couple by the city on the occasion of the Coronation in 1804 (the ships containing the cutlery are an allusion to the Parisian coat of arms). The 'Salle du Conseil' was restored in 1867; the library is the only room which has survived in its original condition. 'Salon de Billard' with Coronation portrait after Fran-

çois Gérard and with furniture by Jacob-Desmalter. 'Salon Doré' with old ceiling painting and portraits by Gérard and Girodet. Music room with items from the Empress's art collection.

First floor: The left wing of the first floor is occupied by four museum rooms devoted to Napoleon (including pictures, reports and documents, imperial Sèvres porcelain, table from Austerlitz), on the right are the Empress's private apartments.

Pavillon des Voitures: Carriages and coaches belonging to the imperial family, including the 'Opale' in which Josephine returned to Malmaison after signature of the divorce; the coach lost by Napoleon at the Battle of Waterloo etc.

Pavillon Osiris: Memorabilia of Napoleon's stay in St.Helena (clothes, iron bedstead, account book, death mask of the Emperor, who died on 5 May 1821).

Château Bois-Préau: This little château also belonged to Josephine, and in the course of constant changes of ownership and sales in the 19C it

Malmaison, dining room

passed to an American; in 1929 Edward Tuck returned it to the French state. It is now part of the Malmaison museum, housing memorabilia of Napoleon's son, the King of Rome (cradle), paintings, and objects associated with the Emperor and his family.

Rueil-Malmaison: The Empress Josephine and her daughter Hortense are interred in *Saint-Pierre et Saint-Paul*, founded in 1585 and built by Jacques Lemercier in the town of Rueil-Malmaison, which now has 633,000 inhabitants. The *tomb of Josephine* is in the chapel on the right of the choir and has a figure by Pierre Cartellier; the *cenotaph of Hortense* in the chapel on the left of the choir is the work of Jean Auguste Barre (1858).

Environs: Buzenval: *Château* between Rueil-Malmaison and Saint-Cloud, the scene of one of the last battles for Paris in the Franco-Prussian War (19 January 1871). The Romantic painter Henri Regnault fell in the Battle of Buzenval.

Mantes-la-Jolie
78 Yvelines   p.256□A 2

Mantes was badly damaged during the Second World War in 1944 and rebuilt as an industrial town; it is an overflow town from Paris and with Mantes-la-Ville, Magnanville, Bouchelay, Guerville, Rosny-sur-Seine and Porcheville forms the Mantes group of towns. Despite bomb damage the important Gothic cathedral has survived.

Mantes remained a bone of contention between the English and the French until well into the 15C. In August 1087 the English king William the Conqueror attacked the French territory, took Mantes by storm and destroyed the town; however, on the following day he fell so heavily from his horse that he died of his wounds in Rouen. King Philippe II Auguste conducted his Norman and Vexin campaigns from Mantes.

Collegiate church of Notre-Dame: Work started *c.* 1170 and was completed in the early 13C (resto-

Malmaison, Josephine's shoes and cushion

ration in the 19C); the church shares not only its name with Notre-Dame de Paris, but its design was directly influenced by the Parisian cathedral. It was originally just a nave with two aisles and choir with ambulatory; the choir chapels and side chapels are 14C additions.

Façade: Despite the ravages of the French Revolution the high artistic quality of the portal figures is still recognizable. The theme of the oldest, left-hand portal (*c.* 1170) is the Resurrection; it shows the three women at the tomb and the Risen Christ on the lintel. The wide central portal (*c.* 1180) is the Porte d'Or, on the theme of the Virgin Mary with scenes from the Life of Mary in the lintel, above it the Coronation of the Virgin. The right-hand portal (*c.* 1300), topped with a lavishly decorated pediment, shows scenes from the Life of Christ. The open arcature connecting the two façade towers dates from the 19C.

Interior: The vaults, streaming with light, reach a height of almost 100 ft. Pilasters alternate with round columns; above them is a gallery with three small arches and blind arches.

Gassicourt church: This church in the NW area of Mantes dates from the 12&13C. The crossing of the old Cluniac priory is dominated by a Romanesque bell tower with saddleback roof.

Tour Saint-Maclou: This tower built in the early 16C was originally the bell tower of a church destroyed during the Revolution.

Environs: Rosny-sur-Seine, Château (6 km. W.): This *château* built *c.* 1595 by Maximilien de Béthune, Baron of Rosny and later Duke of Sully in the Louis-Treize style is set in an extensive *park* with ancient avenues of elms and thousands of mulberry trees planted by the agronomist Olivier de Serre for the culture of silkworms. Work on the two low wings was broken off by order of the Duc de Sully when Henry IV died, but building, based on the original plans, continued after the restoration of the monarchy for the Duchesse de Berry, the new owner. The new wings were pulled down again in 1840 because they did not harmonize with the building as a whole. Some of the furniture is the work of cabinet-maker Georges Jacob, leading exponent in this field of the Directoire style *c.* 1800. Original furnishings have survived in some of the rooms (Salon Henry IV, Chambre de Sully). The 'Salon de Tapisseries' is an example of restoration style.

Marly-le-Roi
78 Yvelines   p.256☐C 2[3x]

All that has survived of the magnificent *château* built by Hardouin-Mansart for Louis XIV, who moved in in 1686, is the *park*, which has been restored, and some slabs in the ground in a garden of limes. During the French Revolution the château, which the king had built as a 'Hermitage', was sold to a manufacturer and pulled down in the 19C. The buildings originally consisted of a central pavilion for the king and his immediate family, and two sets of six smaller side pavilions, each with two apartments, separated by a pool. The Roi Soleil's pavilion symbolized the sun, twelve smaller pavilions stood for the signs of the zodiac.

Saint-Victor: Built in 1688 by Hardouin-Mansart, original interior, high altar from the chapel of Versailles.

Château Monte-Cristo: This privately-owned château in the Renaissance style was commissioned by Alexandre Dumas, successful author of the novel 'The Count of Monte Cristo' which appeared in 18 volumes in 1845&6, and is still read today.

Mantes-la-Jolie, collegiate church ▷

The château is not open to the public. The building, which cost 500,000 francs, was inaugurated in 1848; in 1850 the property was compulsorily auctioned for 30,000 francs to cover its debts.

Meaux
77 Seine-et-Marne   p.256☐F 2

The town of Meaux, on the Marne and the Canal de l'Ourcq, is rich in tradition; its inhabitants are known as 'Meldois', after the Gauls who lived here in ancient times. It is the seat of a Catholic bishop and the principal town of northern Brie with an important market for cattle and dairy produce; there are also numerous industrial establishments.

History: In Roman times Meaux was the capital of the Gallic Mendi, a Gallia Lugdunensis tribe on the lower Marne; Caesar commissioned ships from them in 55&4 BC for his expedition to Britain. In Roman times the town was called *Civitas Meldorum* or simply *Meldis*. Little has survived from the Celtic and Roman period (coins, inscriptions, water supply). A Gaul called Orgetorix offered his fellow-citizens a theatre, which his sons built in the 1C AD; this building has not yet been unearthed. The town became the seat of a bishop in the 4C and as such was soon capital of the Brie area. From the 10C onwards the later county of Meaux was dependent on the counts of Champagne, who granted the town a charter in 1179. In 1314 Philip the Fair united Meaux with the French crown. Late medieval fortifications were added to the Gallo-Roman town wall, of which sections have survived, in the 15C. The town suffered a great deal in the Huguenot Wars. In the Franco-Prussian War Meaux was the headquarters of the King of Prussia from the 15 to 19 September 1870.

The most famous bishops of Meaux were Guillaume Briçonnet and Jacques Bénigne Bossuet. Briçonnet became Bishop of Meaux in 1516, and his views soon placed him under suspicion of heresy. He established the reforming 'Meaux Group' (Cenacle

Meaux, view of the cathedral

de Meaux, also known as Fabristes) in association with the theologian and humanist Jacobus Faber (Jacques Lefèvre d'Estaples), who came to Meaux in 1520 and became Vicar General in 1523, and the Swiss reformer Guillaume Farel. Faber had to flee from Meaux in 1525, after his Bible commentaries had been placed on the index of books forbidden to Catholics; he also translated the Bible into French ('La Sainte Bible en François', 1530).

In 1681 Jacques Bénigne Bossuet, theologian, orator and tutor of princes, born in Dijon, became Bishop of Meaux. Here the preacher, known as the 'Eagle of Meaux', wrote the 'Declaratio cleri Gallicani' (Four Gallican Articles), which were assimilated into French law, and prescribed for instruction in theological colleges. 1) The Popes received only spiritual authority from God, thus kings and princes are independent of the power of the church in secular matters and cannot be deposed, and their subjects cannot be dispensed from allegiance to them. 2) The Pope's absolute authority is limited by the decrees of the Council of Constance concerning the authority of the General Councils. 3) The liberties of the kingdom of France and the Gallican church are inviolable. 4) Papal decisions only have force by the consent of the church as a whole. The acceptance of Bossuet's 'Gallican Articles' by a General Assembly of the French clergy in 1682 was a decisive victory for the Roi Soleil, Louis XIV, in his struggle against the power of the Pope.

Saint-Etienne Cathedral: Meaux' incomplete Gothic cathedral was started in the 12C, the main sections were built in the late 12 and early 13C and not completed until the 16C. The choir was completed c. 1200; Marie, daughter of Louis VII and wife of Count Henri de Champagne was buried here in 1198. The architect Villard de Honnecourt visited Meaux during his journeys through France c. 1230–5, and sketched the ground plan of the cathedral: round apse with ambulatory and three chapels. The sketch book in which Villard made his drawings is the only Gothic record of

Meaux, cathedral of Saint-Etienne, tympanum of the S. portal

a stonemasons' lodge extant (now in the Bibliothèque Nationale in Paris). Two further choir chapels were added in the 14C, and two bays to the nave; work also started on the façade. The N. tower was completed *c.* 1500, but the slate-clad S. tower, the 'Tour Noire' is still a stump with a make-shift roof.

Portals: Despite damage in the Huguenot Wars important carving has survived. The left-hand portal (14C) has scenes from the life of John the Baptist. The central portal dates from *c.* 1300 and depicts the Last Judgement; the tympanum on the right (late 14C) has scenes from the life of Mary.

Interior: The most striking feature of the interior is its height (105 ft. to the vaulting). A tablet in front of the choir stalls indicates Bossuet's tomb. The organ above the late Gothic arch is 17C. The Porte Maugarni (15C) on the left in front of the choir is named after a bandit who was hanged here in 1372; this execution on consecrated ground caused great agitation at the time. Excavations under the choir revealed remains of an older church.

Meaux, cathedral, S. portal, detail

Former Bishop's Palace (Musée Bossuet): The Bossuet Museum is housed in the 17C Bishop's Palace (heavily restored), and has a wide range of collections: pre-history, local history, painting, 17C apothecaries' vessels etc.

Melun
77 Seine-et-Marne   p.256☐E 3

Melun is sited on both banks of the Seine and is the administrative capital of the Département of Seine et Marne and an important centre of trade and industry (musical instruments, brewing and textiles, car bodywork, aero engines, radiators etc.). The new town of Melun-Sénart, due to have about 300,000 inhabitants by 1988, is between Melun and the wooded area of Sénart; it covers an area of 17,000 hectares and was established in 1969.

Melun is the ancient *Melodunum*, inhabited by the Celtic Senoni tribe. The old town, like Paris, was founded on an island in the Seine. In 53 BC Melodunum became Roman, later the first Capetian kings had a residence here. In Frankish times the town was the capital of a county, united with the French crown in 1016. Melun was conquered by the English in 1420, but they handed the town over to Charles VII in 1430.

Notre-Dame: This church built on an island in the Seine in the first third of the 11C was rebuilt on numerous occasions (nave with Gothic vaults, Renaissance façade). In the interior are two notable *paintings:* 'Descent from the Cross' by the Dutch painter Jacob Jordaens and a 'Rescue of Moses' attributed to Francesco Primaticcio, one of the principal masters of the School of Fontainebleau.

Saint-Aspais: A medallion in the apse of this church commemorates the relief of Meaux by Joan of Arc in 1430. The church was built in the first half of the 16C, but still shows Gothic influence.

Town Hall: The town hall is housed in a Renaissance building, the left-hand side of which was extended in the 19C. In the courtyard is a statue of Bishop Jacques Amyot, the humanist born in Melun in 1530. Amyot's translations from the Greek (Heliodor, Plutarch) are graceful works of classical literature.

Environs: Dammarie-les-Lys (2 km. SW): Site of the ruins of *Lys Abbey*, a Cistercian abbey founded in the 13C.

Méréville
91 Essonne   p.256□C 4

Méréville, which also has an 11&13C church, is best known for its château.

Château: Shortly before the Revolution the 17&18C château came into the possession of the banker de Laborde, father of the poetess Nathalie de Noailles, later Duchesse de Mouchy, immortalized by Chateaubriand in his novel 'Le Dernier des Abencérages' as Blanca. He described the Château de Méréville as 'an oasis created by the smile of a Muse, but a Muse of the kind which Gallic poets call learned fairies'.

Méry-sur-Oise
95 Val-d'Oise   p.256□C 1

The little town of Méry, near the new town of Cergy-Pontoise, still has the 15&16C *Saint-Denis*, and a magnificent 16C *château*, restored in the 18C. Buffon was involved in designing the gardens.

Environs: Former du Val Abbey (4 km. E.): The ruins of this *Cistercian abbey*, with buildings dating from

the 12,13&17C and pulled down in the 19C, are on a private plot of land on the edge of the forest of L'Isle-Adam.

Meudon
92 Hauts-de-Seine   p.256□C 2

The Château de Meudon was almost completely destroyed in 1871; its remains stand on the famous 'Terrasse de Meudon', (there is now an observatory in the former château), from which there is the most magnificent view over the valley of the Seine and Paris. The Forest of Meudon is much visited by the inhabitants of Paris.

Meudon was lived in and visited by world-famous artists, poets, politicians and musicians: the Pléiade poet Pierre de Ronsard (1524–85), the surgeon Ambroise Paré (1510–90), the early Renaissance poet François Rabelais (1494–1553), who became canon in Meudon in 1551, the philosopher and author Jean-Jacques Rousseau (1712–78), the novelist

Méry-sur-Oise, château park

Honoré de Balzac (1799–1850). Richard Wagner wrote his early opera 'The Flying Dutchman' in a modest house at 27 Avenue du Château in 1841; the villa occupied by the sculptor Auguste Rodin is now a Rodin Museum (see below); the Franco-German painter, graphic artist, sculptor and poet Hans Arp moved to Meudon with his wife Sophie Taeuber-Arp in 1926, and he lived here until he moved to Grasse, near Nice, in 1941; the controversial novelist and essayist Louis-Ferdinand Céline died in Meudon in 1961.

History: Anne de Pisselieu, Duchesse d'Etampes, daughter of Anton de Meudon, was lady of the town 1527–52, and commissioned the old château on the S. section of the present Terrasse. The Duchesse d'Etampes was one of Francis I's most influential mistresses. Anne de Pisselieu was originally a lady-in-waiting of the Queen Mother Louise of Savoy and from 1526 (a year before she became the owner of Meudon) she captivated the King with her beauty and intellect for 20 years. In 1536 the King had her marry Jean de Brosse to keep up appearances, and conferred upon her the duchy of Etampes in the modern Département of Essonne. Her jealousy of Diane de Poitiers, the Dauphin's mistress, moved her to set up an opponent to him in the person of the Duke of Orléans, which split court and state into two parties. After the death of Francis I in 1547 she was confined to her estates, and transferred her allegiance to the Reformed church in consequence of her opposition to Diane de Poitiers.

After the death of the Duchesse d'Etampes, Charles de Guise, Cardinal of Lorraine, became Lord of Meudon 1552–74. Charles de Guise, who had been Archbishop of Rheims at the age of nine, and a cardinal at 21, was the effective head of state under Francis II, and ruled cruelly and despotically, with the vain aim of acquiring the crown for his House. He commissioned a grotto on the sight of the modern observatory from Francesco Primaticcio c. 1555, and built the upper supporting walls of the terrace. Finance Minister Abel Servien, who owned the château until 1659, entrusted rebuilding work to the architect Louis Le Vau, and had the first terraces laid out. Louvois, the Minister of War, the next owner of Meudon, had the park landscaped by Le Nôtre, and the Avenue du Château to Bellevue was laid out.

In 1695 Louis XIV presented Meudon to the Grand Dauphin, for whom Jules Hardouin-Mansart built the new château over the grotto of 1555; work proceeded 1706–9. When the Grand Dauphin died in 1711 Meudon was diminished in importance, although distinguished 18C guests included Peter the Great and King Stanislaus Leszczynski. After the Revolution an establishment for fire-arm research was housed here in the late 18C, the officers of which included Choderlos de Laclos, author of the succès de scandale 'Les Liaisons Dangereuses'.

A fire resulting from an explosion caused extensive damage, which Napoleon I had magnificently repaired. After the coup d'état of 1852, under the Second Empire, Jérôme Bonaparte, the former 'merry king' of Westphalia, took up residence in the château, and after his death in 1860 it was taken over by Prince Napoleon. During the siege of Paris 1870&1 the Prussians established their artillery on the Heights of Meudon, the château was burned down, and the wings were later demolished. Only the central pavilion has survived; it now houses astrophysicist Jules Janssen's observatory.

Musée de Meudon: The country house at 11 Rue des Pierres, occupied in the 17C by Armande Béjart, wife of the comic playwright and actor Molière, now houses a museum with exhibits on the history of the château, memorabilia of famous inhabitants of the town (including Béjart, Wagner, Rodin). The bronze bust of Helvetia in the garden is the work of Gustave Courbet, created in exile in Switzerland (Courbet was involved in the Paris Commune uprising in 1871, was accused of having knocked over the Vendôme column, and fled to Switzerland in 1875, where he died two years later).

Musée Rodin (Villa des Brillants): The country house into which Rodin moved in 1895 and in which he worked until his death is open to the public as a museum. Rodin died on 17 November 1917 in Meudon and was buried in the park of his country house beside his lifelong companion Rose Beuret who died six months before him (the sculpture 'The Thinker' stands above the tomb). The most striking works from the artist's late period are 'Porte de l'Enfer' (1880), 'The Burghers of Calais' (1884), 'Victor Hugo' (1890) and 'Honoré de Balzac' (1891).

Bellevue: Château Bellevue, built for Madame de Pompadour over a relatively brief period (1748–50) and with a very great deal of effort, was the most famous of all the European palaces called 'Bellevue' until well into the 19C. Louis XV, who visited it on 24 November 1750, four days after it was completed, was so impressed by its situation and furnishings that he acquired it for himself, but allowed his favourite to use it. The most famous artists of the period were involved in beautifying the château, and it was soon considered the finest of its kind in Europe (artists included rococo sculptors Guillaume Coustou the Younger, Etienne-Maurice Falconet and Jean-Baptiste Pigalle, and also painters François Boucher and Charles van Loo). In the course of the Revolution it fell into the hands of the so-called 'Bande Noire', who had it pulled down. 'Bande Noire' was a term used under the Revolution for companies of builders and other capitalists who acquired ecclesiastical possessions, émigrés' property and also buildings which had been put on sale as a result of the dissolution of entails and majorats. They were known perjoratively as 'Bandes

Méry-sur-Oise, view of château from park

Noires' because they usually pulled down old buildings of historical importance without any consideration for their importance either historically or as works of art, in order to split up and sell land and building materials. The last surviving section of this château was the Villa Brambor-ion, an important strategic point during the siege of Paris by the Prussians 1870&1.

In 1823 a M.Guillaume bought the land and split it into parcels. Subsequently a number of fine villas and other houses were built, and they now make up the village of Bellevue, which is part of the commune of Meudon.

Milly-la-Forêt
91 Essonne   p.256□D 4

The little town of Milly-la-Forêt is on the edge of the Forest of Fontaine-bleau. The poet and author Jean Cocteau died here (1889–1963).

Chapelle   Saint-Blaise-des-

Simples: Cocteau was a man of many talents who also drew and painted, and he decorated this chapel S. of Milly-la-Forêt when the Romanesque building was restored in 1959. The name of the little church, in which Cocteau is buried, refers to the medicinal herbs ('simples') growing around Milly-la-Forêt.

Also worth seeing: Gothic *church* (12,13&15C) with fine bell tower. 14C *market halls*.

Montfort-l'Amaury
78 Yvelines   p.256□B 2

This little town was the seat of a medieval dynasty originating from Amaury (Amalrich), Count of Henne-gau (*c.* 952). The most famous representatives of this race were Count Simon IV, his son Count Amaury VI and his younger brother Simon de Montfort, Earl of Leicester. Simon IV, who took part in a crusade to Palestine 1190–1200, gave orders in

Milly-la-Forêt, Saint-Blaise-des-Simples, tomb of J.Cocteau (l), detail from his painting (r)

1208 initiating the crusade against the Albigensians, against whom he campaigned with unimaginable cruelty, particularly in Béziers in 1209. In 1213 he defeated Peter II of Aragon and Count Raymond VI of Toulouse at Muret, upon which Pope Innocent conferred the possessions of the counts of Toulouse upon him. He died in 1218 at the siege of Toulouse. His son Amaury VI continued the campaign against the Albigensians, but was pressed so hard that he resigned his rights in the county of Toulouse to King Louis VIII in 1226. In 1312 Montfort was acquired by the dukes of Brittany through marriage. Montfort came to the French crown when Anne, the rich daughter of the last Duke of Brittany, married King Charles VIII in 1491 and then entered into a second marriage with King Louis XII in 1499. The various castles in the town have survived only as ruins.

Saint-Pierre: This church, rebuilt by Anne de Bretagne in the late 15C, has magnificent *Renaissance stained glass* (16C). The late Gothic cemetery gate leads to the *ossuary* ('Ancien Charrier', 16&17C) with three walks, rather like a cloister.

Maurice Ravel house: There is a *Ravel museum* in 'Le Belvédère', the house in which the composer Maurice Ravel (1875–1937) lived from 1920.

Environs: Pontchartrain (10 km. NE): The extensive *château*, built in the mid 17C and attributed to François Mansart, is reflected in the waters of the Mauldre. André Le Nôtre designed the large park.

Montlhéry
91 Essonne   p.256□D 6

Montlhéry, once the possession of mighty liege lords, is famous for the battle of 16 July 1465 between King Louis XI and Count Charles de Charolais (later Duke Charles the Bold of Burgundy). Charles had placed himself at the head of the Ligue du Bien

Montfort-l'Amaury, late Gothic cemetery gate (l), Saint-Pierre, Renaissance stained glass (r)

Public, a group of French noblemen opposed to the king's despotic behaviour. As King Louis left the battle-field during the night, he was considered to have lost. Montlhéry was and remains a centre of vegetable and tomato growing.

Tower: The famous 13&14C tower is Montlhéry's principal sight; it was part of a castle of which the ring walls have fallen into complete disrepair.

Also worth seeing: 17C *church* with parts from the original 13C building. 12C *town hall*.

Montmorency
95 Val-d'Oise   p.256☐D 2

This town owes its fame to the philosopher Jean-Jacques Rousseau, who lived in Montmorency from 1756–62 at the invitation of Madame d'Epinay, and here wrote his novel 'Emile ou de l'Education' and his sensitive bestseller 'Julie ou La Nouvelle Héloïse'

Montmorency, Saint-Martin, W. portal

(in Rousseau's honour the town was not called Montmorency under the Revolution, but Emile). Rousseau lived in Madame d'Epinay's Château la Chevrette 1752–5, and after a brief stay in Paris he then moved in the the Eremitage (10 Rue de l'Eremitage; since rebuilt) in the gardens of the château, with his mistress Thérèse Lavasseur and her mother. Here he was visited by Madame d'Houdetot (she lived in nearby Eaubonne), who served as model for Julie in 'La Nouvelle Héloïse'.

Montmorency took its name from the famous Franco-Dutch aristocratic family of Montmorency, whose members bore the title 'First Baron of France' from 1327. Lesbius was the founding father; he had been converted by St.Dionysius and is said to have been martyred with him. Bouchard I of Montmorency (d.*c.* 980) is the earliest proven holder of the barony of Montmorency. Mathieu II, known as the 'Golden Constable', forced the Albigensians into submission in 1226. After his death (1230) the house split into two principal lines, the older one of the barons of Montmorency and the more recent line of Montmorency-Laval. The even later Nivelle line transplanted itself to the Netherlands, where it came to a bloody end with the execution of the Count of Hoorne and his brother Floris (1568&70). The title of duke fell to the barons of Montmorency in 1551.

Saint-Martin: 16C Renaissance church, restored in the 19C, with interesting stained glass windows.

Montreuil-sous-Bois
93 Seine-Saint-Denis   p.256☐D 2

Industrial town to the E. of Paris. *Saint-Pierre-et-Saint-Paul* has been refurbished and rebuilt; 12&16C sections. *Historical Museum* specializing in the social movement in France.

Mont-Valérien

92 Hauts-de-Seine   p.256☐C 2

To the W. of Paris on the left bank of
the Seine is Mont Valérien, 528 ft.
above the surface of the river, a lonely
hill on which the Mémorial de la
Résistance has stood since 1960.

Mont Valérien has been a cult site
since Gallic times, from the 15C
numerous hermits established themselves here, and a chapel built in 1634
was a popular place of pilgrimage
for Parisians until the French
Revolution.

In 1830 the hill became part of the
defensive ring around Paris, and in
1840 Adolphe Thiers provided it with
strong fortifications; the Forteresse
du Mont-Valérien was the most
important of Paris' inner defences.
Because of its height and heavy
artillery (including 'Valérie', a 21 cm
naval gun) the hill was of great
strategic significance in the Franco-
Prussian War. During the siege of
Paris the positions of the Third
German Army were fired upon from
here from September 1870 to January
1871, and the château at Saint-Cloud
and the Sèvres porcelain factory destroyed. The decisive battle for Paris
also took place here: on 19 January
1871 (King Wilhelm I of Prussia had
had himself proclaimed German
Emperor in Versailles on the previous
day) General Trochu launched his
last sortie from Mont-Valérien with
100,000 men; the Paris national guard
also came under fire in large numbers
for the first time in the course of this
battle. The sortie ended in total
retreat by the French on the same
day. Trochu resigned immediately as
a consequence of this, and Paris capitulated on 28 January. On the next
day troops of the Fifth Prussian Army
corps occupied Mont-Valérien.

In the confusion surrounding the
Commune uprising Mont-Valérien
remained in the power of French
government troops; they bombarded
the inner suburbs from here, Neuilly
in particular.

The clearing between the ramparts of
the fortress played a horrifying role
during the Nazi occupation 1941–44:
about 4,500 Resistance fighters from
all over France were killed here, some

Mont-Valérien, Mémorial de la Résistance

of them shot as hostages at mass executions.

Mémorial de la Résistance: Designed under Charles de Gaulle in 1959&60 by the architect Félix Bruneau. 16 reliefs on a façade of red Vosges sandstone over 100 yards long commemorate the French struggle for freedom; the Cross of Lorraine with two horizontal bars became the symbol of the free French in 1940 under de Gaulle's government in exile and was the emblem of the Gaullistes from 1959. (De Gaulle chose this emblem on the false assumption that the French national heroine Joan of Arc had borne the Cross of Lorraine on her banners in her struggle against the English). The 16 reliefs correspond to 16 coffins of unknown Resistance fighters in the crypt. Those condemned to death had to await their execution in the *chapel* at the top of the hill.

Moret-sur-Loing
77 Seine-et-Marne   p.256□F 4

This picturesque little town on the Loing, a tributary of the Seine, is, like Barbizon, one of the places on the edge of the Forest of Fontainebleau much visited by the inhabitants of the capital on summer weekends. The Impressionist landscape painter Alfred Sisley, who spent his last years in Moret (9 Rue du Donjon) and died here on 29 January 1899, made the little town and its half-timbered houses world-famous by his paintings.

Before Champagne became part of France (before 1314&61) Moret was one of the most important of the kings' fortresses against the counts of Champagne. The impressive remains of the medieval *ring wall* date from this period (12&13C); the two fortified *gates* (Porte de Paris and Porte de Bourgogne) were also part of this system. Moret was also strategically

important in the Hundred Years War in the struggle against the English.

Church: Started in the early 13C (choir)and completed in the 14&15C. Fine 16C organ.

Maison de François Premier: Attributed to Jean Goujon and Pierre Lescaut (first half of the 16C). Francis I's lavishly decorated residence is in the courtyard of the Hôtel de Ville; it was moved to Paris and rebuilt there, but was brought back in 1958.

Nanterre
92 Hauts-de-Seine   p.256□C 2

Nanterre is the administrative capital of the Hauts-de-Seine Département and an expanding new town; the intention is to create 28,000 dwellings in circular high-rise towers (architect of the coloured residential towers already standing: Emile Aillod).

However, Nanterre is not just an ultra-modern town in which the not-so-rosy future has become the present (Paris X University in Nanterre was one of the centres of disquiet in May 1968, a sign of the isolation of these new parts of the city superimposed on the decaying older suburbs of Paris), but also has a past going back to the time of the Celts, when the town was called *Nemetodorum*. In the Middle

Nanterre, coloured tower blocks

Ages it belonged to the monastery of St.Geneviève, the patron saint of Paris, who according to tradition was born in Nanterre.

Basilique Nationale de Sainte-Geneviève: This Catholic pilgrimage church has 13,17&20C sections: nave, modern transept and choir.

Environs: Courbevoie: Directly to the N. of Nanterre is the industrial town of Courbevoie with 59,000 inhabitants (opposite Neuilly, on the other bank of the Seine). 18C *Saint-Pierre-Saint-Paul.*
La Défense: The new business quarter of La Défense between Courbevoie, Puteaux and Nanterre, aligned with the Champs-Elysées, is the largest town-planning project in the Paris area. Almost 105,000 people come to work in this ghost town each day, though 20,000 people do actually live here. The centre is the 'Dalle', a gigantic square 1.2 kilometres long and between 260 and 820 yards wide; under it are the station, parking facilities etc. La Défense is still far from complete, and building has slowed down under pressure of the world economic crisis in the eighties and massive protests from the population.

Nemours
77 Seine-et-Marne   p 258☐E 4

The town of Nemours on the Loing, a tributary of the Seine, is a popular resort for Parisians and a tourist attraction in its own right.
Nemours became an important feature of the political scene as a result of the agreement between King Henry II and the Sacred League of Péronne against the Huguenots (Edict of Nemours): this forbade Reformed

Nemours, Saint-Jean-Baptiste

worship, expelled Reformed priests from the land and presented Protestants with the choice of being converted to Catholicism or leaving France. Nemours enjoyed changing fortunes: in 1404 the town and environs were raised to the rank of duchy and then to the peerage in favour of the counts of Evreux. After the possessions had reverted to the crown in 1425, Louis XI restored the duchy of Nemours in favour of Jacques d'Armagnac, Count of La Marche (1461). In 1503 Nemours fell to the Crown once more, whereupon Louis XII presented the duchy to his cousin Gaston de Foix in 1507 and after his death in 1512 to Julian de'Medici, the husband of his aunt Philiberte of Savoy. In 1528 Francis I conferred it upon Philippe of Savoy. his mother's brother. The female descendants of the House of Savoy-Nemours (the male line died out in 1659) sold the town to Louis XIV in 1666, and he granted it to the Orléans family, who kept it until 1789. Louis Philippe, the Citizens' King, gave his second son Louis Charles Philippe Raphael (1814–96) the title of Duke of Nemours once more.

Nemours is the birthplace of the mathematician Etienne Bézout (1730–83) and the Polish revolutionary Ludwik Mieroslawski (1814–78).

Town: Nemours has retained its medieval and Renaissance character to some extent; it has narrow streets running parallel to the river and the Gothic church of *Saint-Jean-Baptiste*, rebuilt under the Renaissance. The great *Loing bridge* was opened on Pope Pius VII's journey to Napoleon's Coronation as Emperor in 1804.

Former Château: The former town

château has a free-standing, almost square *keep*; it was originally a medieval castle, rebuilt in the 15&16C, the portal and staircase were modernized in the 18C. It now houses the *municipal museum*

Neuilly-sur-Seine
92 Hauts-de-Seine   p.256☐D 2

Neuilly, or Neuilly-sur-Seine, W. of Paris and N. of the Bois de Boulogne, likes to think itself part of Paris as it is so near the capital (formerly it was directly by the ring wall), but is a town in its own right (largely residential; there is also machine and chemical industry).
The town developed after the rebuilding of the bridge with five broad arches, almost three hundred yards long, which Perronet built over the Seine (altered in the 20C). This bridge, before it was rebuilt in the 18C, is said to have been the scene of an incident which caused the philosopher, mathematician and physicist Blaise Pascal to renounce the life of the world: while he was out driving for pleasure the first two horses of the four pulling his carriage shied on the bridge, and would have pulled the other pair and the carriage into the Seine if the harness had not broken by a happy chance.
The château of the Orléans family, in which Louis Philippe accepted the crown after the July revolution of 1830 and from which he later took the name of Duke of Neuilly, was almost completely destroyed in 1848; in 1853 the property was sold by the state, parcelled and redesigned as a small estate for well-to-do Parisian families. Neuilly is the birthplace of the winner of the Nobel Prize for Literature Roger Martin du Gard (cycle of novels 'Les Thibault'). The writer Anatole France (1844–1924) is buried in the cemetery in the Rue Victor-Noir. The writer Georges Bernanos died after an operation for cancer of

Nemours, former château

the liver in the American Hospital (Hôpital Américain de Paris, 63 Boulevard Victor Hugo) on 5 July 1948. There is a memorial plaque to the poet Théophile Gautier at 30–32 Rue de Longchamp, the house in which he lived from 1826 until his death in 1872.

Environs: Levallois-Perret: This industrial town with 60,000 inhabitants is due NE of Neuilly-sur-Seine. Levalloisien, a technique of stone tool manufacture used above all in the mid-Palaeolithic Age in Eurasia and the Middle Stone Age in Africa, is named after a prehistoric excavation site in Levallois-Perret.

Nogent-sur-Marne
94 Val-de-Marne   p.256☐D2

Nogent-sur-Marne, in which Jean-

Antoine Watteau, the great master of French 18C painting, died in 1721, is still closely connected with art today: Art Museum with library; Maison Nationale de Retraite des Artistes. The town, which has an 11,13&15C church (Saint-Saturnin), and is popular with visitors from Paris: cafés with gardens, Foire à la Ferraille ('Junk market'), Fête du Petit Vin Blanc, etc.

Environs: Beauté: Charles V built the château of Beauté between Nogent and Vincennes in 1375, and died here in 1380. In 1448 Charles VII presented it to his mistress Agnès Sorel, who was thereafter known as the 'Dame de Beauté'. Louis XIII had the château pulled down in 1622.

Bry-sur-Marne (2 km. E.): Restored 17C *church*. The painter and pioneer of photography J.Daguerre, inventor of the daguerrotype, died in Bry in 1851.

Fontenay-sous-Bois (2 km N.): *Saint-Germain-l'Auxerrois* with 15C sections.

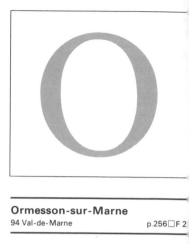

Ormesson-sur-Marne
94 Val-de-Marne   p.256☐F 2

Château: The little town is named after the Lefèvre d'Ormesson family, who bought the château, built *c.* 1580 by Jacques II Androuet du Cerceau. It is reflected in the water of a pool. The new owners commissioned Le Nôtre to landscape the park. When Olivier Lefèvre fell from favour with Louis XIV, he withdrew here and received the great minds of his age:

Ormesson-sur-Marne, château

Madame de Sévigné, Racine, Boileau, la Fontaine, Bossuet among others.

Also worth seeing: 18C *church of the Ascension*, restored in the 20C.

Palaiseau
91 Essonne   p.256☐C 3

Palaiseau, seat of the sub-prefecture of the Département of Essonne, owes its name to a Merovingian building rather like a palace; its history is thus a long one. From 754 until the 10C it belonged to the monastery of Saint-Germain, in the 17C it became capital of the county of the same name. Most of the *church* in Palaiseau dates from the 15C. The authoress Georges Sand lived in the *villa* which bears her name 1864–9. The *Rue de la Pie-Voleuse* ('Thieving Magpie') became world-famous through the melodrama 'The Thieving Magpie or the Servant of Palaiseau' by Louis-Charles Caigniez (the basis of Rossini's opera of the same name).

Environs: Orsay (3 km. SW): *Saint-Martin-et-Saint-Laurent* (12&18C). *University*.

Pantin
93 Seine-Saint-Denis   p.256☐D 2

Industrial and harbour town on the Canal de l'Ourcq on the NE borders of Paris. *Saint-Germain-l'Auxerrois* (17&18C). The *'Les Courtilières' estate* (Avenue de la Division Leclerc) was built 1957–60 by Emile Aillaud.

Poissy
78 Yvelines   p.256☐C 2

This industrial town in a loop of the Seine in the W. suburbs of Paris was once a royal residence. King Louis IX, St.Louis, was born here on 25 April 1214, and so was his son Philippe III, on 3 April 1245. The most striking building in Poissy is the originally Romanesque church of Notre-Dame.

Notre-Dame: Only the W. portal and central tower of the former collegiate church of Notre-Dame (12C) are Romanesque; the church was radically rebuilt in the 15C and restored in the 19C by the historicist Eugène Emmanuel Viollet-le-Duc. The S. porch with double portal is late Gothic; the tympanums are decorated with foliage, and a fleur-de-lys as a symbol of the Virgin, rays issue from a cloud, symbolizing the Holy Ghost. These symbols combine to form an allegorical representation of the Annunciation. In one of the chapels is the font said to have been used for the baptism of St.Louis.

Former abbey: All that remains of the abbey is the fortified entrance. There is now a park on the site of the building in which the so-called Colloquium of Poissy took place in September 1561. This was a religious discussion under King Charles IX, the last peaceful attempt to unite the Catholic and Reformed churches in France. A *toy museum* has been established in the open space in which the painter Ernest Meissonier owned land.

Villa Savoye (Parc du Lycée): Le

Poissy, Ville Savoye by Le Corbusier

Corbusier completed this villa on stilts for a well-to-do Parisian family in 1931. The building fell visibly into disrepair until it was listed under André Malraux in 1965.

Environs: Grignon 13.5 km. S.): The Scottish financial reformer and economist John Law acquired a huge fortunes as a successful gambler in France, Holland, Germany and Italy. His plans for reorganization of the financial system on the basis of paper money was a failure in Scotland, London and Turin, but found receptive ears in Versailles. In May 1715 the Regent gave him permission to set up a private bank with shares. When it became clear that the notes were backed by sound credit, the Regent then gave permission, in 1718, to put his ideas into practice on a larger scale, but, for reasons of greed (Louis XIV had left the state coffers empty) forced him into an area of unlimited speculation. Law's bank became a state bank issuing banknotes en masse (3,071 million in all) The use of metal money was made difficult in every possible way, and finally it was forbidden to own it, along with gold and silver crockery and jewels, and all metal objects of value were to be handed over to the royal bank.

Law then, still with the support of the Regent, founded the trading company 'Compagnie d'Occident', to the end of exploiting the colonies; after merging with other trading companies it became known as the 'Compagnie des Indes'.

The public were practically forced to buy shares, and the Rue Quincampoix in Paris became synonymous with frantic speculation on a hitherto unheard-of scale: the value of the Mississippi shares rose from a nominal value of 500 livres to 5,000

Poissy, Notre-Dame, Entombment (16C)

and finally 20,000 livres. This rapid rise was fuelled by the issue of new shares, only issued to holders of the old ones.

The 'Compagnie des Indes' finally took over state debts and the levying of taxes, the government had more money than it could spend, Law was made Director General of Finance (Finance Minister) in 1720, after becoming a Catholic, and the Academy of Sciences elected him as a member. But everything collapsed in the same year: professional speculators began to have doubts, and these soon spread to the general public. In May 1720 the bank declared itself bankrupt, suspended cash payments, the shares sank to a tenth of their value, and on 10 October 1721 the notes had to be withdrawn from circulation completely; countless people had been reduced to penury. John Law had to flee to Venice.

Triel-sur-Seine: (6 km. NW): This little town in the Arrondissement of Saint-Germain-en-Laye has a fine 13,15&16C *church*. 15C late Gothic portal on the right-hand side; Gothic nave; Renaissance choir with notable 16C stained glass.

Pontoise
95 Val-d'Oise   p.256☐C 1

As a Vexin fortress, protecting the city against raids from Normandy, Pontoise was one of the kings' most favoured resorts. In the late 19C Pissarro lived here from 1872–84, and Cézanne also painted the Pontoise countryside. Pontoise, with its steep, twisty, narrow streets and steps above the Oise and the Viosne is now part of the new town of Cergy-Pontoise. It is the home town of Duke Philip the

Poissy, former abbey

Pontoise, Notre-Dame, Madonna (10C)

Bold of Burgundy (1342–1404), the architect Jacques Lemercier (1585–1564) and the Empire architect Pierre François Léonard Fontaine (1762–1853).

In ancient times the town was known as *Briba Isarae* (Celtic 'Oise bridge'), in the Middle Ages *Pons Isarae* or *Pontisara*, (also *Pond Hyserae*, *Pontesia* and *Pons Äsiä*). A fortress was built in 844, in 885 it was conquered by the Normans. The abbey of Saint-Mellon was founded *c.* 899. Later Pontoise, whose owners called themselves the counts of Pontoise, was the capital of the Vexin and had a royal residence. Charles VI of France conducted peace negotiations with Charles II of Navarre here on 21 August 1359; on 31 July 1413 the Dauphin Charles (VII) made peace with the other princes. The English conquered the town in 1419, were dri-

ven out in 1423, but took it again under Talbot in 1437.

Charles VII conquered it after a three-month siege on 19 September 1441. In 1560 an Imperial Diet was held in Pontoise; during the Fronde uprising Louis XIV sought refuge here, and in 1672, 1720 and 1751 the Parisian parliament met in Pontoise. The *château* was destroyed in the Revolution, and nothing but the high retaining walls have survived.

Saint-Maclou cathedral: Pontoise's importance in the Middle Ages can be seen from the fact that in 1140, shortly after Saint-Denis, one of the first Gothic cathedrals in the Ile de France, was built in the town. The juxtapostiton of Gothic and Renaissance elements is explained by the fact that the building was not completed until the 16C (significant rebuilding

Pontoise, Saint-Maclou cathedral

in the 15C). Most of the transept and choir and also the ambulatory and apsidioles date from the 12C (with the exception of the vaults, which have fine Romanesque capitals). The choir furnishings date from the 17C. In the *chapel of the Passion* near the N. tower is a notable mid-16C Holy Sepulchre.

Notre-Dame: This Renaissance church rebuilt in the 16C still has Gothic vaulting. In a modern chapel with ex-votos on the wall is a 10C statue of Notre-Dame-de-Pontoise. In the nave on the right under an arch is the tomb of St.Walter. St.Walter of Rebais, born in the late 11C in Andainville in Picardy, was first a Benedictine monk in Rebais in the bishopric of Meaux and *c.* 1060–9 became the first abbot of the newly-founded monastery of Pontoise. He escaped the burden of monastery administration by fleeing to Cluny, but was compelled to return to Pontoise on the orders of Gregory VII. He died on 8 April 1099, Good Friday, and was buried in Pontoise, and his mortal remains were placed in his tomb in 1153.

Musée Tavet-Delacour: The municipal museum is housed in a charming late Gothic palace dating from the late 15C. Exhibits include paintings, drawings, sculpture and objects of local interest. The museum also houses the Otto Freundlich bequest; he was one of the first exponents of geometrical abstraction. Freundlich lived mainly in Paris from 1909, and was murdered in the concentration camp at Maidanek in 1943.

Environs: Pierrelaye (3 km. SE): 17&18C *château.*

Saint-Ouen-l'Aumône: In the suburb across the river from Pontoise are ruins of the *former Cistercian abbey of Maubuisson*. It was founded by Blanca of Castile, the mother of Louis IX, six days before her death and formerly contained the Queen's tomb and those of many other princes, but was abandoned during the Fronde uprising and destroyed under the Revolution.

Port-Royal des Champs
78 Yvelines   p.256☐C 3

The only evidence of the former magnificence of the mighty Cistercian abbey of Port-Royal, the centre of Jansenism, is the National Museum in the buildings to the N. of the former abbey, where the 'lords of Port-Royal' lived in the 17C.
Port-Royal was founded not far from Versailles in 1204. In the late 16C it was restored by the family of the advocate Antoine Arnauld. In 1602 Arnauld's eleven-year-old daughter Jacqueline, one of his 22 children, took over direction of the convent under the name Mother Angelica and in 1609 she carried out reforms on the principles of Jansenism, a moral and religious reform movement inspired by the Dutch theologian Cornelius Jansen (d.1638). In 1626 Angelica tightened links with Parisian theology by founding a daughter house in the Parisian suburb of Saint-Jacques, and thereafter the original convent was known as Port-Royal 'des Champs', and the new convent as 'Port-Royal de Paris'.
In about 1640 male advocates of Jansenism moved into a special building at the mother house, the so-called Granges (barns). They shared the penances and work of the nuns, and established a monastery school giving the lax Jesuit Rule purer morality and a more thorough grounding in scholarship; they also introduced improved teaching methods.
Famous Jansenists or sympathizers with the movement included the writer and 'Pope of Art' Nicolas Boileau-Despréaux, the fabulist Jean de

Pontoise, Musée Tavet-Delacour, sculpture by O.Freundlich (l), cathedral, capital (r)

la Fontaine, the dramatist Jean Baptiste Racine, the linguist Claude Lancelot, the philosopher Pierre Nicole, the theologian Louis Sebastian Le Nain Tillemont. The most famous Jansenist was the philosopher Blaise Pascal who, after an accident in 1654 and the mystical conversion associated with it, lived in Port-Royal until his death. He continued his mathematical work but devoted himself particularly to asceticism and meditation. He wrote his famous letter against the Jesuits, the 'Provinciales' in Port-Royal, and his main work, the 'Pensées'.
After a clash with Pope and King the convent was dissolved in 1709, and the building destroyed by the Parisian police in 1710.

Musée National de Port-Royal: The museum is in the former Granges and documents the history of Jansenism in France with drawings, engravings, documents, paintings (including work by the court painter Philippe de Champaigne, a supporter of Jansenism, and 'Peintre de Port-Royal').

Environs: Dampierre (5 km. SW): The *château*, restored in 1840, was built in 1675 by Jules Hardouin-Mansart on the site of a Renaissance building (some surviving outbuildings). The present building is in brick, set in a park landscaped by André Le Nôtre. The lavish interior decoration dated in part from the time at which the château was built, and some has been retained in Louis-Treize style.
Magny-les-Hameaux (3 km. E.) The former *parish church* (12C choir, 15C nave) contains fragments from the convent building which was destroyed, choir stalls from the abbey of Vaux-de-Cernay, tombstones from the desecrated cemetery etc.
In the *cemetery* is a monument to the Symbolist poet Albert Samain, one of the co-founders of the 'Mercure de France', who died in Magny in 1900.

Saint-Lambert-des Bois (1.5 km. S.): In the *cemetery* near the church (13C) is a mass grave containing bones removed from Port-Royal.
Vaux-de-Cernay (10 km. SW): Near the little town of Cernay-la-Ville in the Chevreuse valley are the ruins of the *Cistercian abbey of Vaux de Cernay*. It was founded in the 12C by monks from Savigny.

Provins
77 Seine-et-Marne   p.258□H 3

Provins, surrounded by fields and about 90 km. SE of Paris on the Durentin and the Voulzie, has declined considerably in importance since the Middle Ages, when it was for a time the third-largest city in France, but its appearance is still more medieval than that of any other town in the Ile de France. Provins is now the administrative centre of an Arrondissement and still an important market for agricultural produce. Ceramics and earthenware are also manufactured here.

History: Provins, the ancient *Pruvinum*, was the principal town of a county in Frankish times and in the late 12C became the principal residence of the counts of Champagne, who established two markets here (May and September), attended by merchants from all over Europe. Edmond de Lancaster, one of the lords of Provins, made cultivated red roses famous from here; they were a rarity at the time. Edmond, the brother of the English king, incorporated the rose into the arms of the House of Lancaster, while the House of York chose the white rose, emblems later to achieve notoriety in the Wars of the Roses (1455–85). Provins was granted a charter in 1230.

Town: The town has been divided into two since the Middle Ages, and this division is still a striking feature.

The 'Ville Haute' is surrounded by ramparts on a ridge, and was formerly the residence of the counts, while the 'Ville Basse' below was the area occupied by merchants, markets and tradespeople.

Ville Haute: The Ville Haute is dominated by the massive *Tour de César*, the emblem of the town. The upper town clusters around both sides of the steep Rue Saint-Thibault with its half-timbered houses on a mountain ridge surrounded by ramparts. In the centre the old fountain, the cross and the old houses in the Place du Châtel form a picturesque group.
Saint-Quiriace: This former collegiate church was built on the site of a former temple. The ambulatory is early Gothic (late 12C). The nave has only two bays, the façade is 15C. The crossing dome dates from the 17C.
Tour de César: The lower section of this massive 144 ft. high keep dates from the early 12C, the upper from the 16C. The first floor houses a guard room, with an opening for the provision of ammunition and food for the soldiers in the high vaults. The turrets were used as dungeons, with the exception of the one intended for the governor.
Grange aux Dîmes: This simple 12C military building was later used as a storeroom. It is above a room in which several underground passages meet.
Porte Saint-Jean: This massive fortified gateway (12&13C) at the entrance to the upper town has two side defensive towers. The defences also included a drawbridge, a portcullis and a gate. The *ramparts* are fortified with towers and have survived in the best condition between the Porte Saint-Jean and the Porte de Jouy (12C).

Ville Basse: The lower town was formerly the province of merchants and the ordinary people. The Provins fairs, known throughout Europe in the Middle Ages, were held here in

May and September. There are still numerous old palaces throughout the old town.
Saint-Ayoul: This old abbey church dates from the 12C, but was much restored in the 15C. The (damaged) portal with façade figures (heads knocked off) and the transept have Romanesque features. The tower is all that remains of a former collegiate church and the monastery attached to it.
Sainte-Croix: This church was extended and embellished in the 13C and owes its name to the fragments, said to be from the Cross of Christ, brought back from the Holy Land by Crusaders. It burned down in the 15C and was rebuilt in the 16C. The Romanesque tower (with modern spire) has survived. The W. façade has a Renaissance portal, and the portal on the N. side is Gothic. The baptismal chapel (left of the entrance) has a 13C carved *font*. Fine *screen* in front of the 16C choir with double ambulatory.
Hôtel-Dieu: This 11&12C former palace is essentially a reconstruction but has some original carving. Its cellars are connected to a network of underground passages.
Ancient Couvent des Cordeliers: The Franciscans were known as 'Cordeliers' ('girdle-wearers') in France from the 13–19C. This ancien monastery was founded in 1248 by Count Thibaut IV, and the surviving sections are two galleries of the *cloister* (14&15C), the Gothic, vaulted *chapterhouse* and the *chapel*. A small 13C *tomb* contains the heart of Thibaut IV (1201–53), Count of Champagne and King of Navarre, one of the best French troubadours and an important French medieval lyric poet, admired by Dante and Petrarch. Of his 66 surviving songs 39 are love songs, and the others war songs, hymns etc.

Environs: Nogent-sur-Seine (1 km. SE): 15&16C *church*.

Provins, Saint-Ayoul, portal ▷

Saint-Loup-de-Naud (8 km. SW): The *church* in Saint-Loup-de-Naud is one of the oldest surviving churches in the Ile de France. It dates from the 11&12C, and was originally part of a Benedictine priory. Choir, parts of the crossing, and nave are Romanesque; the W. bays and the *portal*, which is reminiscent of the King's Portal in Chartres, are early Gothic: in the tympanum of the portal is Christ enthroned as Judge of the World, with symbols of the Evangelists; Mary and the Apostles are on the lintel, and the archivolts have representations of scenes from the life of St.Loup, bishop of Sens (d.623); a statue of St.Loup decorates the central pier, and there are figures in the jambs. Remarkable also are the siren birds, based on the harpies of ancient legend, originally demons of the storm, later seen as ugly giant birds with women's heads, and in medieval art above all a symbol of greed. In the right apsidiole is a 14C *statue of the Virgin.* Fine 12C *font.*

Voulton (*c.* 9 km. N.): Voulton *priory church*, built in the late 12 and early 13C.

Le Raincy
93 Saint-Denis   p.256☐E2

Notre-Dame de Raincy: This church built by Auguste Perret in 1922&3 was considered a landmark in the history of modern church architecture: it is in reinforced concrete, with no attempt to conceal the character of the material. The bell tower is over 140 ft. high.

There is a remarkable Romanesque font in front of the church.

Le Raincy, Notre-Dame de Raincy, tower

Rambouillet

78 Yvelines   p.256☐B 3

Château: The forest of Rambouillet has been used by hunting parties for centuries, and the château has been the summer residence of the French president since 1897 (Félix Faure). Limited public access when the president is not in residence.

The château was built in 1375 on the foundations of an earlier fortress, of which only the massive *round tower*, in which Francis I died during a hunting party in 1547, has survived. Louis XIV acquired Rambouillet for his illegitimate son the Count of Toulouse, who rebuilt it and had the parks landscaped in 1706.

In 1783 Louis XVI bought Rambouillet, started a dairy for his wife Marie-Antoinette and began to breed Rambouillet sheep. The English Garden was designed by Hubert Robert. In 1830 Charles X signed his abdication papers here. The château has been state property since 1870. *Interior:* 18C wood panelling. *Napoleon I's bathroom* was painted with mock ancient frescos in 1807. It is adjacent to the room in which the dethroned Emperor spent the night of 29–30 June 1815 on his long journey into exile in St.Helena. The *Salle des Marbres* on the ground floor was once part of the old château. It was faced with coloured marble for Charles d'Angenner, Marquis de Rambouillet, in 1556.

Park: The park has a complex system of small roads and canals, with areas for parking and recreation. Feasts used to be held on the artificial islands.

Laiterie de la Reine: The dairy, built in 1785, is in the form of a circular temple with artificial grotto.

Bergerie Nationale: The Rambouillet breed of sheep, now well known, developed from an experiment by Louis XVI. He acquired Spanish merino sheep and crossed them with local animals. They were kept first of all in the open air, then moved into covered accommodation, to acclimatize the merinos, spoilt by

Le Raincy, Romanesque font, detail

the sun, to the harsher climate. Rambouillet sheep, domestic animals with fine wool, are bred for eating particularly in dry areas of the world (the USA for example) because of their resistance to heat and dry conditions.

English Garden: The *pavilion*, completely covered with mother-of-pearl and shells and built by the Duc de Penthièvre *c.* 1778 for his stepdaughter the Princess de Lamballe, is a particularly decorative feature of the gardens, designed by Hubert Robert, with streams and tropical trees.

Rampillon
77 Seine-et-Marne   p.258☐G 3

Church: This 13C building with nave and two aisles in the little village of Rampillon on the Brie has two remarkable portals dating from the early Gothic period. The church originally belonged to the Templars, and for this reason the floor of the nave is covered with numerous gravestones of Knights Templar and Hospitaller, some of them very fine.

W. portal: Christ appears in the tympanum as Judge of the World, with angels, the Virgin and St.John. The lintel shows the Resurrection of the Dead at the Last Judgement, with angels blowing trumpets, the weighing of souls, and Abraham's Bosom. On the jambs statues of the Apostles, with reliefs below them showing tasks performed in the various months of the year.
S. portal: The tympanum of the smaller S. portal shows Christ crowning Mary, surrounded by angels. Worth seeing in the *interior* are the triforium, the polygonal choir and a 16C altarpiece with a 14C statue of the Virgin.

Environs: Nagis (4.5 km. NW): 13C church, later rebuilt. *Château* with two surviving medieval towers. One of the wings now houses the *town hall.*

Royaumont, abbey
95 Val-d'Oise   p.256☐D 1

The Cistercian abbey of Royaumont,

Rampillon, church, Apostle carvings on the W. portal

highly influential in the Middle Ages, was founded by Saint Louis in 1228; tradition has it that he was personally involved in the work of building, and himself served the monks in the refectory.

From the 16C onwards numerous prominent personalities were abbots of Royaumont, including Mazarin, and several princes. The abbey was dissolved in 1791 and passed to the Marquis de Travannet, who had the church pulled down and set up a cotton mill in the monastery. The buildings are now a cultural centre.

Monastery: The monastery buildings date from the 12C. Cloisters, chapterhouse, great hall and the sacristy of the church have survived. The former *refectory* is impressive, and contains the tomb of Marshall Henri de Lorraine by Antoine Coysevox, originally in the church. The kitchens have been restored to their medieval condition.

Ruined church: The once lavishly furnished abbey church was stripped of its *objets d'art* during the Revolution, and demolished. All that has survived are the bases of the piers, the S. wall and the N. staircase tower. The ruins give an impression of the original dimensions of the building.

Abbot's palace: The so-called abbot's palace was built in 1785, shortly before the Revolution, in the monastery gardens.

Environs: Asnières-sur-Oise: Administratively Royaumont is now attached to the nearby town of Asnières-sur-Oise, which has a charming 12&13C *church*.

This is also the site of the world-famous *dogs' cemetery*, containing the bodies not just of dogs, but of various quadrupeds of which their owners were particularly fond; best-known is the memorial to the St.Bernard Berry, who saved the lives of 40 people.

Rampillon, church, W. portal, detail

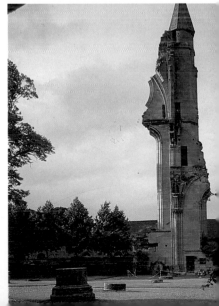

Royaumont abbey, ruined church

Saint-Cloud

92 Hauts-de-Seine   p.256☐C 2

Saint-Cloud, on the Seine in the W. suburbs of Paris, had, until the Franco-Prussian War, a château which was one of the finest in France and the scene of numerous important historical events. The park, considered to be André le Nôtre's masterpiece, has survived, and is now a popular destination for excursions from Paris.

Saint-Cloud, sculpture in the park

History: The name of town and château is derived from *Chlodovald*, one of the three sons of the Frankish King Chlodomer, who founded a monastery here and died *c.* 560. Bishop Gregory of Tours records in his 'Frankish History': 'The third brother, however, Chlodovald by name, they could not seize, he being rescued by the loyalty of mighty men. He renounced this earthly kingdom and turned to the Lord, cut off his hair with his own hands and became a clergyman. His life was all good works and he departed this world as a priest'. The Frankish historian Fredegar adds in his 'Chronicles' that miracles occurred at the tomb of Chlodovald. The place remained a possession of the bishops of Paris, to whom it had been left by Chlodovald. Saint-Cloud was twice burned down, in 1346 by the English and in 1411 by the Armagnacs. When King Henry III laid siege to Paris in 1589, he established a camp in Saint-Cloud, where he was mortally wounded with a poisoned knife on 1 August by the fanatical Dominican Jacques Clément; the king died on the following

day. Servants, attracted by the king's cries, rushed to the spot and stabbed the murderer; his body was torn to pieces by four horses on the way to the place of execution, and then burned.

In 1685 Louis XIV acquired the property for his brother, Duc Philippe d'Orléans, known as Monsieur. The latter had it extended and rebuilt as a château for himself and his second wife Liselotte von der Pfalz by Jules Hardouin-Mansart and Jean Girard. The park was designed by Le Nôtre.

Duc Philippe II Joseph d'Orléans, who later became the wealthiest landowner in France, attached himself to the Third Estate in 1789 (he acquired the name 'Philippe Egalité') and died on the scaffold in 1793, was born in Saint-Cloud in 1747. In 1785 Louis XVI acquired the château for Queen Marie Antoinette, who built numerous extensions (including some designed by Johann Heinrich Riesener).

Under the Revolution the château was let to a restaurateur, who held dances here until, in the last days of the Dir-

ectoire, the two councils used it for their meetings. Napoleon Bonaparte unseated the Directoire in Saint-Cloud by the coup d'état of 18 Brumaire (9&10 November 1799), made the château habitable again at great expense, and spent a great deal of time here. He proclaimed the Empire here on 18 May 1804 and subsequently dealt with affairs of state in Saint-Cloud more frequently than in Paris; In 1810 he celebrated here his marriage to Marie-Louise, daughter of the last Holy Roman Emperor Franz II and first Austrian Emperor (Franz I). Schwarzenberg and Blücher made Saint-Cloud their headquarters in 1814 and 1815, and the details of the surrender of Paris to Blücher and Wellington were signed here on 3 August 1815. King Charles X was in residence in the château when the July Revolution broke out in 1830. It was also here that he signed the ill-fated Ordonnances which led to the outbreak of the Revolution. Under the July Monarchy the château was the residence of the royal family. Napoleon III proclaimed the Second Empire here in 1852. In July 1870

Saint-Cloud, park with view of Paris

Napoleon III signed the declaration of war against Prussia in Saint-Cloud, and set out on the campaign from here. During the siege of Paris the château was set on fire by bombardment from the Mont-Valérien fortress (q.v.); the outer walls were demolished in 1891.

Park: Although only outbuildings of the château have survived and the sculptural decoration has almost all disappeared, Le Nôtre's park is still one of the most beautiful of those surviving from the 17C. There is a wonderful view of Paris and the Seine plain from the terrace on which the château stood (marked out with topiary-work yews). The *Grande Cascade*, the work of Antoine Lepautre (upper section) and Hardouin-Mansart (second pool) is one of the most inventive of 17C jeux d'eau. Above the terrace is the pool with 24 fountains. Elias Robert was responsible for the group 'France Crowns Art and Industry' (1855).

Environs: Marnes-la-Coquette (3 km. SW): 2,000 inhabitants. *Sainte-*

Eugénie (19C). There is a branch of the Institut Pasteur in the château at *Villeneuve-l'Etang*. The chemist and microbiologist Louis Pasteur died here in 1895.

Saint-Denis
93 Seine-Saint-Denis   p.256☐D 2

In the grey but important industrial town of Saint-Denis, N. of Paris, is the former abbey church of the same name, the place of anointing and entombment of the kings of France from Hugh Capet onwards (exceptions: Philip I, Louis VII and Louis IX) and also one of the most important cathedrals in the West. It is named after the French national saint Denis.

Basilica of Saint-Denis: As a symbol of kingship, Saint-Denis was the object of the mob's blind lust for destruction under the Revolution. Only fragments remain of the magnificent interior decoration, now in the Galerie d'Apollon in the

Saint-Denis, basilica, tower

Louvre (coronation insignia) and the Cabinet des Médailles in the Bibliothèque Nationale (throne of Dagobert, some of the treasure). Inexpert restoration in the 19C caused further damage: among other things the N. tower was cracked, destroying the symmetry of Suger's magnificent W. façade. Restoration on historical principles did not start until Viollet-le-Duc took over the project. The royal tombs are of great cultural interest, and some of high artistic quality.

Origins: The existence of St.Denis is not historically authenticated. According to tradition he was sent to France as a missionary bishop by Pope Fabian (236–250), where as first bishop of Paris he was beheaded *c.* 250 on Montmartre and buried in Catuliacum, later Saint-Denis (or alternatively walked from Montmartre to Catuliacum with his head in his hand).

It is said that the first church containing the tomb of the saint was commissioned by St.Genevieve *c.* 475; this was a lavishly furnished basilica with nave and two aisles (fragments sur-

vive). For a long time the Merovingian King Dagobert I was held to be the actual founder of Saint-Denis; in accordance with his own wishes he was buried on his death in 639 in the church 'which he had himself earlier caused to be decorated and in every place ornamented in a most worthy fashion with gold, precious stones, and many exceedingly valuable objects' (Fredegar).

Carolingian pillared basilica: The pact between the Popes and the Frankish kings, a decisive factor in the history of the West, was concluded in Saint-Denis in 754. Pope Stephen III was under pressure from the Lombards and had travelled to the kingdom of the Franks especially to enlist the help of King Pépin the Short. After Pépin had sworn an oath of friendship with the Pope and his successors in Quierzy, and promised to free Ravenna from the Lombards and return the town to the Pope (so-called Gift of Pépin: established the temporal authority of the Pope), Stephen anointed Pépin king once more in Saint-Denis and granted him the title 'Patricius Romanus'. The Pope

Saint-Denis, basilica, portal tympanum

Saint-Denis, basilica, choir, detail

Saint-Denis, nave and choir

anointed Pépin's sons Charles (Charlemagne) and Karlmann at the same time, so that the grace of God should be transferred to the new race of kings.

A new cathedral was built under Pépin the Short and abbot Fulrad (749–84), and consecrated in the presence of Charlemagne in 775: a pillared basilica with nave and two aisles, semicircular choir and two towers over a narthex in the W. (presumed to have been the first façade of its kind) and a ring crypt in the E. (earliest example N. of the Alps). In the 9C the apse was rebuilt (consecrated 832).

Suger's early Gothic church: The ever-increasing stream of pilgrims necessitated a new building in the early 12C, and this was realized by Abbot Suger. The abbey church corresponded largely with the present church, and marks the beginning of French Gothic. Suger was a prince of the church and statesman (1081–1151), and one of the most important minds in 12C France; he had considerable political influence under Louis VI and Louis VII. During Louis VII's crusade of 1147–9 he was imperial regent. The new building was started in 1157 with the twin-towered façade in the W., almost 100 ft. in front of the Carolingian basilica, and the tower chapel was consecrated in 1140.

Nave and transept: It was not until the 13C that work began under Abbot Eudes-Clement on rebuilding the Carolingian nave and transept in high Gothic style. In 1231 work began on the upper section of the choir, which led to the destruction of Suger's vaulting. The transept was complete by 1245; this was to house the royal tombs. The entire building was consecrated in 1281. The architect of nave and transept is not known; he is designated 'master of Saint-Denis'.

Royal tombs: The famous tombs of Saint-Denis were rescued and stored

Saint-Denis, basilica, bishop's throne▷

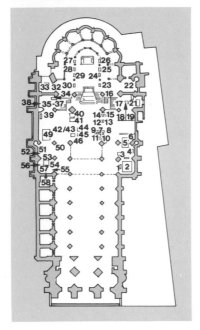

Saint-Denis The figures on the plan are referred to in the main text

during the Revolution (but not before 49 bronze recumbent figures had been melted down). In 1806 Napoleon designated Saint-Denis as funerary church for his dynasty, had the rescued monuments returned to the church, and assembled other royal monuments from various churches and abbeys here. The monuments are not arranged in chronological order, and are of variable artistic quality. They include Renaissance masterpieces:

1) Charles d'Evreux, Comte d'Etampes (d.1336); recumbent figure from the monastery of the Cordeliers in Paris.

2) The contract for the tomb of Louis d'Orléans (d.1407), his consort Valentine Visconti (d. 1408) and that of Charles d'Orléans (d.1465) and Philippe de Vertus (d.1420), was awarded by Louis XII to Italian artists, demonstrating an increasing inclination towards the art of the Italian Renaissance. Louis d'Orléans, a prince as intelligent and gifted as he was extravagant and unscrupulous, was the founder of the Orléans-Valois line.

Saint-Denis, S. window (Gregorian calendar)

3) Marguerite, Countess of Flanders (d.1382), daughter of Philip V.

4) Urn created by Pierre Bontemps 1550–5 for the heart of Francis I, the father of the French Renaissance (see under Fontainebleau), who died in Rambouillet in 1547. The column which originally supported the urn was designed by Primaticcio.

5) Pierre Bontemps followed Philibert de l'Orme's designs to create the tomb of Francis I (d.1547), his first wife Claude (d.1524) and their children Charlotte (d.1524; Bontemps), Francis and Charles (d.1536 and 1545; François Carmoy), a masterpiece of the French Renaissance. The base is decorated with reliefs of scenes from Francis' Italian Wars against the Holy Roman Emperor, Charles V.

6) Béatrice de Bourbon (d.1338), from 1334 consort of John, the blind King of Bohemia, a member of the Luxemburg dynasty.

7) Philip III, the Bold (d.1285); first portrait statue representing an individual (a departure from the previous ideal of a ruler of timeless appearance); white marble (Pierre d'Echelles in association with Jean d'Arras). Philip the Bold, son of Saint Louis, waged countless unsuccessful wars and died of sorrow in Perpignan, after his fleet had been destroyed in the war against Catalonia.

8) Isabelle d'Aragon (d.1271), first consort of Philip III, the Bold; she died on the journey back from a crusade in Cosenza at the age of 24; marble.

9) Philip IV, the Fair (d.1314); memorial created in the same studio as Nos. 34 and 39, 1327–9.

10) Charles Martel ('the Hammer'), d.741; idealized portrait created c. 1265 of the last Frankish mayor of the palace, sole ruler of the Frankish Empire without the title of king from 737. He defeated the Moslems in 732 at a battle fought between Tours and Poitiers, and stopped their advance into the European interior; Charles Martel is wearing 13C costume.

11) Clovis II (d.657); idealized portrait dating from c. 1265 of the King of Neustria and Burgundy, and, after removal of the Austrasian mayor of the palace Grimobald, of the entire Frankish Empire; he died in a state of mental collapse at the age of 23.

Saint-Denis, N. window of the basilica

12) Louis III (d.882); idealized portrait dating from c. 1265 of the eldest son of Louis the Stammerer. The 'Song of Louis', the first historic song in German (Rhine Frankish) takes Louis III's victory over the Normans at Saucourt as its theme.

13) Karlmann (d.884); idealized portrait dating from c. 1265 of the Frankish king (second son of Louis the Stammerer) who died at the age of 18.

14) Pépin the Younger, usually known as the Short (d.768); idealized portrait dating from c. 1265 of the first Carolingian King of the Franks.

15) Berthe au grand pied, (d.783), daughter of Count Cheribert of Laon, consort of King Pépin the Short. Bertha's beauty was marred by an excessively large foot; legend has it that, while travelling to marry Pépin, she was handed over by her escort the court stewardess to vassals who had been bribed to murder her. The stewardess's own ugly daughter was substituted for Bertha. The disappointed Pépin later met Bertha near a forest mill, recognized her by her deformity, and married her; this marriage produced Charlemagne.

16) Dagobert I (d.638); 13C tabernacle with scenes from the life of Dagobert restored by Viollet-le-Duc in the 19C.

17) Louis de Sancerre (d.1402), Constable of France.

18) Charles V, the Wise (d. 1380); realistic portrait by André Beauneveu (1364, almost 15 years before the death of the king).

19) Jeanne de Bourbon (d.1377); recumbent figure of the consort of Charles the Wise from the tomb which contained her entrails (indicated by a bag on the breast of the figure) in the Celestine Convent in Paris.

20) Charles VI, the Mad, (d.1422) and his consort Isabeau de Bavière (d.1435); both figures by Pierre de Thury 1429. Isabeau, daughter of Duke Stephen of Bavaria, married the seventeen-year-old Charles in 1385 and from 1392, when he became mad, she conducted the affairs of state with her brother-in-law, Duke Louis d'Orléans (see above, No. 2) and the Duke of Burgundy. The former became her lover, and together they oppressed the country with heavy taxes to satisfy

Saint-Denis, tomb of Louis XII (l), tomb of Louis XVI and Marie Antoinette

Isabeau's extravagance and love of show.

21) Bertrand Du Guesclin (d.1380), Constable of France under Charles V; realistic portrait of the ugly, squat warrior by Thomas Privé and Robert Loisel (1379). Du Guesclin was already on outstanding performer at tournaments at the age of seventeen, and in 1361 entered the service of the Dauphin Charles, who, after his accession to the throne, made Du Guesclin Governor of Pontorson. His victory over Charles the Bad of Navarre at Cocherel in 1364 gained him the further titles of Count of Longueville and Marshall of Normandy.

22) Louis XVI and Marie-Antionette (executed 1793); created by Gaule and Petigot (1816).

23) Leo VI or Léon de Lusignan (d.1393), last ruler of the Latin kingdom of Armenia. He came from the Royal House of Cyprus, and the Lusignan family. He was taken prisoner in Egypt and went to Paris after his release, and later died there; the sculptor did not give him a sceptre.

24) Unknown (13C).

25) Charles de Valois, Comte d'Alençon (d.1346) and Maria of Spain. Figures, attributed to Jean de Liège, from the Jacobite monastery in Paris.

26) Blanche de Bretagne (d.c. 1327).

27) Blanche (d.1243) and Jean (d.1268), children of Saint Louis; from the monastery of Royaumont.

28) Robert d'Artois (d.1317), tomb figure of Jean Pépin of Huy for the monastery of the Cordeliers in Paris.

29) Fredegunde (d.597), the blood-thirsty and extravagant queen of the part of the Frankish empire known as Neustria; slab with mosaics, 11&12C, originally in Saint-Germain-des-Prés.

30) Clovis I (d.511), founder of the Frankish empire; tomb slab (mid 13C) from the church of Sainte-Geneviève, which he founded (now demolished).

31) Childebert I (d.558), son of Clovis I, king of the part of the Frankish empire which had its capital in Paris; tomb slab (mid 12C) from Saint-Germain-des-Prés.

32) Henry II (d.1559) and Catharine de'Medici (d.1589); figures by Ger-

Saint-Denis, tomb of Charles d'Evreux

Saint-Denis. tomb of Henry II and Catharine de'Medici (1583 by G.Pilon)

main Pilon (first tomb; see second tomb: No. 39).

33) Marie de Bourbon (d.1538), aunt to Henry IV; originally in Notre-Dame in Soissons.

34) Philip VI of Valois (d.1350), founder of the Valois dynasty; 12C, studio of André Beauneveu; Jean II, the Good (d.1364), died in English captivity during the Hundred Years War; 12C, studio of André Beauneveu.

35) Philip V, the Tall (d.1322), king.

36) Charles IV, the Fair (d.1328), king, brother of Philip V.

37) Jeanne d'Evreux (d.1371), Queen of France as the third consort of Charles IV.

38) Blanche de France, Duchesse d'Orléans (d.1392), tomb figure by Robert Loisel.

39) Henry II (d.1559) and Catharine de'Medici (d.1589), second tomb (see No. 32); one of the most important tombs in Saint-Denis; figures by Germain Pilon and Jacquio Ponce to designs by Primaticcio; originally in the Valois funerary chapel.

40) Karlmann (d.771), king of the Franks 768–771, brother of Charlemagne and Ermentrudis (d.869), consort of Charles the Bald.

41) Philip (d.1131), son of Louis VI, died at the age of fifteen, and Constanza of Castile (d.1160), consort of Louis VII.

42) Louis X, the Quarrelsome (d.1316) and his son Jean, who died at the age of five (1316); tomb 1327.

43) Jeanne de France (d.1349), Queen of Navarre, daughter of Louis the Quarrelsome; tomb 1327.

44) Henry I (d.1060) and his grandson Louis VI, the Fat (d.1137).

45) Robert II, the Pious (d.1031) and his consort Constance of Arles (d.1032).

46) Column for the urn containing the

Saint-Denis, crypt, stoup (l), cloak of a Prince of the Blood (r)

heart of Henry III (d.1589); the work of Jean Pagot (1635).

47) Column for the urn containing the heart of Louis de Bourbon (d.1556), abbot of Saint-Denis.

48) Guillaume du Chastel (d.1441), knight from the entourage of Charles VII.

49) Louis XII (d.1515) and Anne de Bretagne (d.1514); early Renaissance masterpiece, co-operative work by Italian artists; studio of the Giusti family from Tours.

50) Philippe-Dagobert (d.1235), brother of St.Louis.

51) Louis (d.1260), eldest son of St.Louis.

52) Blanche de France (d.1243), daughter of St.Louis.

53) Louis and Philip (d.c. 1272), grandsons of St.Louis (copy by Viollet-le-Duc).

54) Charles d'Anjou (d.1285), King of Naples and Sicily. Charles is buried in Naples, but his heart was interred in the Jacobin church in Paris (heart in his left hand).

55) Blanche d'Evreux (d.1398), Queen of France, second wife of Philip V (in mourning as a widow; she survived Philip by 48 years), and her daughter Jeanne de France (d.1371), who died at the age of 20.

56) Charles, Comte de Valois, (d.1325), son of Philip the Bold; originally in the Jacobin monastery in Paris.

57) Clémence de Hongrie (d.1328), queen as second consort of Louis X; originally in the Jacobin monastery.

58) Louis de France, Comte d'Evreux (d.1319) and his consort Marguerite d'Artois (d.1311).

Musée d'Art et d'Histoire de Saint-Denis: The collection of documents relating to the history of the abbey and the town is in the

Saint-Germain-en-Laye, château seen from the garden

former Carmelite monastery. Documents on the history of the Commune uprising, and also on the life and work of the poet Paul Eluard, born in Saint-Denis in 1895.

Saint-Germain-en-Laye
78 Yvelines   p.256☐C 2

The residential town of Saint-Germain-en-Laye in the W. suburbs of Paris on the Seine and on the S. edge of the Forêt de Saint-Germain, was the residence of numerous French kings before Louis XIV moved to Versailles in 1682. Although the population has increased considerably, the original centre of Saint-Germain has survived, with many fine 17&18C buildings.
The town has a number of distinguished sons and daughters: the poetess and Queen Margaret of Navarre (1492–1549), King Henry II (1519–59), Queen Jeanne d'Albret of Navarre (1528–72), King Charles IX (1550–74), Queen Margarete de Valois, known as la Reine Margot (1553–1615), King Louis XIV (1638–1715), Philip I Duc d'Orléans, known as Monsieur (1640–1701), the archaeologist, art historian and theologian Salomon Reinach (1858–1932) and his brother Théodore, historian, numismatist and philologist (1860–1928), the composer Claude Debussy (1862–1918), the painter and graphic artist Maurice Denis (1870–1943), the dramatist Edouard Bourdet (1887–1945) and the organist and composer Jehan Alain (1911–40).

History: Saint-Germain-en-Laye has been the scene of many historical events. On 8 August 1570 King Charles IX issued the Edict of Saint-

Saint-Germain-en-Laye, Le Nôtre's terrace with view of the Parisian plain

Germain-en-Laye, signed by Catharine de'Medici, permitting the Huguenots freedom of religion in certain places and four secured areas for free worship. The treaty of Saint-Germain-en-Laye (26&27 October 1635) received Duke Bernhard of Sachsen-Weimar into French service during the Thirty Years War; he thereby acquired money for the maintenance of an army and assurance of the county of Alsace and the governorship of Hagenau. The rights of Parliament were limited by an Edict from Richelieu on 21 December 1641. In 1679 Louis XIV concluded a separate peace in Saint-Germain en-Laye with the Great Elector of Brandenburg, according to which the Elector had to return to Sweden all the land acquired in the course of his Pomeranian conquests. In 1847 the town was attached to the railway network. On 10 September 1919 the peace treaty

between Austria and the allies was signed in Saint-Germain-en-Laye; Austria and Hungary were declared independent states, and Austria compelled to recognize Czechoslovakia, Poland, Hungary and Yugoslavia as independent states.

Château and gardens: Saint-Germain grew up around a monastery founded by Robert the Pious in the 10C. In 1122 a fortress was established here to protect Paris from the W. St.Louis endowed the Sainte-Chapelle *c.* 1230. After damage in the Hundred Years War, Charles V had the château rebuilt in five sections *c.* 1370, and the fortress-like lower part of the building, the chapel and the keep dating from this period survived when much of the building was pulled down from 1530 and replaced by the present palace (Château Vieux), designed by Pierre Chambiges. In

Saint-Germain-en-Laye, view of Paris

1557 Henry II commissioned another palace from Philibert Delorme (Château Neuf) as a theatre and bath house on the edge of the plateau. Louis XIV entrusted André le Nôtre with the construction of the famous terrace, almost a mile and a half long, the design of the garden (destroyed by the building of the railway in the 19C) and the reafforestation of the woodland, before turning his attention to Versailles. After Louis XIV moved to Versailles he handed over the château to King James II, who had been exiled from England after the 'Glorious Revolution', and who died here in 1701; his son, the Young Pretender, also lived here. The Château Neuf was pulled down before the French Revolution. Part of the garden was parcelled off under Charles X; Napoleon III had the whole site restored. The Musée des Antiquités

Nationales de France has been housed in the château since 1867.

Musée des Antiquités Nationales: This museum accommodated in the château shows Gallo-Roman antiquities and finds from the area covered by modern France from the Palaeolithic to the Merovingian period; it was established by Napoleon III at the same time as he restored the château. It is one of the most important museums in the world. The numerous important items in the collection include the *Brassempouy Venus* and the *horse from the Espelugues caves*.

Town: The principal houses of Saint-Germain are grouped around the château, and include a number of 17&18C *palaces*. *Saint-Louis-Saint-Germain:* Neoclassical building from the period *c.* 1800 with a pulpit

Saint-Germain-en-Laye, Sainte-Chapelle, keystone (l), No. 15 Rue Henry IV, door (r)

endowed by Louis XIV. organ case early 18C, 14C Madonna, mausoleum of James II. *Saint-Léger:* Church built 1960&1. *Musée Municipale:* The municipal museum, accommodated in an 18C town house, has a fine collection of graphics, and shows drawings, engravings and documents concerned with the history of the châteaux, also paintings (including a copy of 'The Juggler' by Hieronymus Bosch).

Saint-Leu-la-Forêt
95 Val-d'Oise   p.256☐C 1

This town on the SW edge of the forest of Montmorency is a popular summer resort. A cross surrounded by yews in the Rue du Château marks the spot at which the Château Saint-Leu used to stand; it was the property

of King Louis Bonaparte of Holland, the younger brother of Napoleon I.

Church: There is a memorial to Louis Bonaparte, the father of Emperor Napoleon III, in this place of worship built under the Second Empire.

Saint-Mandé
94 Val-de-Marne   p.256☐D 2

Saint-Louis de Vincennes: This church in the town W. of the forest of Vincennes is decorated with *frescos* by the Nabis painter Maurice Denis.

Cemetery: (Avenue Joffre and Rue Lagny): This is the last resting place of the actress Juliette Drouet, Victor Hugo's mistress of long standing, and her illegitimate daughter by the sculptor James Pradier.

Saint-Maur-des-Fossés
94 Val-de-Marne   p.256□E 2

In the 16C Rabelais, doctor and writer, regularly visited Cardinal du Bellay in his magnificent residence in Saint-Maur. The château was built by Philibert Delorme (destroyed during the French revolution), and Rabelais described the place as 'a paradise of health, of noble grace, of cheerful, unsullied content, of peace and comfort, of enjoyment and bliss, and offering all the righteous joys of work in the fields and life in the country'. Since then much has changed: Saint-Maur has 80,000 inhabitants and is the home of numerous industries, but in the villa districts (particularly in La Varenne-Saint-Hilaire) the original idyll has survived to some extent. The town is set in a bend of the Marne which forms a peninsula, with the loop cut off by the Saint-Maur canal, over 1,250 yards long, and in a tunnel for some of its length. Until the Revolution Saint-Maur was an ecclesiastical centre; Saint-Nicolas (12,13&14C) has a miraculous statue of the Madonna (Notre-Dame des Miracles), and in the 19C it was a centre for artists and literati. The writer and critic Sainte-Beuve wrote two of the poems from the 'Consolations' cycle in Saint-Maur, Victor Hugo and Théophile Gautier recorded the joys of the idyllic Marne countryside, Alexandre Dumas the Elder wrote about its restaurants (e.g. 'Père-la-Ruine', 13 Quai de la Varenne), Henri Murger, author of 'Scènes de la Vie de Bohème' spent time here, and the Polish Nobel prizewinner Henryk Sienkiewicz is said to have written part of his world success 'Quo Vadis?' at 86–8 Quai du Parc.

Former abbey of Saint-Maur:
This abbey founded c. 640 (destroyed during the French Revolution) was the royal monastery of the Capetian kings from the 10C. It became world-famous in the 17C through the Benedictine Lorenz Bernard, who introduced a new Rule (1618). After confirmation by Popes Gregory XV (1621) and Urban VIII (1627) the Congregation spread rapidly and by the early 18C had 180 monasteries in six provinces.

Saint-Ouen
93 Seine-Saint-Denis   p.256□D 2

Saint-Ouen, famous for its *château* (and its flea market) came into being in the 8C as a Merovingian possession which grew up around a church dedicated to St.Ouen (now the church of the Sacré-Coeur). The château, built c. 1660, was acquired by Louis XVIII, who rebuilt it and presented it to Madame du Cayla. Before Louis' return to Paris after the fall of Napoleon he stayed in Saint-Ouen and signed a proclamation here on 2 May 1814 which formed the basis of the altered constitution.

Saint-Sulpice-de-Favières
91 Essonne   p.256□C 3

The pilgrimage village of Saint-Sulpice is in a valley of the Renarde, and the relics of St.Sulpice were venerated here. Sulpice, the favourite of the Merovingian King Gunthram, according to the Frankish historian Gregory of Tours 'a man of noble race, born of one of the most respected senatorial families in Gaul, thoroughly instructed in the free sciences, in poetry without an equal', was bishop of Bourges in the early 7C; he died there in 647. According to tradition he brought a drowned child back to life in Saint-Sulpice.

Pilgrimage church: Work on the

nave of this important Gothic church started *c.* 1260 and the building was completed by the addition of choir in the 14C. 16C choir stalls, 17C retable in the Saint-Sulpice chapel on the left. The relics of the saint are kept in the '*Chapelle des Miracles*', the only surviving section of a 12C church. Scenes from the life of Saint-Sulpice in the 14C *stained glass* above the high altar.

Sceaux
92 Hauts-de-Seine   p.256□D 2

Château: In 1670 the château was acquired by chief minister Jean-Baptiste Colbert, who commissioned its extension into a princely baroque residence by the architect Claude Perrault, with sculpture by François Girardon and Antoine Coysevox; work continued until 1677; all that now remains are some outbuildings, the park, designed by André Le Nôtre and restored from his plans in the 19&20C, and also Perrault's Pavillon d'Aurore. The old château was pulled down during the French Revolution, and the present building, housing the fine Musée de l'Ile de France, dates from the 19C.
Pavillon d'Aurore: This little domed, two-storeyed building with flights of steps at the sides is attributed to Perrault. The interior of the central domed room is decorated with Le Brun's ceiling painting 'Aurora Leaving Cephalus in order to bring Light into the World'. Louis XIV favoured the sun as a symbol and had himself venerated in the figure of the (sun) god Apollo, while his chief minister Colbert preferred Aurora, the dawn.
Orangerie: The orangery built in 1683 by Jules Hardouin-Mansart is still used for musical performances. When the Duchesse du Maine was the lady of the château in the first half of the

Sceaux, château park, statue ▷

Sceaux, view of the château

18C, Parisian high society met here for sumptuous balls.

Park: The garden designed by Le Nôtre was largely restored in the 20C. An outstanding feature is the newly designed *cascade*, featuring works by Rodin. The Grand Canal, which runs right through the park, begins in front of the central rear terrace.

Pavillon de Hanovre: The perspective beyond the Grand Canal is completed by the Pavillon de Hanovre; its name derives from the fact that it was paid for with money acquired in the sack of Hanover. It was built in 1760 for the Parisian garden of Cardinal Richelieu's grand-nephew by Jean Michel Chevotet, and transferred here in 1930.

Musée de l'Ile de France: This museum, in the château, contains outstanding material on the châteaux of the Ile de France (plans, models, old views) and also items manufactured in

or near them (porcelain, fabrics). Also paintings, engravings etc.

Sceaux church: 16C, contains the sculpture 'Baptism of Christ' by Jean-Baptiste Tuby.

Sèvres
92 Hauts-de-Seine   p.256□C 2

Sèvres, between the park of Saint-Cloud in the N. and the forest of Meudon in the S., is known above all for its world-famous porcelain and the unique ceramics museum showing porcelain and ceramics from all over the world, from ancient times to the present day. Other notable features of the town are *Saint-Romain* (13&13 and 17C) and the 18C *town hall.* Sèvres is the birthplace of the painter Constant Troyon (1810–65), a

Sèvres, ceramics museum, Gardener (Derby), 1770–84 (l), Vase Etrusque à Rouleaux (1813, r)

member of the Barbizon School and master of animal painting (principal works in the Louvre).

During the Franco-Prussian War, Sèvres was occupied by troops of the German Third Army on 19 September 1870. The bridge over the Seine in Sèvres had been cut off from the right bank, and was the scene of negotiations between the French and the Germans in the course of the siege of Paris, during which the town came under heavy fire from the Mont-Valérien batteries and gunboats on the Seine.

Porcelain factory: The word-famous porcelain factory was founded privately in Vincennes in 1738, then transferred to Sèvres in 1756; it was bought by Louis XV in 1759, at the instigation of Madame de Pompadour. The earliest items produced were marked with two crossed Ls. As well as the L ('Louis'), another letter indicates the year in which the item was produced, a system which started in Vincennes: A = 1753, AA = 1778 running to PP = 1793. The marks changed as time passed. In 1928 the sequence started again with a capital A, until 1940 = M. 1941 saw another fresh start with A. The principal items produced included services, chandeliers, clocks, and, most importantly, magnificent display vases and bisque figures (bisque is unglazed bone china, with a matt, slightly rough surface), based on models provided by the greatest sculptors of the period. The surviving pieces of this 'Vieux Sèvres' are now among the most sought-after items on the antique market. The ground colours of this period are also famous: sky blue 1753, pink c. 1756&7 and also royal blue (bleu du roi or bleu de Sèvres, often with delicate gold veining), Turkish blue, Pompadour red (rose Dubarry) and apple green (vert pomme).

From 1757–66 the rococo sculptor Etienne-Maurice Falconet was director of the Sèvres porcelain factory. Many of his sculptures (in the Louvre) also exist aş Sèvres porcelain, the most famous is the nymph getting out of a bath known as the 'Baigneuse', which became famous through numerous Sèvres porcelain and bronze reproductions. The group 'Annette et Lubin' dates from 1764. Josse François Joseph le Riche's mythological groups followed in 1771&2. The high point of Sèvres production was a 744-piece porcelain service for Catharine the Great of Russia.

After the outbreak of the French Revolution there were fewer aristocratic customers, and in 1792 the title 'Manufacture Royale' was changed to 'Manufacture Nationale'. In 1805 the factory returned to its privileged status as property of the Emperor.

In 1800 the mineralogist, geologist and palaeontologist Alexandre Brongniart became director of the porcelain factory, a post which he retained, despite the changing political situation, until his death in 1847. Brongniart succeeded in manufacturing hard-fired porcelain (kaolin deposits were discovered in France in 1768), and manufacture of bone china ceased in 1804. Brongniart also developed vitrifiable pigments, which 1818–50 were used above all for numerous copies of famous pictures on porcelain. In 1820 Brongniart founded a school for porcelain painters, and in 1824 the ceramics museum, with the assistance of the porcelain painter Riocreux. Brongniart also extended the range of goods produced to include stained-glass windows (1828–55), and enamel painting (until 1872).

After the death of Brongniart a period of decline began (the factory came close to closure in 1872), although production of bone china started up again and cast porcelain products were introduced. Technical director G.Vogt (1880–1909) developed a 'new' hard-fired porcelain' with fired glazes on a basis of copper oxide. Another great success was the bone china developed around the turn of the century; this was very easy to model and contained silicon. Despite all this, the work of the factory aroused little interest at the World Fair of 1889, and its existence was still in jeopardy until a new guiding principle for production was adopted after the First World War: the work of contemporary artists was integrated into the process, the manufacture of furniture plaques was reintroduced, along with lighting and ceramics for the building industry. Important 20C artists who worked for Sèvres include Ossip Zadkine, Raoul Dufy and Giorgio de Chirico. The 39 by 13 ft. glazed earthenware mural was the work of Marcel Gromaire and Henri Laurens.

Musée National du Céramique:
The ceramic museum founded by

Sucy-en-Brie, Saint-Martin

Alexandre Brongniart in 1824 houses an outstanding collection of earthenware and porcelain of all countries and periods, from the oldest Greek and Etruscan clay vases to the most modern products.

Sucy-en-Brie
94 Val-de-Marne   p.256□E 2

This little town is situated in a rural area SE of Créteil.

Saint-Martin: The church dates from the 12&13C and has been restored.

Former Château de Montaleau (now Mairie): The authoress Madame de Sévigné spent time here in the 17C.

Château le Grand Val (17C): In the 18C the château was owned by the mother-in-law of Freiherr von Holbach, who often received his friend Diderot here.

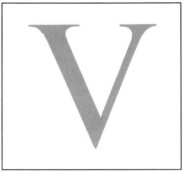

Thoiry
78 Yvelines   p.256□B 2

Château: This château dates from the 16C. The contents include furniture, wall hangings and paintings, in particular by the important Régence portraitist Nicolas de Largillières, and a valuable library.

Wild-life park: The park surrounding the château has a French (18C) and an English garden, and is also a large wild-life park, with wild animals (including elephants) roaming freely (important 'African reserve').

Environs: Maule (7 km. NE): *Saint-Nicolas* with 11C crypt and Renaissance tower.

Vaux-le-Vicomte, Château
77 Seine-et-Marne   p.256□E 3

The château of Vaux-le-Vicomte near Melun, with gardens by André le Nôtre, is a precursor of Versailles and itself one of the most important 17C French châteaux. The interplay of architecture, landscaping and decoration led to artistic coherence of a kind never before realized, making the château one of the finest manifestations of European baroque, and establishing French art as a world force. The artistic triumvirate responsible were architect Louis le Vau, landscape gardener Le Nôtre and the painter, ornamental artist and decorator Charles Le Brun. It is said that Vaux-le-Vicomte stimulated Louis

XIV to build Versailles. Le Vau, Le Nôtre and Le Brun were all involved in the latter project.

History: As no fundamental alterations or extensions have been made to the château and gardens, Vaux-le-Vicomte is one of the best examples of a relatively large 17C building and park to have survived.

Vaux-le-Vicomte, as was the case with many other châteaux of the period, was built by a member of the nobility of office who had acquired wealth as a result of his circumstances: finance minster Nicolas Fouquet, Vicomte de Vaux, Marquis de Belle-Isle, scion of an old family of parliamentarians. Fouquet, an able and ambitious man, attached himself to chief minister Mazarin, who made him army superintendent, and, as a reward for faithful service during the Fronde uprising (see Paris, History: 1650) he was made Procureur Général and in 1653 superintendent of finance and minister of state. While attempting to assuage Cardinal Mazarin's insatiable greed, he also increased his own wealth with huge sums drawn from the public purse. He used the money to secure supporters by bribery and to ensure that he had accommodation to which to retreat, partly to satisfy his need for luxury, and partly to support deserving writers (including La Fontaine and Molière). In 1655 he commissioned Le Vau, who was also a favourite of Mazarin, to build the château, and left him a very free hand at the planning stage. He employed Le Nôtre to landscape the park, and Le Brun to design the interior decoration. The latter established a tapestry studio in the château; it was later transferred to Paris, and became the royal Gobelin factory. The château was completed by 1661 (at times as many as 18,000 workers were employed here).

Cardinal Jules Mazarin died on 9 March 1661, and Fouquet, who anticipated succeeding the cardinal as chief minister, set the consecration of

Vaux-le-Vicomte for 17 August of the same year, a ceremony to which he invited Louis XIV. In the meantime Colbert, Fouquet's rival in the struggle for the lucrative post of chief minister, informed the king of Fouquet's embezzlement. Louis XIV still appeared at the consecration ceremony—it was only with difficulty that his mother prevented him from arresting the minister on the spot. The king had just had to melt down his own cutlery and crockery to pay his debts, but Fouquet served him a supper costing 120,000 livres on 36 dozen golden and 500 dozen silver plates; the feast concluded with a magnificent firework display in the park; Molière's troupe presented the world première of the comédie-ballet 'Les Fâcheux', which had been created within 14 days; design was by Le Brun, and the performance was framed by 1,200 fountains.

This magnificent, extravagant feast cost Fouquet his post: the king returned to Fontainebleau the same evening and had Fouquet arrested on 5 September. After a long investigation he was sentenced merely to

Vaux-le-Vicomte, château seen from the park

banishment in 1664, but brought at Louis XIV's behest to Pinerolo, where he was confined under rigorous conditions, and died in 1680.

In 1701 the château was acquired by Marshall Claude Louis Hector de Villars, the industrialist. Sommier bought it in 1875, and restored the neglected gardens and the fabric of the building.

Exterior: The corner pavilions at the ends of the four side wings and the steep roofs and tall chimneys which are such a feature, particularly on the courtyard side, are clear signs that traditional elements of French château design have been adopted. The central pavilion however, almost baroque in its approach, protrudes slightly, and dominates the rest of the buildings with its domed roof and lantern.

Although the relatively small château is separated from its immediate surroundings by a moat it still dominates the park, which is spacious, divided into several distinct areas, and perfectly balanced in design, with many axes relating directly to the compact château with its tall central section. The *park* was Le Nôtre's first independent creation and represents the beginning of the art of French landscape gardening.

Disposition of rooms: At the centre of the château are the oval, two-storeyed domed room in the central pavilion and the square vestibule facing the cour d'honneur. On both sides of these rooms in the main axis are a staircase separated from the vestibule and then the other rooms in the château. Thus the previous pattern of the 'appartement simple' was dropped in favour of the 'appartement double', which pointed the way for later developments in château building: the state rooms on the garden side are arranged in sequence on the ground and first floors.

Environs: Blandy-les-Tours (5 km. E.): Ruins of a medieval *fortress*, which was rebuilt and then demolished. Romanesque *crypt*. Remains of a *manor house* and *chapel* (16C). *Walls* and *towers*.

Champeaux (3 km. NE of Blandy):

Champeaux is best known for the scholastic theologian William of Champeaux (Guillaume de Champeaux or Guilemus Campellensis, *c.* 1070–1121), who was born here; he was the teacher and later opponent of the celebrated Peter Abelard. Under William of Champeaux the priory became one of the intellectual and spiritual centres of France in the early 12C.

Versailles

78 Yvelines   p.256□C 2

Palace of Versailles

The palace is not only the most important of the French baroque period, but also the largest in Europe, and became the definitive model for the residences of European princes in the 18C. At present the palace is largely as it was immediately before the French Revolution.

History

To Louis XIII: Versailles, unlike many other important palaces, does not have a particularly long history, although the name *Versaliae* appears in writing in the year 1037. It was not until the 16C that the forests in the area were systematically opened up for hunting purposes, and 1631–4 Louis XIII commissioned Philibert Le Roy to build the hunting lodge with corner pavilions and moats which forms the core of the present palace.

Extension of the hunting lodge under Louis XIV: Louis XIV came to the throne at the age of twenty-three in 1661, and subsequently spent a lot of time in Versailles; he therefore decided to extend park and château. The leading artists involved in the project were architect Louis Le Vau, painter and decorator Charles Le Brun and landscape gardener André Le Nôtre; this brilliant trio had already achieved hitherto unheard-of unity of architecture, decoration and landscaping in the baroque château of Vaux-le-Vicomte (1657–61). Work began on the marshy, impracticable site at Versailles, far from ideal for a building on this scale, in 1663; earth was moved to an extent previously not

Versailles, cour d'honneur with equestrian statue of Louis XIV

contemplated in Europe, trees were felled, and other preparatory work undertaken. More than 30,000 workmen, including royal troops, were employed at one time on the project, which proved a heavy burden on the exchequer. But, as the Duc de Saint-Simon remarked, 'Louis XIV took pleasure in subduing nature'.

In 1663 work began on lawns and bosquets in the garden and the building of two wings (now the Cour Royal) in front of the hunting lodge, and in the same year great feasts were held here (e.g. a feast including the world premiere of Molière's 'Tartuffe' on 12 May 1664). In 1666 the three-day Fête de Plaisir was held in honour of twenty-two-year-old Louise de Lavallière; she had been the king's mistress for several years and was the mother of four of his children. While still at war in 1667, Louis gave orders to extend Versailles as a royal residence and to expand the park accordingly.

Royal residence: When Louis XIV was at the height of his political powers after the peace of Nijmegen (end of the Franco-Dutch War), he finally transferred his residence to Versailles (though it did not become the official seat of the court, which included approximately 20,000 people, until 1682). In the same year, 1678, Louis appointed Jules Hardouin-Mansart, who built the Château de Clagny for Louis' mistress Madame de Montespan and the eight children she had borne him, to be superintendent of building. Mansart's lavish rebuilding and extensions gave the palace and its surroundings their final architectural shape: Galerie des Glaces with two corner salons (Salon de la Guerre and Salon de la Paix), extension of the façade to almost 2,000 ft., garden façade, S. wing and finally the chapel(1699–1710), one of Mansart's most mature works) on the courtyard side of the N. wing.

Under Louis XV: After the death of Louis XIV at Versailles, he was succeeded by his grandson Louis XV, a minor, with Duc Philippe d'Orléans as Regent; the latter transferred the residence back to Paris. In 1722, when he took over the reins of government, Louis XV returned to Versailles. In 1736 the Salon d'Her-

Versailles, main building and S. wing

cule was consecrated, the Petits Appartements were furnished from 1739. Ange-Jacques Gabriel intended to rebuild the courtyard façade on neoclassical lines, but the plan was fortunately never realized; all that was built was the Louis XV wing (1771–4; the balancing Dufour wing dates from 1814–29). More significant was the appearance of the long-awaited opera house, consecrated in 1770 on the occasion of the Dauphin's marriage to Marie-Antoinette. In 1774 Marie Antoinette made the Petit Trianon her principal residence.

Revolution: The Palace of Versailles played a leading role in the French Revolution. The States General, an assembly of deputies of the Three Estates (nobility, clergy and the Third Estate, the bourgeoisie) met in the palace for the first time since 1614 on 5 May 1789. The electoral procedure based on the Estates placed the Third Estate in the minority. The Marquis de Ferrières de Marsay, deputy of the nobility to the States General, described the entry of the States General into Versailles in a letter to his wife: 'The deputies of the Three Estates walked in pairs with candles in their hands, the Third Estate in black silk cloaks and batiste cravats, the nobility wearing black silk robes, and also doublets of golden cloth, silk cloaks trimmed with golden fabric and hats with feathers, the brims turned up in the manner of Henry IV, the clergy in soutanes and birettas. They walked past the king and bowed, then turned to the queen and bowed a second time. The streets were decorated with banners of state, the regiment of the French and Swiss guard formed a line from Notre-Dame to Saint-Louis. Enormous groups of people watched us in total silence'.

The Third Estate, which enjoyed the support of certain members of the lower ranks of the clergy and some of the nobility, constituted itself into the Assemblée Nationale on 17 June, and in a motion proposed by Abbé Emmanuel Joseph Sieyès, claimed sole right of expression of the will of the nation and partnership with the crown; they also decided upon a general tax strike. On 20 June the deputies of the Third Estate swore that they would not dis-

Versailles, Parterre d'Eau, bronze figure

perse until a constitution had been established. On 23 June Louis XVI proclaimed to the Assemblée Nationale that no king had ever done as much for a nation as he; without his express confirmation the decisions and suggestions of the Assemblée Nationale could not become law. When he ordered the dissolution of the Assemblée Nationale, Count Mirabeau, deputy of the Third Estate, formulated the Assemblée Nationale's refusal to obey the king's instruction that it should be dissolved in the famous sentence: 'Say to those who sent you that we are here by the will of the nation and that we will only yield to the force of the bayonet.' On 6 July the self-styled Assemblée Nationale declared itself Assemblée Nationale Constituante and proclaimed the sovereignty of the people as against the power of the king. On 11 July Louis XVI dismissed Jacques Necker, the popular Director-General of Finance. There were riots in Paris, groups of popular militia (national guard) were formed. The French Revolution began on 14 July with the storming of the Bastille (state prison and symbol of royal tyranny). On the night of 4–5 August the Assemblée Nationale Constituante proclaimed the end of the feudal sysem and abolition of church tithes. The deputies of the first Two Estates renounced their privileges. This marked the end of the Ancien Régime, the previous social system based on absolute rule. On 26 August the Assemblée Nationale passed the declaration of human and citizens' rights.

As Louis XVI refused to sign the decrees of the Assemblée Nationale, the political left of the assembly organized the procession of the women of Les Halles to Versailles (second great day of the sansculottes): the royal family was compelled to move to Paris; the Assemblée Constituante did the same. The later revolutionary leader Jean-Paul Marat called for the march on Versailles in these words: 'Put this Austrian woman (Queen Marie-Antoinette) in prison!...The heir to the throne has no right to his supper while you have no bread!'.

This was the end of Versailles as the seat of government. The most

Versailles, Orangerie

important works of art were transferred to the Louvre in 1792, the furniture was sold. For a time there was a plan to demolish the Palace.

Restoration: In 1797 a picture gallery was established and war-weary soldiers were accommodated in the palace, and Napoleon I considered rebuilding the complex in Empire style, but the plan was never put into practice. Napoleon, and Louis XVIII under the Restoration, protected the building from falling completely into disrepair. Louis Philippe the Citizen King finally transformed the palace into a national historical museum.

Franco-Prussian War: On 18 September 1870 Versailles was occupied by the Germans and remained the centre of German Army operations. King Wilhelm I of Prussia arrived on 5 October and established quarters in the Préfecture, while the palace was used as a military hospital. The treaties concluded here between the North German Confederacy and Baden and Hessen, Bavaria and Württemberg led to the foundation of the new German Empire, proclaimed here on 18 January 1871 in the Galerie des Glaces.

Late 19&20C: After the Germans had left, Versailles became the seat of President Thiers' government and the French Assemblé Nationale, and headquarters of Marshall MacMahon's army under the Paris Commune. Fighting against the Communards and the capture of Paris were directed from Versailles. After this Paris remained the seat of the president of the French Republic and the two chambers, until they moved back to Paris in 1879.

On 28 June 1919 the Treaty of Versailles was signed in the Galerie des Glaces at Versailles, the same room in which Wilhelm I had been proclaimed emperor in 1871. The treaty marked the defeat of the German Empire. Socialist president François Mitterand forged a link with the

◁ *Versailles, statue in the park*

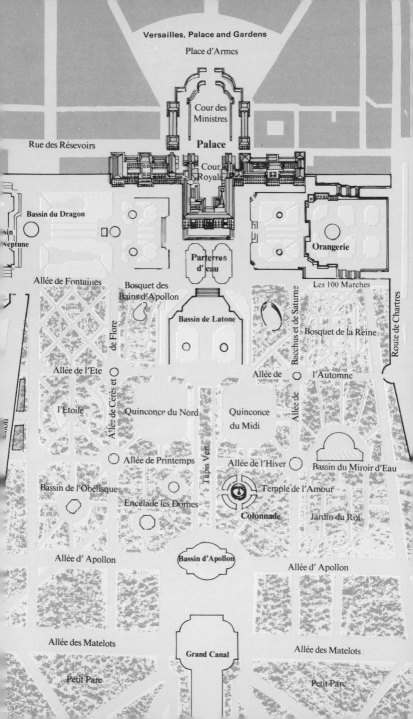

Versailles, Palace and Gardens

Place d'Armes

Cour des Ministres

Palace

Rue des Réservoirs

Cour Royale

Bassin du Dragon

sin
Neptune

Orangerie

Parterres
d'eau

Les 100 Marches

Route de Chartres

Allée de Fontaines

Bosquet des
Bains d'Apollon

de Flore

Bassin de Latone

Bacchus et de Saturne

Bosquet de la Reine

Allée de l'Ete

Allée de Cérès et

Allée de

l'Automne

Allée de

l'Étoile

Quinconce du Nord

Quinconce
du Midi

Tapis Vert

Allée de Printemps

Allée de l'Hiver

Bassin du Miroir d'Eau

Bassin de l'Obélisque

Encelade les Dômes

Temple de l'Amour

Jardin du Roi

Colonnade

Allée d' Apollon

Bassin d'Apollon

Allée d' Apollon

Allée des Matelots

Grand Canal

Allée des Matelots

Petit Parc

Petit Parc

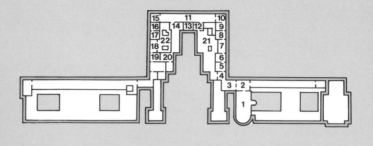

splendours of the past when he summoned his world economic summit to Versailles.

Exterior: The cour d'honneur extends from the railings restored under Louis XVIII to the equestrian statue of Louis XIV (1835), flanked by the so-called Ministre wings by architects Le Vau and Mansart. Adjacent is the Cour Royale. In the middle of Louis XIII's former hunting lodge is the Cour de Marbre, which formerly was set higher. The great façades on the park side are almost 2,000 ft. long. The protruding central section above the Parterre d'Eau encloses Louis XIII's building and is the work of Le Vau and above all Mansart.

Entrance: The state staircase designed by Le Vau as the Escalier des Ambassadeurs and built in 1678 by Orbay and Le Brun was pulled down on the orders of Louis XV in 1752; entrance to the Palace is now via the Vestibule de Gabriel and the Vestibule de la Chapelle.

Chapel: The Chapelle Royale Saint-Louis is in the N. wing on the courtyard side. It was started in 1689, work continued in 1699, but it was not consecrated until 1710 (completed by Robert de Cotte). It is Hardouin-Mansart's last ecclesiastical building and considered to be among his most mature work. The late baroque two-

Versailles, park, Latone fountain

storeyed palace chapel combines medieval ideas on the model of the Sainte-Chapelle in Paris and ancient elements (fluted Corinthian columns on low bases running right round the chapel) in a masterly fashion, and also uses the effect of light and colour with great skill.

Salon d'Hercule: The royal gallery in the chapel is connected with the Salon d'Hercule, built after completion of the chapel; it is the largest room in the palace and shows the first signs of the transition from baroque to rococo. Fireplace by Antoine Vassé; ceiling painting 'Apotheosis of Hercules' by François Lemoyne.

Grands Appartements: Le Brun used an elaborate system of marble, stucco moulding, painting and gilt for the decoration of the state rooms in the N. wing (Salon de l'Abondance, planet rooms from the Salon de Vénus, Salon de Diane, Salon de Mars etc, up to the former throne room, the Salon d'Apollon). The iconographic programme, based on the idea of the planet rooms (cf. the Palazzo Pitti in Florence), reaches its peak in the equation of the king with Apollo; this motif is repeated in Palace and park in numerous variations and expresses the pretentions and greatness of Absolutism.

In Greek mythology Apollo is the son of Zeus and Artemis (Diana). His origins are obscure, it is possible that they were in Asia Minor. His name and thus his essential being are unexplained. Interpretations are the 'Destroyer', 'Turner Away of Misfortune' 'Shining One', 'Prophet', 'Hurdle Watcher', 'the Powerful, Helping One' etc. These various names indicate the broad spectrum of his

Salon de Diane, Louis XIV

Chapelle Royale Saint-Louis

divine functions: plague god, bringer of sudden death, shepherd god, god of healing, of poetry, of song and of string playing, leader of the muses etc. His most important additional name is 'Phoibos': the shining one (or pure, purifying). In the Middle Ages Apollo was equated with the sun god Helios = Sol. In antiquity Helios had been portrayed as a beautiful youth who rose in the E. at dawn with his chariot drawn by four horses, drove them across the sky and plunged in the evening into the western ocean. In the late Middle Ages Apollo and Helios/Sol were clearly perceived as equals. A decisive turing point was reached in the late 15C when the 'Apollo Belvedere' was found, personifying definitively for contemporaries and on into the 19C all that was pure, noble and light. The function of Helios/Sol as guardian and guarantor of world order was transferred to him. This interpretation had repercussions in the art of decoration, in Versailles more than anywhere else. As guardian and guarantor of the world order Apollo/Helios had to be linked with earthly kingship. Examples of this are Le Brun's paintings in Versailles and the Louvre. The high point of the iconography of the planet rooms in Versailles is the equation of the 'Sun King' Louis XIV with the 'Sun' God Apollo/Helios, a motif repeated throughout the Palace.

Galerie des Glaces (Grande Galerie): The Galerie des Glaces is the pinnacle of late baroque/neoclassical architecture. Despite its enormous dimensions, (239 ft. long by 34.ft. wide by 41 ft. high) lucid articulation and decoration give an

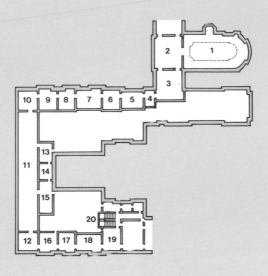

Salon d'Hercule, fireplace by Antoine Vassé

Salon de la Guerre

La Chambre de la Reine

impression of unity, almost of austerity. The architect was Hardouin-Mansart, Le Brun was in charge of decoration. The gallery has 17 windows with 17 corresponding mirrors, and looks out on the Parterre d'Eau. The gallery and adjacent rooms glorify Louis XIV's victories over the German States, Spain and Holland. Trophies; composite capitals with the Bourbon fleur-de-lys, the Gallic cock's head and the head of Apollo, based on an idea by Colbert; stucco relief of the triumphant king on horseback by Coysevox in the Salon de la Guerre.

Appartement du Roi: The Appartement du Roi is connected with the Galerie des Glaces. The king's *bedroom* is at the precise centre of the palace, aligned E. to the rising sun, the scene of the ceremonies of 'lever' and 'coucher', symbolically interpreted through the cult of the ruler as Apollo. The alcove sculptures are by Coustou and Lespingola; 'Sainte-Madeleine' by Dominiquin; 'Self-Portrait' and 'Portrait of the Marquis de Moncade' by van Dyck. This immeasurably luxurious room, in which the king finally died, was the 'Holy of Holies', with entrance granted to the chosen few under the most rigorous etiquette. In the antechamber, the *Salon de l'Oeil de Boeuf* (1701) are portraits of the royal family and allegorical compositions by Jean Nocret (Louis XIV as Apollo surrounded by his family).

Grand Appartement de la Reine: Access to the Grand Appartement de la Reine in the S. wing is through the Salon de la Paix (ceiling by Le Brun, painting by François Lemoyne over the fireplace); most of the Queen's Apartments were altered under Marie-Antoinette.
Chambre de la Reine: Gold, grisaille, wood varving, Lyon silk. The magically luxurious bedroom of the last

Galerie des Glaces ▷

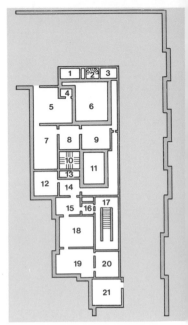

Salon de Mars

Versailles, palace, Petits Appartements 1
Cabinet des Bains **2** Staircase **3** Cabinet Doré **4**
Garde-robe de la Reine **5** Chambre de Louis
XV **6** Cour des Cerfs **7** Cabinet de la Pendule **8**
Antichambre des Chiens **9** Salle à Manger des
Retours des Chasses **10** Escalier du Roi **11** Cour
du Roi **12** Cabinet d'Angle **13** Garde-robe **14**
Arrière Cabinet **15** Salon de Musique de Mme
Adélaïde **16** Très Arrière Cabinet **17** Escalier
Louis-Philippe **18** Louis XVI Library **19** Salle à
Manger aux Salles Neuves **20** Salle de Billard **21**
Salon des Jeux de Louis XVI

queen of the Ancien Régime has been
outstandingly well restored, appear-
ing as it did before the Revolution.
Original decoration by Le Brun,
panelling executed by Robert de
Cotte. *Paintings above the doors* by
Charles-Joseph Natoire and Jean-
François de Troy, *ceiling paintings* by
François Boucher. The bed is a copy;
Marie-Antoinette's fine *jewel cabinet*.
Other rooms are the *Salon des Nobles
de la Reine* with ceiling paintings by
Michel Corneille; the *Antichambre de
la Reine*, complete after lengthy restoration; the *Salle des Gardes de la Reine*
with coloured marble ceiling and
painting by Nicolas Coypel. The
Queen's *marble staircase* is by Har-
douin-Mansart.

Museum of French History: This
museum is distributed throughout
various levels of the N. wing (18C),
the central section (18C, Consulate,

Empire) and S. wing (Galerie des
Batailles); the exhibits cover the
history of the French monarchy from
the time of the Crusades to the beginning of the Third Republic. Adjacent
is the *Appartement de Madame de
Maintenon* with 16&17C collections.

Petits Appartements: In the 18C
Louis XV found the Grands Appartements furnished by Louis XIV too
old-fashioned, uncomfortable and
impractical, and so from 1738 he built
the so-called Petits Appartements for

Salon de Mercure, details of wall and ceiling paintings

himself and the Queen (on the opposite side of the Cour de Marbre). They reflect the change in domestic culture from the 17 to the 18C. The rooms consist of the Chambre du Roi (Louis XV died here in 1774), with wardrobe, bathroom, Cabinet de la Pendule with astronomical clock dating from 1754 and equestrian statue of the king, study (Cabinet d'Angle) with a secret room for the king's correspondence; the Cabinet de Madame Adélaïde was occupied by Louis XIV's favourite Madame de Montespan. Louis XVI's library used to contain a gallery for the king's collection of paintings by Leonardo da Vinci ('Mona Lisa'), Titian, Correggio and others (now all in the Louvre). This gallery and the Escalier des Ambassadeurs were pulled down in 1752 and replaced by the library. Also dining room, billiard room and card room.

Opéra: Built 1769&70 by Jacques-Ange Gabriel, opened on 17 May 1770 on the occasion of the Dauphin's wedding to Marie-Antoinette, the daughter of the Austrian emperor. For reasons of haste, wood was used in the interior; the painting suggests more valuable materials.

Orangerie: The subterranean Orangery, with arcades to the S. and framed with two flights of steps is the work of Hardouin-Mansart (1684–6). Thousands of orange trees and exotic decorative plants can survive the winter here.

Park: A walk through Le Nôtre's park, according to a guide to the correct approach to walking in the gardens at Versailles written by Louis XIV, should begin at the terrace in front of the central building of the palace, from which the eye can range freely over the entire park. The spacious grounds stress the axiality and symmetry of the palace in its natural surroundings, everything is a component of the iconography of the worship of the absolute ruler in the age of rationalism: flat, carpet-like lawns alternate with bosquets, artistic architectural creations, and pools; fountains and statues are symmetrically arranged around main and side axes. At the end of the lawn in front of the N. façade (kneeling Venus by Coysevox) with François Girardon's Fontaine de la Pyramide (four basins one above the other) and the nymphs' bath, is the Bassin de Neptune (started by Le Nôtre and completed by Gabriel) with sculptures by Lambert-Sigisbert Adam; this is the finest fountain in Versailles and plays during the Fêtes de Nuit; the picture is completed by the Orangery.

The central axis is three km. long and starts with the *Parterre d'Eau* with two large pools and 16 bronze statues representing the rivers of France; in front of the palace façade are bronze versions of ancient sculptures (Apollo, Bacchus, Antinous, Silenus)

and, corresponding to the Salon de la Guerre and the Salon de la Paix in the palace, the *Vase de la Guerre* by Coysevox (French victory over the Ottomans in 1664, homage of Spain to France) and the *Vase de la Paix* by Jean-Baptiste Tuby (Peace of Aix-la-Chapelle and Peace of Nijmegen).

The *Parterre de Latone* below the terrace was designed by Hardouin-Mansart, and is decorated with gilded broze sculptures and Balthazar Marsy's statue of Latona with her Children. The huge expanse of lawn with statues and vases (Tapis Vert) extends to the *Bassin d'Apollon* (by Tuby, designed by Le Brun).

The *Grand Canal* is the central element in the organization of perspective; it was excavated 1667–80 and is just under a mile long. Adjacent to the canal is the *Petit Parc*; other green areas are part of the Trianon gardens and the Grand Parc.

Grand Trianon: Louis XIV commissioned Hardouin-Mansart to build the little palace of Grand Trianon (1687&8) in the village of Trianon on the N. arm of the Grand Canal

Sculpture in the park at Versailles

for his mistress, Madame de Maintenon, as a refuge for use in intimate hours away from the demands of etiquette, and as a counterbalance to the official state palace. The single-storeyed marble building has two residential sections for the king and his favourite, connected by a colonnade of double Ionic columns (Robert de Cotte). Some of the interior has been altered: in the right wing are the circular Louis-Quatorze drawing room, the heavy family salon built under Louis-Philippe, the Napoleonic study and bedroom. The *Grande Galerie* is decorated with views of the gardens and bosquets in their original condition. Botanical gardens were laid out under Louis XV; Gabriel built the Pavillon Français in 1750; it is still in the baroque tradition. Hardouin-Mansart created the wonderful *Buffet d'Eau* (1703). There is a *carriage museum* in a 19C building. On 4 June 1920 the Grand Trianon was the scene of the conclusion of peace between the Allies and Hungary who, as a successor in law of the Danube monarchy, had to hand over more than two thirds of her territory to Romania, Yugoslavia and Czechoslovakia.

Petit Trianon: The unified, block-like building of the Petit Trianon by Gabriel (1764–8), a masterpiece of the neoclassical style, was built for Madame de Pompadour, who died before it was completed. After that Louis XV presented it to Madame Dubarry.

Hameau: Marie-Antoinette had the park of the Petit Trianon redesigned as an English garden with buildings showing English influence: Belvedere (1777), Temple d'Amour (1778), theatre (1780). The theatrically laid-out village ('hameau') reflects playful acceptance of Rousseau's ideas by a queen of the late absolute period. It is in the style of Norman peasant architecture; around the village pond are grouped a mill, two farmhouses (one for the queen, the other for billiards), a dovecote and a building for fishing ('Tour de Marlborough'). A farmer was employed to perform rural tasks to complete the illusion that the queen led a natural life in the country.

Bassin d'Apollon in the park

Versailles town

From the Place d'Armes in front of the palace three roads lead like rays to the town of Versailles, planned and built in the initial stages by Le Vau, and completely centred on the palace. Hardouin-Mansart built the *Royal Mews* (Ecuries) between the three roads. The roofs of the buildings were not allowed to stand higher than the then level of the Cour de Marbre. The layout of the town of Versailles influenced the planning of numerous European residence towns (including Karlsruhe, St.Petersburg, Mannheim). Near the *Grand Commun* (domestic buildings by Hardouin-Mansart, 1628–84) on the left of the courtyard in front of the palace are the 18C *Hôtel de la Guerre* and the *Hôtel de la Marine et des Affaires Etrangères*. The latter building houses an important *library* and works by the modern painter and graphic artist André Dunopyer de Segonzac. The deputies of the Third Estate swore not to disperse until they had given France a constitution in the *Jeu de Paume* in 1789. On the right of the palace are the 18C *Hôtel de Pompadour* and *Théâtre Montansier*.9

Churches: The NE part of Versailles around *Notre-Dame* (1684–6, Hardouin-Mansart) dates from the reign of the Roi Soleil; the quarter dating from the reign of Louis XVI grew up around *Saint-Louis*, built 1743–54 by Hardouin-Mansart de Sangonne, a grandson of the famous architect.

Musée Lambinet: Various collections accommodated in an 18C palace: works by the sculptor Jean-Antoine Houdon, weapons from the Versailles factory, fans, copper plates for printing on material by Jouy, souvenirs of General Hoche, who was born here, and also works of the painter and graphic artist Dunoyer de Segonzac with Versailles themes.

Vétheuil

95 Val-d'Oise   p.256□A 1

This little village was made famous by Claude Monet, who painted 'La Seine

Sculpture in the Flora fountain

à Vétheuil' and other pictures here in 1901.

Former collegiate church: This 12C building has a lavish 16C W. façade and a magnificent Renaissance portal on the S. side. The interior has numerous statues, largely 16C. The Chapelle de la Confrérie de la Charité is decorated with wall paintings, some of which are 16C.

Environs: Haute-Isle (4 km. N.): Village partly cut into the rock above the Seine (cave dwellings). *Church* with tiny bell tower.
Roche-Guyon, La (2 km. W. of Haute-Isle): The *castle* dates from the 10C, rebuilt in the 12C. All that has survived are the ruins of the keep. The residence beneath it (restored after damage in the Second World War) has 12–18C sections.

Ville-d'Avray
92 Hauts-de-Seine   p.256☐C 2

This residential town SW of Paris on

the edge of the Bois de Fausses Reposes achieved world fame through the painter Corot, who painted the ponds and also lived here for a time. He painted the frescos in Saint-Nicolas (17C).

Villa 'Les Jardies' (14 Avenue Gambetta): The villa came into the possession of Honoré de Balzac in 1837, but he had to sell it four years later because he was so heavily in debt. The house now contains memorabilia of the politician Léon Gambetta, who on 26 November 1882 was seriously injured by a revolver shot fired by a former mistress; he died on 31 December in Villa-d'Avray. His heart is in the memorial behind the villa.

Villeneuve-Saint-Georges
94 Val-de-Marne   p.256☐D 3

On a hill behind Saint-Georges (12–15C) is the former *Château de Beauregard*, now used as an old people's home. The château was the property

Ile des Enfants, fountain sculpture, detail

of the Polish Countess Evalina Hanska-Rzewuska, whom Balzac married near Kiev shortly before his death in the Ukraine. Balzac did not have a very high opinion of the Villeneuve area, which he described as 'rough, poor land, a country of heavy soil and woods' with 'nothing of the lightheartedness of Champagne and the amiability of the wine-growing villages slumbering under the good sun in the mild valley of the Marne'.

Vincennes
94 Val-de-Marne   p.256☐D 2

The former royal residence of Vincennes in the E. suburbs of Paris is now largely a residential town. The university in the Bois de Vincennes founded in 1968 (Paris-VIII) is part of the University of Paris.

Château: According to tradition St.Louis used to deliver judgement under the giant oaks in the woodland E. of Paris. He built a castle here which Philip VI fortified in 1337 by the addition of a keep; this was extended under Charles V to become the most modern fortress in Europe (nine towers); work was completed in 1373, possibly to plans by Raymond du Temple. In 1379 the foundation stone of the chapel was laid, but it was not completed until 1552 by Philibert de l'Orme, who retained the Gothic character of the building. Maria de'-Medici had the complex rebuilt, Le Vau was responsible for the Pavillon du Roi (for a time the home of the young Louis XIV) and the Pavillon de la Reine. In 1668 a state gaol was set up, and remained here until 1784. The porcelain factory founded in 1738 was transferred to Sèvres. In 1808 Napoleon had the fortress towers pulled down level with the height of the walls, and established an arsenal. Louis-Philippe the Citizen King commissioned casemates and included Vincennes in the fortifications of Paris. restoration of the castle began under Viollet-le-Duc.

Interior: The 138 ft. high Tour du Village was the seat of the sergeants of the castle in the Middle Ages. The square keep is a fortress in its own

Versailles, mock village Le Hameau

right; it houses a small *historical museum*. The court chapel with late Gothic façade was influenced by the Sainte-Chapelle in Paris (cycle of Renaissance stained glass, restored). Triumphal arch by Louis le Vau.

Cultural history: The state prison of Vincennes had numerous distinguished inmates, including Count Mirabeau, detained here 1777–80 for the abduction of his mistress Sophie Monnier; he wrote his famous 'Lettres à Sophie' while in the prison. The philosopher Denis Diderot was arrested in 1746 for corruption and imprisoned in Vincennes, and this occurred a second time in 1749 on publication of his 'Lettre sur les Aveugles'. Jean-Jacques Rousseau visited him here frequently, and was relieved by the conditions afforded to the editor of the 'Encyclopédie': 'On returning to Paris I was greeted by the pleasant news that Diderot had left the tower and had been assigned the château and park of Vincennes as his prison, also that he is permitted to receive his friends'. On one of his lengthy walks from Paris to Vincennes in summer 1749 (Rousseau could not afford to hire a carriage) he read in the 'Mercure de France' of the essay subject set by the Academy in Dijon: 'Has progress made in science and the arts contributed to the refinement of morals?' Rousseau replied in the negative, and became famous as a result of his essay. The notorious Marquis de Sade was also imprisoned in Vincennes on numerous occasions, before ending his life in the Bastille. He wrote to his wife on the subject of his imprisonment in Vincennes: 'I am locked in a tower behind 19 iron doors. Light is admitted through two little windows, each sealed with 20 bars.'

Bois de Vincennes: The Bois de Vincennes covers 921 hectares (bought back by Paris) and contains a *zoological garden* (the most important zoo in France), a *floral garden*, a *tropical garden*, a *racecourse*, various *sports facilities*, the *Musée national des Arts Africains et Océaniens* and *university buildings*.

Versailles, Temple d'Amour

Vincennes, château, keep

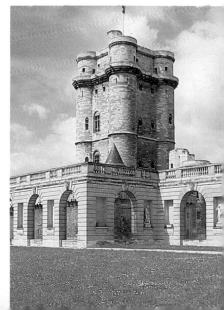

Alphabetical list of the sights of Paris

Index of places described in the guide

Glossary

Acanthus: Decorative element found especially on → Corinthian capitals; it developed from the stylized representation of a sharply serrated, thistle-like leaf.

Aedicule: Wall niche housing a bust or statue; usually with a → gable, → pillars or → columns.

Aisle: Longitudinal section of a church or other building, usually divided from other such sections by an → arcade.

Altar: Sacrificial table of Greeks and Romans. The Lord's table in the Christian faith. Catholic churches often have several side altars as well as the high altar.

Ambo: Stand or lectern by the choir screen in early Christian and medieval churches; predecessor of the → pulpit.

Ambulatory: A corridor created by continuing the side aisles around the choir; often used for processions.

Antependium: Covering for the front of the altar.

Apse: Large recess at end of the → choir, usually semicircular or polygonal. As a rule it contains the → altar.

Apsidiole: Small apsidal chapel.

Aquamanile: Pouring-vessel or bowl for ritual washing in the Catholic liturgy.

Aqueduct: Water pipe or channel across an arched bridge; frequently built as monumental structures by the Romans.

Arabesque: Stylized foliage used as a decorative motif.

Arcade: A series of arches borne by columns or pillars. When the arcade is attached to a wall (and is purely decorative), it is called a blind arcade.

Arch: A curved structure of support employed in spanning a space.

Architrave: Main stone member on top of the columns; lowest part of the → entablature.

Archivolt: The face of an arch in Romanesque and Gothic portals; often more than one.

Ashlar: Hewn block of stone (as opposed to that straight from the quarry).

Atrium: In Roman houses a central hall with an opening in the roof. In Christian architecture, a forecourt usually surrounded by columns; also known as a → paradise.

Attic: A (usually richly decorated) storey above the main → entablature; intended to conceal the roof.

Baldacchino: Canopy above altars, tombs, statues, portals, etc.

Baluster: Short squat or shaped column.

Balustrade: Rail formed of → balusters.

Baptistery: Place of baptism; may be a separate building.

Baroque: Architectural style from c.1600–c.1750. Distinguished by powerfully agitated, interlocking forms.

Bartizan: A small corner turret projecting from the top of a building.

Base: Foot of a column or pillar.

Basket arch: A flattened round arch.

Basilica: Greek hall of kings. In church architecture, a church with nave and two or more aisles, the roof of the nave being higher than the roofs above the aisles.

Bay: Vertical division of a building between pillars, columns, windows, wall arches, etc.

Blind arcade: → Arcade.

Blind tracery: → Tracery.

Bosquet: Clumps of trees and bushes, particularly common in French gardens and parks.

Bracket: A projection from the wall used as a support -for a bust, statue, arch, etc.

Calotte: Half dome with no drum.

Calvary: Sculpture of the Crucifixion and Mount Calvary.

Campanile: Bell tower; usually a free standing building.

Capital: Topmost part of a column. The shape of the capital determines the style or → order.

Cartouche: Decorative frame or panel imitating a scrolled piece of paper, usually with an inscription, coat-of-arms, etc.

Caryatid: A carved figure supporting the entablature.

Cella: Main room of ancient temple containing divine image.

Cenotaph: Monument to dead buried elsewhere.

Chapterhouse: Assembly room in which monks or nuns discuss the community's business.

Charnel house: House or vault in which bones are placed.

Choir: That part of the church in which divine service is sung. Shorter and often narrower than the nave, it is usually raised and at the E. end. In the Middle Ages the choir was often separated from the rest of the church by a screen.

Ciborium: Canopy over high altar; usually in the form of a dome supported on columns.

Classicism: Revival of Greek and Roman architectural principles.

Clerestory: Upper part of the main walls of the nave, above the roofs of the aisles and pierced by windows.

Cloister: Four sided covered walk (often vaulted) and opening inwards by arcades.

Coffered ceiling: A ceiling divided into square or polygonal panels, which are painted or otherwise decorated.

Column: Support with circular cross-section, narrowing somewhat towards the top; the type of column is determined by the → order. → Pillar.

Compound pillar: Often found in Gothic buildings. A central shaft has attached or detached shafts or half-shafts clustered around it.

Conch: Semicircular recess with a half-dome.

Confessio: Chamber or recess for a relic near the altar.

Corinthian order: → Order with richly decorated → capitals; the base has two or more tiers and is similar to that of the → Ionic order.

Cornice: Projecting upper limit of a wall; topmost member of the → entablature of an → order.

Cosmati work: Decorative technique involving the use of marble inlay, mosaics etc.; many Roman marble workers had the family name Cosma.

Crocket: Gothic leaf-like decoration projecting from the sides of pinnacles, gables etc.

Crossing: The intersection of the nave and transept.

Crypt: Burial place, usually under the → choir. Churches were often built above an old crypt.

Curtain wall: Outer wall of castle.

Cyclops wall: Ancient wall made of large rough bocks of stone of irregular shape.

Dipteros: Temple in which porticoes are connected by a double row of lateral columns.

Diptych: A painted hinged double (altar) panel.

Directoire style: French style under the Directoire (1795–9), influenced by Antiquity.

Dolmen: Chamber tomb lined and roofed with megaliths.

Doric order: → Order in which the columns lack a base and bear flat, pad-shaped → capitals.

Dormer window: Window in sloping roof which projects and has its own gabled roof.

Drum: Substructure of a dome; as a rule either cylindrical or polygonal.

Dwarf Gallery: Romanesque feature; wall passage of small arches on the outside of a building.

Empire style: Classical style in France at the beginning of the 19C, with Graeco-Roman and Egyptian models.

Enclos Paroissal: Enclosed churchyard in France, often with a → Calvary.

Entablature: Upper part of an → order; made up of → architrave, → frieze and → cornice.

Eremitage: Pavilion in park or garden, lonely castle or palace.

Exedra: Apse, vaulted with a half-dome; may have raised seats.

Façade: Main front of a building, often decoratively treated.

Facing: Panelling in front of structural components not intended to be visible.

Faience: Glazed pottery named after the Italian town of Faenza.

Fan vault: Looks like a highly decorated rib vault; Concave-sided cone-like sections meet or nearly meet at the apex of the vault.

Filigree work: Originally goldsmith's work in which gold and silver wire were ornamentally soldered on to a metal base. Also used in a more general sense for intricately perforated carvings and stucco.

Finial: Small decorative pinnacle.

Flying buttress: Very large Gothic windows made it necessary to buttress or strengthen the outer walls by half-arches and arches. This support transmitted the thrust of the vault to the buttress.

Foliate capital: Gothic capital in which the basic form is covered with delicate leaf ornaments.

Fosse: Artificially created ditch; often separated castles from the surrounding land with access by a drawbridge.

Fresco: Pigments dispersed in water are appplied without a bonding agent to the still-damp lime plaster. While the mortar dries, the pigments become adsorbed into the plaster.

Frieze: Decorative strips for the borders of a wall. The frieze can be two- or three-dimensional and can consist of figures or ornaments.

Gable: The triangular upper section of a wall. Normally at one end of a pitched roof but it may be purely decorative.

Gallery: Intermediate storey; in a church it is usually for singers and the organ. Arcaded walkway.

Gobelin: Pictorial tapestry woven in the Gobelins factory in Paris.

Gothic: Period in European art and architecture stretching from the mid 12C to the 16C.

Grisaille: Painting in various shades of grey.

Groin vault: Vault in which two → barrel vaults intersect at right angles. The simple groin vault is to be distinguished from the rib vault, in which the intersecting edges are reinforced by ribs.

Half-timbering: Beams are used as supporting parts with an infill of loam or brick.

Hall church: In contrast to the → basilica, nave and aisles are of equal height; no → transept.

Hermitage: Pavilion in parks and gardens; originally the residence of a hermit.

Holy Sepulchre: Structure representing Christ's tomb as discovered by Constantine, who later encased it in a miniature temple.

Iconostasis: In the Eastern church, a screen of paintings between the sanctuary and the nave.

Intarsia: Inlaid work in wood, plaster, stone etc.

Ionic order: → Order in which the columns stand on a base of two or more tiers; the → capital has two lateral → volutes.

Jamb: Vertical part of arch, doorway or window.

Keep: Main tower of a castle; last refuge in time of siege.

Lantern: Small windowed turret on top of roof or dome.

Loggia: Pillared gallery, open on one or more sides; often on an upper storey.

Lunette : Semicircular panel above doors and windows, often with paintings or sculptures.

Mandorla: Almond shaped niche containing a figure of Christ enthroned.

Mannerism: Artistic style between → Renaissance and → baroque (c .1530–1630). Mannerism neglects natural and classical forms in favour of an intended artificiality of manner.

Mansard: An angled roof in which the lower slope is steeper than the upper. The area gained is also called a mansard and can be used to live in. Named after the French architect F.Mansart.

Mausoleum: A splendid tomb, usually in the form of a small house or temple; from the tomb of Mausolus at Halicarnassus.

Menhir: Rough-hewn prehistoric standing stone.

Mensa: Flat surface of the altar.

Mezzanine: Intermediate storey.

Miniature: Small picture, hand illumination in old manuscripts.

Monks' choir: That section of the choir reserved for the monks, frequently closed off.

Monstrance: Ornamented receptacle in which the consecrated Host is shown (usually behind glass).

Mosaic: Decoration for wall, floor or vault, assembled from small coloured stones, pieces of glass or fragments of other materials.

Mullion: Vertical division of a window into two or more lights.

Narthex: Vestibule of basilica or church.

Nave: Central aisle of church, intended for the congregation; excludes choir and apse.

Neo-baroque: Reaction to the cool restraint of → classicism. Re-uses baroque forms; developed in the last part of the 19C as a historicizing, sumptuous style with exaggerated three-dimensional ornamentation and conspicuous colours.

Neo-Gothic: Historicizing 19C style, which was intended to revive Gothic structural forms and decorative elements.

Net vault: Vault in which the ribs cross one another repeatedly.

Nuns' choir: Gallery from which nuns attended divine service.

Nymphaeum: Roman pleasure house, often with statues and fountains.

Obelisk: Free-standing pillar with square ground plan and pyramidal peak.

Odeum: Building, usually round, in which musical or other artistic performances were given.

Onion dome: Bulbous dome with a point, common in Russia and E.Europe; not a true dome, i.e. without a vault.

Opisthodomos: Rear section of Greek temple; behind the cella.

Orangery: Part of baroque castles and parks originally intended to shelter orange trees and other southern plants in winter. However, orangeries often had halls for large court assemblies.

Oratory: Small private chapel.

Order: Classical architectural system prescribing decorations and proportions according to one of the accepted forms: → Corinthian, → Doric, → Ionic, etc. An order consists of a column, which

usually has a base, shaft and capital, and the entablature, which itself consists of architrave, frieze and cornice.

Oriel: Projecting window on an upper floor; it is often a decorative feature.

Pallium: A cloak worn by the Romans; in the Middle Ages, a coronation cloak for kings and emperors, later also for archbishops.

Pantheon: Temple dedicated to all gods; often modelled on that in Rome, which is a rotunda. Building in which distinguished people are buried or have memorials.

Paradise: → Atrium.

Pavilion: Polygonal or round building in parks or pleasure grounds. The main structure of baroque castles is very often linked by corner pavilions to the galleries branching off from the castle.

Pedestal: Base of a column or the base for a statue.

Pendentive: The means by which a circular dome is supported on a square base; concave area or spandrel between two walls and the base of a dome.

Peripteros: Greek temple in which the porticoes are connected laterally by single rows of columns.

Peristyle: Continuous colonnade surrounding a temple or open court.

Pilaster: Pier projecting from a wall; conforms to one of the → orders.

Pilaster strip: Pilaster without base and capital; feature of Anglo-Saxon and early Romanesque buildings.

Pillar: Supporting member, like a → column but with a square or polygonal cross section; does not conform to any order.

Plinth: Projecting lower part of wall or column.

Polyptych: An (altar) painting composed of several panels or wings.

Porch: Covered entrance to a building.

Portico: Porch supported by columns and often with a pediment; may be the centre-piece of façade.

Predella: Substructure of the altar. Paintings along lower edge of large altarpiece.

Pronaos: Area in front of ancient temple (also of churches); sides enclosed and columns in front.

Propylaeum: Entrance gateway, usually to temple precincts. The Propylaeum on the Acropolis at Athens, 437–432 BC, was the model for later buildings.

Prothyra: Railing before door of Roman house.

Pseudoperipteros: Temple in which porticoes are connected laterally by → pilasters and not → columns.

Pulpit: Raised place in church from which the sermon is preached. May be covered by a → baldacchino or → sounding board.

Putto: Figure of naked angelic child in → Renaissance, → baroque and → rococo art and architecture.

Pylon: Entrance gate of Egyptian temple; more generally used as isolated structure to mark a boundary.

Quadriga: Chariot drawn by four horses harnessed abreast.

Refectory: Dining hall of a monastery.

Régence style: French style transitional between the → baroque and the → rococo.

Relief: Carved or moulded work in which the design stands out. The different depths of relief are, in ascending order, rilievo stiacciato, bas-relief and high relief or alto-rilievo.

Reliquary: Receptacle in which a saint's relics are preserved.

Renaissance: Italian art and architecture from the early 15C to the mid 16C. It marks the end of the medieval conception of the world and the beginning of a new view based on classical antiquity (Ital. rinascimento = rebirth).

Retable: Shrine-like structure above and behind the altar.

Rib vault: → Groin vault.

Rocaille: Decorative ornaments adapted from the shell motif; chiefly late → Renaissance and → Rococo.

Rococo: Style towards the end of the → baroque (1720–70); elegant, often dainty, tendency to oval forms.

Romanesque: Comprehensive name for architecture from 1000–c. 1300. Buildings are distinguished by round arches, calm ornament and a heavy general appearance.

Rood screen: Screen between → choir and → nave, which bears a rood or crucifix.

Rose-window: A much divided round window with rich → tracery; found especially in Gothic buildings, often above the portal.

Rotunda: Round building.

Rustication: Massive blocks of stone separated by deep joints.

Sanctuary: Area around the high altar in a church.

Sarcophagus: Stone coffin, usually richly decorated.

Scroll: Spiral-shaped ornament.

Secularization: Transfer of ecclesiastical possessions to secular use, especially in the Napoleonic period (1803).

Sedilia: Seats for clergy; usually in the wall of the S. side of the choir.

Sgraffito: Scratched-on decoration.

Sounding board: → Pulpit.

Spandrel: The triangular space between the curve of an arch, the horizontal drawn from its apex, and the vertical drawn from the point of its springing; also the area between two arches in an arcade, and that part of a vault between two adjacent ribs.

Springer: The first stone in which the curve of an arch or vault begins.

Squinch: An arch or system of arches at the internal angles of towers to form the base of a round drum or dome above a square structure. → Pendentive.

Stela: Standing block.

Strapwork: Renaissance carved work modelled on fretwork or cut leather.

Stucco: Plasterwork, made of gypsum, lime, sand and water, which is easy to model. Used chiefly in the 17&18C for three-dimensional interior decoration.

Synagogue: Jewish place of worship.

Tabernacle: Receptacle for the consecrated host.

Tambour: Lower section, or 'drum' of a dome, usually cylindrical or polygonal.

Telamon: Support in the form of a male figure (male caryatid).

Terracotta: Fired, unglazed clay.

Thermal baths: Roman hot-water baths.

Tracery: Geometrically conceived decorative stonework, particularly used to decorate windows, screens, etc. If it embellishes a wall, it is known as blind tracery.

Transenna: Screen or lattice in openwork found in early Christian churches.

Transept: That part of a church at right angles to the nave; → basilica.

Triforium: Arcaded wall passage looking on to the nave; between the arcade and the clerestory.

Triptych: Tripartite altar painting.

Triumphal arch: Free-standing gateway based on a Roman original.

Trompe l'oeil: Special kind of image which the eye is deceived into viewing as three dimensional.

Tunnel vault: Simplest vault; continuous structure with semicircular or pointed cross section uninterrupted by cross vaults.

Tympanum: The often semicircular panel contained within the lintel of a doorway and the arch above it.

Volute: Spiral scroll on an Ionic capital; smaller volutes on Composite and Corinthian capitals.

Winged altar: Triptych or polyptych with hinged, usually richly carved or painted, wings.

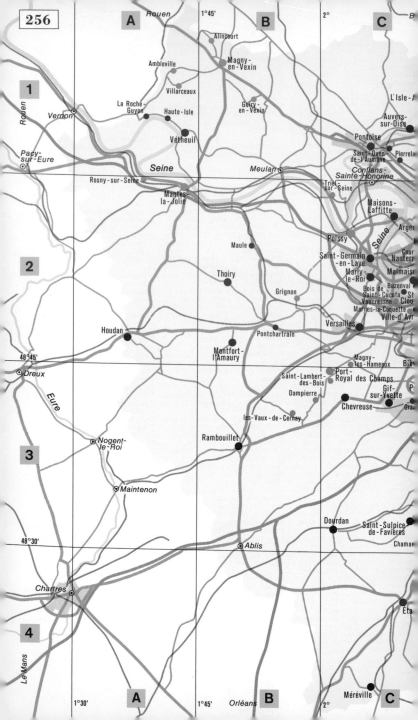

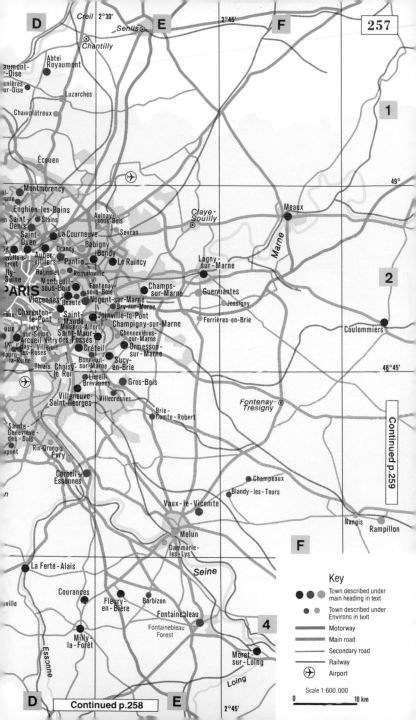

D
Creil 2°30'
Senlis
Chantilly
E
2°45'
F

Abtei
Royaumont
aumont-
-Oise
snières-
ur-Oise
Luzarches
Champlâtreux

1

Écouen

49°

Montmorency
Enghien-les-Bains
en Saint-
Denis
Stains
La Courneuve
Saint-
Ouen
Aubervilliers
Drancy
Bobigny
Bondy
Le Raincy
Aulnay-
sous-Bois
Sevran
Claye-
Souilly
Meaux
Marne

Lagny-
sur-Marne

Pantin
Romainville
Ragnolet
Montreuil-
sous-Bois
Fontenay-
sous-Bois
Champs-
sur-Marne
Guermantes
Jossigny

PARIS
Vincennes
Beauté
Nogent-sur-Marne
Bry-sur-Marne
Champigny-sur-Marne
Ferrières-en-Brie

2

Charenton-
le-Pont
Saint-
Mandé
Joinville-le-Pont
Chennevières-
sur-Marne
Coulommiers

Ivry-
sur-Seine
Arcueil
Villejuif
Maisons-Alfort
Saint-Maur-
des-Fossés
Créteil
Ormesson-
sur-Marne

Thiais
Bonneuil-
sur-Marne
Sucy-
en-Brie
48°45'

Choisy-
le-Roi
Limeil-
Brévannes
Gros-Bois
Fontenay-
Tresigny

Villeneuve-
Saint-Georges
Villecresnes
Brie-
Comte-Robert

Sainte-
Geneviève-
des-Bois
Ris-Orangis
Fviy

Corbeil-
Essonnes
Champeaux
Blandy-les-Tours

Vaux-le-Vicomte

Nangis
Rampillon

Melun

La Ferté-Alais
Dammarie-
les-Lys
Seine

F

Courances
Fleury-
en-Bière
Barbizon

Fontainebleau

4

Milly-
la-Forêt
Fontainebleau
Forest

Essonne

Moret-
sur-Loing
Loing

D
Continued p.258
E
2°45'

Continued p.259

Key

Town described under
main heading in text

Town described under
Environs in text

Motorway

Main road

Secondary road

Railway

Airport

Scale 1:600,000

0   10 km

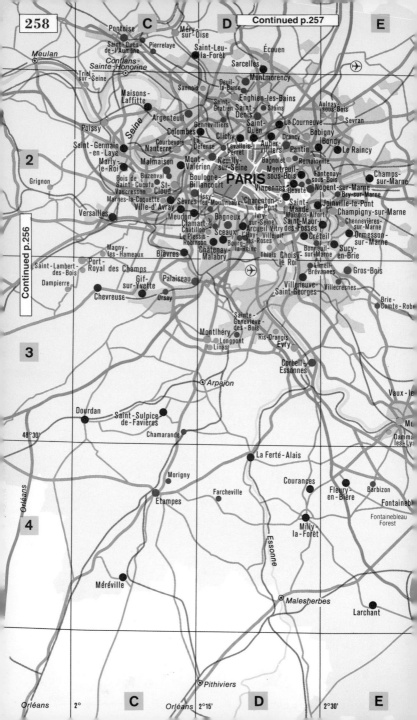

Continued p.257

C
D
E

Meulan

Pontoise

Saint-Ouen-de-l'Aumône
Pierrelaye
Saint-Leu-la-Forêt
Écouen

Conflans-Sainte-Honorine
Triel-sur-Seine

Sarcelles

Mery-sur-Oise

Montmorency

Deuil-la-Barre

Sannois
Enghien-les-Bains
Aulnay-sous-Bois

Maisons-Laffitte
Saint-Gratien
Saint-Denis
Stains
Sevran

Argenteuil
Gennevilliers
La Courneuve

Poissy
Seine
Colombes
Clichy
Saint-Ouen
Bobigny
Le Raincy

Saint-Germain-en-Laye
Courbevoie
La Défense
Levallois-Perret
Drancy
Bondy

Nanterre
Auber-villiers
Pantin

Marly-le-Roi
Malmaison
Mont-Valérien
Neuilly-sur-Seine
Bagnolet
Romainville

Grignon
Bois de Saint-Cucufa
Buzenval
PARIS
Montreuil-sous-Bois
Fontenay-sous-Bois
Champs-sur-Marne

Vaucresson
Boulogne-Billancourt
Vincennes
Beauté
Nogent-sur-Marne
Bry-sur-Marne

Marnes-la-Coquette
St-Cloud
Sèvres
Issy-les-Moulineaux
Charenton-le-Pont
Saint-Mandé
Joinville-le-Pont
Champigny-sur-Marne

Versailles
Ville-d'Avray
Meudon
Bagneux
Ivry-sur-Seine
Saint-Maur-des-Fossés
Chennevières-sur-Marne

Clamart
Chatillon
Arcueil
Vitry
Villejuif
Créteil
Ormesson-sur-Marne

Le Plessis-Robinson
Sceaux
Bourg-la-Reine
L'Haÿ-les-Roses
Thiais
Bonneuil-sur-Marne
Sucy-en-Brie

Magny-les-Hameaux
Bièvres
Châtenay-Malabry
Choisy-le-Roi
Limeil-Brévannes
Gros-Bois

Port-Royal des Champs
Palaiseau
Villeneuve-Saint-Georges
Villecresnes

Saint-Lambert-des-Bois
Gif-sur-Yvette
Brie-Comte-Rob

Dampierre

Chevreuse
Orsay

Sainte-Geneviève-des-Bois

Montlhéry
Ris-Orangis

Longpont
Évry
Vaux-le

Linas

Corbeil-Essonnes

Dourdan
Me

Saint-Sulpice-de-Favières
Damm-les-Ly

48°30'
Chamarande

La Ferté-Alais

Morigny
Courances
Fleury-en-Bière
Barbizon

Étampes
Farcheville
Fontainebl

Milly-la-Forêt
Fontainebleau Forest

Essonne

Méréville

Malesherbes
Larchant

Orléans

Pithiviers

Orléans
2°
C
Orléans
2°15'
D
2°30'
E

Continued p.256

2

3

4

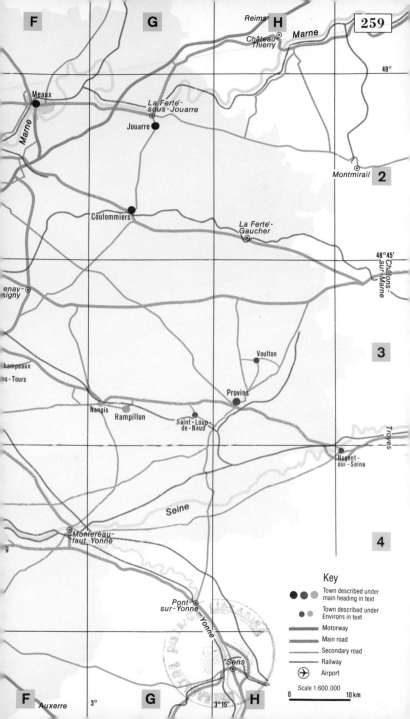

F	G	H

Reims
Marne
Château-Thierry ⊙

49°

Meaux ●

Marne

La Ferté-sous-Jouarre ⊙

Jouarre ●

Montmirail ⊙ **2**

Coulommiers ●

La Ferté-Gaucher ⊙

48°45'

Châlons-sur-Marne

enay-signy ⊙

3

hampeaux
es-Tours

Voulton ●

Provins ●

Nangis Rampillon ●

Saint-Loup-de-Naud ●

Troyes

Nogent-oui-Seine ⊙

Seine

Montereau-faut-Yonne ⊙

4

y

Pont-sur-Yonne ⊙

Yonne

Sens ⊙

Key

●●● Town described under main heading in text

●● Town described under Environs in text

━━ Motorway

━━ Main road

━━ Secondary road

━━ Railway

⊙ Airport

Scale 1:600,000

0 ——————— 10 km

F	G	H

Auxerre   3°   3°15'